www.EZmethods.com

EZ SOLUTIONS

TEST PREP SERIES

MATH PRACTICE

ADVANCED WORKBOOK

EZ SIMPLIFIED SOLUTIONS – THE BREAKTHROUGH IN TEST PREP!

LEADERS IN TEST PREP SOLUTIONS – WE MAKE IT EZ FOR YOU!

AUTHOR: PUNIT RAJA SURYACHANDRA

EZ Solutions
P O Box 10755
Silver Spring, MD 20914
USA

EZ SOLUTIONS
P.O. Box 10755
Silver Spring, MD 20914
USA

Conceived, conceptualized, written, and edited by:
Punit Raja SuryaChandra, EZ Solutions

PRINTED AND MANUFACTURED IN THE UNITED STATES OF AMERICA

TABLE OF CONTENTS

THIS PAGE HAS BEEN INTENTIONALLY LEFT BLANK

PREFACE

HIGHLIGHTS:
- About EZ Solutions
- About Our Author
- About EZ Books
- About This Book

▪ABOUT EZ SOLUTIONS

EZ Solutions – *the breakthrough in test-preparation*!

EZ Solutions is an organization formed to provide **simplified solutions** for test-preparation and tutoring. Although EZ Solutions is a fairly new name in the publishing industry, it has quickly become a respected publisher of test-prep books, study guides, study aids, handbooks, and other reference works. EZ publications and educational materials are highly respected, and they continue to receive an unprecedented amount of praise from professionals, instructors, librarians, parents, and students.

OBJECTIVE: Our ultimate objective is to help you **achieve academic and scholastic excellence**. We possess the right blend and matrix of skills and expertise that are required to not only do justice to our programs and publications, but also to handle them most effectively and efficiently. We are confident that our state-of-the-art programs/publications will give you a completely **new dimension** by enhancing your skill set and improving your overall performance.

MISSION: Our mission is to foster continuous knowledge to develop and enhance each student's skills through innovative and methodical programs/publications coupled with our add-on services – leading to a **better career and life** for our students.

OUR PHILOSOPHY: We subscribe to the traditional philosophy that everyone is equally capable of learning and that the natural, though sometimes unfulfilled and unexplored impetus of people is towards growth and development. We know that the human brain is undoubtedly a very powerful and efficient problem-solving tool, and every individual is much more capable than they realize. We strive to implement this philosophy throughout our books by helping our students explore their **potential** so that they can **perform at their optimum level**.

OUR COMMITMENT TOWARDS YOUR SATISFACTION: Reinventing, Redesigning, and Redefining Success: We are committed to providing **total customer satisfaction** that exceeds your expectations! Your satisfaction is extremely important to us, and your approval is one of the most important indicators that we have done our job correctly.

Long-Term Alliance: We, at EZ, look forward to forming a **long-term alliance** with all our readers who buy our book(s), for the days, months, and years to come. Moreover, our commitment to client service is one of our most important and distinguished characteristics. We also encourage our readers to contact us for any further assistance, feedback, suggestions, or inquiries.

EZ Solutions publishing series include books for the following major standardized tests:
- GMAT
- SAT
- PSAT
- ASVAB
- PRAXIS Series
- GRE
- ACT
- CLEP
- TOEFL
- Other (national and state) Standardized Tests

EZ Solutions aims to provide good quality study aides in a wide variety of disciplines to the following:
- Students who have not yet completed high school
- High School students preparing to enter college
- College students preparing to enter graduate or post-graduate school
- Anyone else who is simply looking to improve their skills

Students from every walk of life, of any background, at any level, in any field, with any ambition, can find what they are looking for among EZ Solutions' publications.

FOREIGN STUDENTS: All of our books are designed, keeping in mind the unique needs of students from North and South America, U.K., Europe, Middle East, Far East, and Asia. Foreign students from countries around the world seeking to obtain education in the United States will find the assistance they need in EZ Solutions' publications.

CONTACT US: Feel free to contact us, and one of our friendly specialists will be more than happy to assist you with your queries, or feel free to browse through our website for lots of useful information.
E-Mail: info@EZmethods.com
Phone: (301) 622-9597
Mail: EZ Solutions, P.O. Box 10755, Silver Spring, MD 20914, USA
Website: www.EZmethods.com

FEEDBACK: The staff of EZ Solutions hopes that you find our books helpful and easy to use. If you have any specific suggestions, comments, or feedback, please email us at: feedback@EZmethods.com

BUSINESS DEVELOPMENT: If you are interested in exploring business development opportunities, including forming a partnership alliance with us, kindly email us at: partners@EZmethods.com.

PRODUCT REGISTRATION: In order to get the most up-to-date information about this and our other books, you must register your purchase with EZ solutions by emailing us at: products@EZmethods.com, or by visiting our website www.EZmethods.com.

ERRORS AND INACCURACIES: We are not responsible for any typographical errors or inaccuracies contained in this publication. The information, prices, and discounts given in this book are subject to change without prior notice. To report any kind of errors or inaccuracies in this publication, kindly email us at: errors@EZmethods.com.

▪ABOUT OUR AUTHOR

The name of the man behind EZ publication series is **Punit Raja SuryaChandra**, who is also the founder of our company. He holds a Bachelors in Business and an MBA. It took him many years to write and publish these unique books. He researched every single book available in the market for test-preparation, and actually realized there is not even one book that is truly complete with all the content and concepts. This was the single most important reason that prompted him to write these books, and hence our **EZ prep guidebooks were born**. He has made every effort to make these books as comprehensive and as complete as possible. His expertise and experience are as diverse as the subjects that are represented in our books. He has the breadth and depth of experience required to write books of this magnitude and intensity. Without his unparalleled and unmatched skills and determination, none of this would have been possible.

In developing these books, his primary goal has been to give everyone the same advantages as the students we tutor privately or students who take our classes. Our tutoring and classroom solutions are only available to a limited number of students; however, with these books, any student in any corner of the world can benefit the same level of service at a fraction of the cost. Therefore, you should take this book as your personal EZ tutor or instructor, because that's precisely how it has been designed.

ACKNOWLEDGEMENTS:
Our author would like to extend his vote of appreciation and gratitude to all his family members for their unconditional and continuous support, to all his close friends for their trust and confidence in him, and to all his colleagues for their helpful consultation and generous advice.

Our EZ books have benefited from dedicated efforts and labors of our author and other members of the editorial staff. Here at EZ, we all wish you the best as you get comfortable, and settle down with your EZ tutor to start working on preparing for your test. In pursuing an educational dream, you have a wonderful and an exciting opportunity ahead of you. All of us at EZ Solutions wish you the very best!

-ABOUT EZ BOOKS

THE EZ NAME:
All our books have been written in a very easy to read manner, and in a very easy to understand fashion, so that students of any background, of any aptitude, of any capacity, of any skill-set, of any level, can benefit from them. These books are not specifically written for the **dummies** or for the **geniuses**; instead, they are written for students who fit into any category of intellectual acumen. This is how we acquired the name **"EZ Solutions"** for our publications – and as the name itself suggests, **we make everything EZ for you**!

THE EZ TUTOR:
Like any good tutor, EZ Tutor will work with you **individually and privately**, providing you with all the tools needed to improve your testing skills. It will assist you in recognizing your weaknesses, and enlighten you on how to improve upon them while transforming them into strengths. Of course, it will also point out your strengths as well, so that you can make them even stronger. By employing innovative techniques, EZ tutor will **stimulate, activate, and accelerate your learning process**. Soon after you start working with your EZ tutor, you will see **remarkable and noticeable improvement** in your performance by utilizing your newly acquired learning skills.

Whenever, Wherever, and However: EZ tutor also has the **flexibility** to work with you whenever you like – day or night, wherever you like – indoors or outdoors, and however you like – for as long or as short. While working with your EZ tutor, you can work at your own pace, you can go as fast or as slow as you like, repeat sections as many times as you need, and skip over sections you already know well. Your EZ tutor will also give you explanations, not just correct answers, and it will be **infinitely patient and adaptable**. Hence, our EZ Tutor will make you a more intelligent and smarter test-taker, and will help you maximize your score!

ADD-ON OPTIONS: *Turn your EZ Virtual Tutor into a Real Tutor!*

EZ TUTORING OVER THE PHONE:
Along with buying the entire series of our modules, students can also add on services like email/online support and/or telephone support. In fact, you can get the best preparation for your test by blending our professional 1-on-1 tutoring with our state-of-the-art books. The most important feature of our add-on features is our individualized and personalized approach that works toward building your self-confidence, and enhancing your ability to learn and perform better. This will also invigorate your motivational, organizational, as well as your learning skills. Our phone specialists are highly qualified, experienced, innovative, and well trained. You can do all this in the exclusivity and comfort of your home. Students can get in touch with one of our specialists anytime they need help – we'll be there for you, whenever you need us! We offer several packages with different levels, features, and customizations for tutoring over the phone to suit your individualized needs. Contact us for more details.

EZ 1-ON-1 TEST-TAKING & ADMISSION CONSULTATION:
We understand that standardized tests and school/college admissions can sometimes become very stressful. Our 1-on-1 Test-Taking & Admission Consulting Program can dramatically reduce your stress and anxiety. One of our consultants can personally guide you through the entire process, starting from familiarizing you with a test to getting you successfully admitted into a school/college of your choice. Again, you can do all this in the exclusivity and comfort of your home. We offer several packages with different levels, features, and customizations for test-taking and admission consultation over the phone to suit your individualized needs. Contact us for more details.
The following are some of the features of our EZ 1-on-1 Test-Taking & Admission Consulting Program:
- Familiarize you with a particular test
- Equip you with test-taking skills for each section of your test
- Reduce test-taking anxiety, stress, nervousness, and test-fever with personal counseling
- Draft and edit your essays
- Re-design your resume
- Prepare you for a telephone or personal interview
- Select the right school/college & help with admission application procedures
- Presentation Skills – how to present and market yourself

EZ UNIQUE FEATURES:

Your EZ Tutor offers you the following unique features that will highlight important information, and will let you find them quickly as and when you need to review them.

EZ STRATEGIES: It provides you with many powerful, effective, proven, and time tested strategies for various concepts, and shows you exactly how to use them to attack different question types. Many of these test-taking strategies cannot be found in any other books!

EZ SHORTCUTS: It gives you many time-saving shortcuts you can apply to save yourself some very valuable testing-time while solving a question on your actual test.

EZ TACTICS: It shows you several important tactics to use so that you can solve problems in the smartest way.

EZ DEFINITIONS: It defines all the key definitions in an easy to understand manner so that you get a clear description and concise understanding of all the key terms.

EZ RULES: It presents all the important rules in an orderly manner so that you can learn the basic rules of all the concepts.

EZ STEPS: It walks you through hundreds of concepts, showing you how to tackle every question type in an organized user-friendly step-by-step easy-to-understand methodology that adapts to your understanding and needs so that you get the best procedural knowledge.

EZ MULTIPLE/ALTERNATE METHODS: It gives you a choice of multiple methods of answering the same question so that you can choose the method that seems easiest to you.

EZ SUMMARIES: It lists a complete summary of all the important concepts in an ordered and organized manner so that you will never have to hunt for them.

EZ FACTS: It provides you with numerous key facts about various principles so that you know all the facts-and-figures of the material you are reviewing.

EZ HINTS: It supplies you with innumerable hints and clues so that you can use them to become a smarter and wiser test-taker.

EZ TIPS: It also presents you with many tips and pointers that will prevent you from making any careless mistakes or falling into traps.

EZ NOTES: It reminds you to make notes of some important points that will come handy while answering a question.

EZ WARNINGS/CAUTIONS: It warns you of some obvious mistakes that will prevent you from making them while answering a question.

EZ EXCEPTIONS: It makes you aware of the exceptions and exclusions that apply to any particular rule.

EZ REFERENCES: It gives you references of related materials that you may want to refer to in other parts of the same or different modules, while learning a specific concept.

EZ SPOTS: It lists buzzwords and phrases that will help you easily spot some specific question types.

EZ PROBLEM SET-UP: It converts even some of the most complex problems into an easy to understand mathematical statement so that you understand accurately how to interpret the problems.

EZ PROBLEM EXPLANATIONS: It provides easy to understand explanations within square brackets for each step of the problem so that you know exactly what you need to do in each step.

EZ SOLVED EXAMPLES: It also throws several realistic solved examples with easy to understand detailed explanations for each and every question type explained so that you can understand and learn how to apply the concepts.

EZ PRACTICE EXERCISES: Last but not the least; it also includes intensive realistic practice exercises with easy to understand detailed explanations for each and every question type explained so that you can put to practice what you learned in an actual test question – solved examples will help you understand the concepts & practice will make you perfect!

GUESS WHAT!! No other book offers you so much. Your EZ tutor strives to provide you with the **best possible training** for your test, and **best value for your time and money**; and it is infinitely committed to providing you with **state-of-the-art** material.

Advantages: Amazing results in the first few days of the program!

Disadvantages: Only if you don't make use of our programs and publications!

THE EZ ADVANTAGE:

EZ TEST-PREP PROGRAM BROKEN INTO MODULES:
Instead of having a **big fat ugly scary all-in-one gigantic book**, we have broken our entire test-prep program into **small easy-to-use modules**.
- **Exclusivity:** Each module is exclusively dedicated to covering one major content area in extensive depth and breadth, allowing you to master each topic by getting an in-depth review.
- **More Content:** You will find many more topics and many more pages per topic than what you can find in all other books combined.
- **Tailored and Customized:** Separated modules offer test-takers of all levels with a more tailored and customized approach towards building specific foundational and advanced skills, and successfully preparing for the test.

EZ TO READ, CARRY, AND MANAGE:
EZ Modules are convenient – they are **easier to read, carry, and manage**.
- **EZ to Read:** EZ Modules are easier to read with text in spacious pages with a bigger font size than those other books with overcrowded pages with a small print.
- **EZ to Carry:** EZ Modules are easier to carry and hold than those other big fat bulky gigantic books.
- **EZ to Manage:** EZ Modules are overall easier to manage than those other all-in-one books.

BUY ONE MODULE OR THE ENTIRE SERIES:
The individually separated modules give you the flexibility to buy only those modules that cover the areas you think you need to work on; nevertheless, we strongly suggest you buy our entire series of modules. In fact, the most efficient and effective way to get the most out of our publications is to use our entire set of modules in conjunction with each other, and not just a few. Each module can be independently bought and studied; however, the modules are somehow connected with and complement the other modules. Therefore, if you are serious about getting a good score on your test, we sincerely recommend you purchase our entire series of modules. Contact us to order, or go to www.EZmethods.com, or check your local bookstore (look at the EZ Book Store on the last page for more information).

NO NEED TO REFER TO ANY OTHER BOOK:
Almost all other test-prep books contain a small disclaimer in some corner. They themselves spell it out very loud and clear, and admit that their book is only a brief review of some important topics; hence, it should not be considered to be an overall review of all the concepts. Most other test-preparation guides only include information for you to get familiar with the kind of topics that may appear on the test, and they suggest that you refer to additional textbooks, or consult other reference books if you want more detailed information and to get an in-depth knowledge of all the concepts. These books are not designed to be a one-stop book to learn everything you must know; instead, they are more like a

summary of some important points. Moreover, they assume that you already know everything, or at least most of the concepts.

However, if you are using our EZ modules to prepare for your test, it's the opposite case, you don't need to refer or consult any other book or text or any other source for assistance. On the contrary, we, in fact, discourage you from referring to any other book, just because there is absolutely no reason to. Our EZ modules contain everything that you need to know in order to do well on your test. We haven't left anything out, and we don't assume anything. Even if you don't know anything, you will find everything in our modules from topics that are frequently tested to topics that are rarely tested, and everything in between. The only topics that you won't find in our books are the topics that will probably never appear on your test!

Frequently Tested: Included in our review – topics that are repeatedly tested on your test, on a regularly basis
Occasionally Tested: Included in our review – topics that are sometimes tested on your test, every now and then
Rarely Tested: Included in our review – topics that are seldom tested on your test, very infrequently
Never Tested: Not included in our review – since these topics are never tested on your test, we don't even mention them anywhere in our review

The bottom line is, if something can be on your test, you'll find it in our modules; and if something is not going to be on your test, it's not going to be in our modules. Each and every math concept that even has the slightest possibility to be on the test can be found in our modules.

THE OFFICIAL REAL PRACTICE TESTS:
Although we don't suggest you refer to any other book, the only time we recommend using other books is for practicing previously administered tests to exercise your skills. The best resources for actual practice tests are the official guides published by the test makers that have several actual previously administered tests. One can **replicate** these tests as closely as one can, but no one other than the test administrators can **duplicate** them, and have the ability to reproduce or publish them. Therefore, to get the maximum effect of our approach, you must practice the actual tests from the official guide. You can also take a free online practice test by going to their website. EZ's practice tests are also based upon the most recently administered tests, and include every type of question that can be expected on the actual exam.

HOW OUR BOOKS CAN HELP YOU:
Our books are designed to help you identify your strengths and the areas which you need to work on. If you study all our modules, you will be fully equipped with all the tools needed to take your test head-on. Moreover, you'll also have the satisfaction that you did all you possibly could do to prepare yourself for the test, and you didn't leave any stone unturned. The amount of content covered in our books is far more than what you would learn by studying all the other test-prep books that are out there, put together, or by even taking an online or an actual prep course, and of course, spending thousands of dollars in the process. This will give you an idea of how material we have covered in our books.

STRUCTURE OF OUR MODULES:
All our modules are **structured in a highly organized and systematic manner**. The review is divided into different modules. Each module is divided into units. Each unit is further subdivided into chapters. Each chapter covers various topics, and in each specific topic, you are given all that you need to solve questions on that topic in detail – explaining key concepts, rules, and other EZ unique features. Also included in some topics are test-taking strategies specific to the topics discussed. Following each topic are solved sample examples with comprehensive explanations, which are exclusively based on that topic, and utilizing the concepts covered in that topic and section. Finally, there are practice exercises with thorough explanations containing real test-like questions for each topic and section, which are very similar to actual test questions. All units, chapters, and topics are chronologically numbered for easy reference.

Moreover, the modules, units, chapters, and topics are all arranged in sequence so that later modules, units, chapters, and topics assume familiarity with the material covered in earlier modules, units, chapters, and topics. Therefore, the best way to review is to work through from the beginning to the end.

SERIES > MODULES > UNITS > CHAPTERS > TOPICS > SUB-TOPICS > SOLVED EXAMPLES > PRACTICE EXERCISES

THE EZ DIFFERENCE:

DIFFERENCE BETWEEN EZ SOLUTIONS' PUBLICATIONS AND OTHER BOOKS:

Most of the other test-prep books suggest that your exam only tests your ability to take the test, and it does not test any actual content knowledge. In other words, they claim that your test is all about knowing the test-taking strategies, and it has very little to do with the actual knowledge of content; others claim that your test is all about knowing a few most commonly tested topics. While we have great respect for these books and the people who write or publish them, all these books have one thing in common: they all want to give their readers a quick shortcut to success. They actually want their readers to believe that just by learning a few strategies and memorizing some key formulas, they'll be able to ace their test. We are not sure if it's the fault of the people who write these books or the people who use them; but someone is definitely trying to fool someone – either those test-prep books for making the readers believe it, or the readers for actually believing it (no pun intended).

With a test as vast as this, it's simply not possible to cover the entire content in just a few pages. We all wish; however, in life, there really aren't any shortcuts to success, and your test is no exception to this rule. Nothing comes easy in life, and that is also precisely the case with your test. You have to do it the hard way by working your way through. Unfortunately, there is no magic potion, which we can give you to succeed in math! Therefore, if you want to do well on your test – be mentally, physically, and psychologically prepared to do some hard work. In this case, efforts and results are directly proportional, that is, greater the efforts you make, better your results are going to be.

While most test-preparation books present materials that stand very little resemblance to the actual tests, EZ's publication series present tests that accurately depict the official tests in both, degree of difficulty and types of questions.

Our EZ books are like no other books you have ever seen or even heard of. We have a completely different concept, and our books are structured using a totally different model. We have *re-defined the way test-prep books should be*.

STRATEGIES SEPARATED FROM CONTENT:
What we have done in our modules is, *separated the actual content-knowledge from the test-taking strategies*. We truly believe that a test-prep program should be more than just a *cheat-sheet of tricks, tips, and traps*. The test you are preparing for is not a simple game that you can master by learning these quick tactics. What you really need to do well on your test is a program that builds true understanding and knowledge of the content.

PERFECT EQUILIBRIUM BETWEEN STRATEGIES AND CONTENT:
In our modules, we've tried our best to present a *truly unique equilibrium* between two competing and challenging skills: test-taking strategies and comprehensive content-knowledge. We have *blended* the two most important ingredients that are essential for your success on your test. We have *enhanced* the old traditional approach to some of the most advanced forms of test-taking strategies. To top all this, we have *refined* our solved examples with detailed explanations to give you hands-on experience to real test-like questions before you take your actual test.

Other Books: Most of the other test-prep books primarily concentrate on teaching their readers how to *guess* and *use the process of elimination,* and they get so obsessed with the tactics that in the process they completely ignore the actual content. Majority of the content of these books consists of pages of guessing techniques.

EZ Books: With our EZ Content-Knowledge Modules, you'll find *100% pure content* that has a highly organized and structured approach to all the content areas, which actually teaches you the content you need to know to do well on your test. Therefore, if you are looking to learn more than just guessing by process of elimination, and if you are serious about developing your skills and confidence level for your exam, then our highly organized and structured test-prep modules is the solution. By studying our books, you'll learn a systematic approach to any question that you may see on your test, and acquire the tools that will help you get there.

EZ Solutions' publications are packed with important information, sophisticated strategies, useful tips, and extensive practice that the experts know will help you do your best on your test.

You should use whichever concept, fact, or tip from that section that you think is appropriate to answer the question correctly in the least possible time. If you've mastered the material in our review modules and strategy modules, you should be able to answer almost all (99.99%) of the questions.

LEARN BACKWARDS AND MOVE FORWARD: Smart students are the ones who make an honest attempt to learn what they read, and also learn from their mistakes, but at the same time, who moves ahead. Therefore, you should learn backwards, that is, learn from your past experiences, and move forward, that is, keep moving ahead without looking back!

ONE CONCEPT, EZ MULTIPLE METHODS:
Our books often give you a *choice of multiple methods* of answering the same question – you can pick the method that seems easiest to you. Our goal is not to *prescribe* any *hard-and-fast* method for taking the test, but instead, to give you the *flexibility and tools you can use to approach your test with confidence and optimism*.

STRATEGIES OR CONTENT?

In order to do well on your test, it is absolutely essential that you have a pretty good grasp of all the concepts laid out in our review modules. Our review modules contain everything you need to know, or must know to crack your test. They cover everything from basic arithmetic to logical reasoning, and everything in between. Nonetheless, that's not enough. You should be able to use these concepts in ways that may not be so familiar or well known to you. This is where our EZ Strategies kick in.

CONTENT VERSUS STRATEGIES:

There is a *succinct* difference between knowing the math content and knowing the math strategies.

Hypothetically speaking, let's assume there is a student named Alex, who learns only the test-taking strategies; and there is another student named Andria, who learns only the math-content. Now when the test time comes, Andria who learns only the math-content is extremely likely to do a lot better than Alex, who learns only the test-taking strategies.

The truth is that someone who has the knowledge of all the math content, but doesn't know anything about the strategies, will almost always do better on the test than someone who knows all the strategies but doesn't know the content properly.

Now let's assume there is another student named Alexandria, who learns both, the test-taking strategies and the math-content. Yes, now we are talking! This student, Alexandria, who knows both the strategies and the content, is guaranteed to do a lot better than Alex, who only knows the strategies, or Andria who only knows the content.

This brings us to our conclusion on this topic: don't just study the strategies, or just the content; you need to know both simultaneously – the strategies and the content, in order to do well on your test. How quickly and accurately you can answer the math questions will depend on your knowledge of the content and the strategies, and that will have an overall effect on your success on the test.

Hence, the equation to succeed on your test is: **Strategies + Content = Success!**

We are confident that if you study our books on test-taking strategies along with our books on content-knowledge, you'll have everything you possibly need to know in order to do well on your test, in fact, to ace your test, and come out with flying colors!

The good thing is that you made the smart decision to buy this book, or if you are reading this online, or in a bookstore, or in a library, you are going to buy one soon!

CONTENT-KNOWLEDGE REVIEW MODULES:

THOROUGH IN-DEPTH REVIEW:
Most other test-prep books briefly touch upon some of the concepts sporadically. On the other hand, our books start from the basics, but unlike other books, they do not end there – *we go deep inside, beyond just touching up the surface* – all the way from fundamental skills to some of the most advanced content that many other prep books choose to ignore. *Each concept is first explained in detail, and then analyzed for most effective understanding* – each and every concept is covered, and we haven't left any stone unturned. Overall, our program is more challenging – you simply get the *best-of-the-best*, and you get more of everything!

COMPREHENSIVE REVIEW:
Our Content-Knowledge Review Modules provide the *most comprehensive and complete review* of all the concepts, which you need to know to excel in your test. Each module is devoted to one of the main subject areas so that you can focus on the most relevant material. The ideal way to review our modules is to go through each topic thoroughly, understand all the solved examples, and work out all of the practice exercises. You must review each topic, understand every solved example, and work out all of the practice exercises. If you don't have enough time, just glimpse through a section. If you feel comfortable with it, move on to something else that may potentially give you more trouble. If you feel uncomfortable with it, review that topic more thoroughly.

Moreover, if you carefully work through our review, you will probably find some topics that you already know, but you may also find some topics that you need to review more closely. You should have a good sense of areas with which you are most comfortable, and in which areas you feel you have a deficiency. Work on any weaknesses you believe you have in those areas. This should help you organize your review more efficiently. Try to give yourself plenty of time and make sure to review the skills and master the concepts that you are required and expected to know to do well on your test. Of course, the more time you invest preparing for your test and more familiar you are with these fundamental principles, the better you will do on your test.

There is a lot of content reviewed in our modules. Although the amount of material presented in our books may appear to be overwhelming, it's the most complete review to get prepared for your test. To some of you, this may seem like a great deal of information to assimilate; however, when you start reviewing, you'll probably realize that you are already comfortable with many concepts discussed in our review modules. We also suggest that you spread your use of our modules over several weeks, and study different modules at your own pace. Even if you are sure you know the basic concepts, our review will help to warm you up so that you can go into your test with crisp and sharp skills. Hence, we strongly suggest that you at least touch up on each concept. However, depending on your strengths and weaknesses, you may be able to move quickly through some areas, and focus more on the others that seem to be troublesome to you. You should develop a plan of attack for your review of the wide range of content. Work on your weaknesses, and be ready to take advantage of your strengths.

Finally, our main objective in the content review modules is to refresh your knowledge of key concepts on the test and we attempt to keep things as concrete and concise as possible.

PRACTICE MODULES:

BASIC WORKBOOK:
Our math practice basic workbook contains a variety of questions on each and every topic that is covered in our review modules. The best way is to first learn all the concepts from our review modules and then apply your skills to test your knowledge on the actual test-like questions in our basic workbook.

ADVANCED WORKBOOK:
Our math practice advanced workbook also contains a variety of questions on each and every topic that is covered in our review modules. Once you become comfortable with the questions in our basic workbook, you should try your hands on our advanced workbook so that you can gain more experience with some of the most difficult questions. For students who are aiming for a very high score, practicing from our advanced workbook is very important. For students who are aiming for a mediocre score, practicing from our advanced workbook is not so important.

▪ABOUT THIS BOOK

In order to excel on your test, it's important that you master each component of your test. That's why we have broken the entire test into different sections and each book focuses only on only one component. It's important to learn the art of tackling the questions you'll see on the test; nevertheless, it's equally important to get a strong hold of the mathematical fundamentals and principles. Apparently it's not enough to only know the test taking strategies, you also need to have a solid knowledge of the math content, and know how to solve the problems mathematically. This book is exclusively dedicated to the **Advanced Problems** that apply to the math section of your test.

WHAT'S COVERED IN THIS BOOK:
In this book, you will learn everything related to **Advanced problems** content that can be used on different types of questions throughout the math section. Mastering the content of this book will not only improve your performance on the math section, but will also make you a smarter and wiser test-taker. In this book, you'll learn all the strategies and the content related to advanced problems, so that you can solve the advanced quickly, correctly, and more efficiently. In fact, being able to solve advanced problems is one of the most important factors to succeed on the math section.

WHAT'S NOT COVERED IN THIS BOOK:
This book does not cover any content other than Advanced Problems – to learn about the content areas, you must refer to the other books in the series.

PRE-REQUISITES FOR THIS BOOK:
The pre-requisite for this book is your thorough familiarity with all the principles and concepts covered in all the review modules and the basic workbook in the series. Hence, when you go through this book, you are already expected to know all the content covered in all of the other books in the series.

RELATED MODULES FOR THIS BOOK:
You will get the best out of this book if you use it in conjunction with some of the other related books in the series that are listed below.

List of related modules for this book:
- EZ Solutions – Test Prep Series – Math Strategies
- EZ Solutions – Test Prep Series – Math Review – Arithmetic
- EZ Solutions – Test Prep Series – Math Review – Algebra
- EZ Solutions – Test Prep Series – Math Review – Applications
- EZ Solutions – Test Prep Series – Math Review – Geometry
- EZ Solutions – Test Prep Series – Math Review – Word Problems
- EZ Solutions – Test Prep Series – Math Review – Logic & Stats
- EZ Solutions – Test Prep Series – Math Practice – Basic Workbook
- EZ Solutions – Test Prep Series – Math Practice – Advanced Workbook

Note: Look at the back of the book for a complete list of EZ books

PART 0.0: INTRODUCTION TO ADVANCED WORKBOOK:

Our Math Practice Advanced Workbook also contains a variety of questions on each and every topic that is covered in our review modules.

Once you become comfortable with the questions in our basic workbook, you should try your hands on our advanced workbook so that you can gain more experience with some of the most difficult questions.

In our Math Practice Advanced Workbook, you'll get to practice all the skills that you learned in our review books. All questions are given for each review book, and are arranged in the same order as in our review books.

After you get a firm control on all the concepts given in our math review books and basic workbook, its important that you practice the actual test-like questions given in this book. Each question is explained in detail.

THIS PAGE HAS BEEN INTENTIONALLY LEFT BLANK

PART 1.0: ARITHMETIC:

TOPICS COVERED:

- Integers

- Fractions

- Decimals

- Exponents

- Radicals

PRACTICE EXERCISE:

Question #1:   What is the value of $\dfrac{7.00007}{8.00008}$?

Question #2:   What is the value of $\dfrac{5.0505}{2.0202}$?

Question #3: $\dfrac{\dfrac{1}{2}+\dfrac{3}{4}}{\dfrac{1}{2}+\dfrac{5}{6}}$

Question #4: $\dfrac{\left[\dfrac{\dfrac{9}{7}}{\dfrac{8}{7}}\right]\left[\dfrac{\dfrac{5}{2}}{\dfrac{9}{2}}\right]}{\left[\dfrac{\dfrac{7}{9}}{\dfrac{7}{8}}\right]\left[\dfrac{\dfrac{2}{5}}{\dfrac{2}{9}}\right]}$

Question #5: $\dfrac{1}{2+\dfrac{3}{4+\dfrac{5}{6}}}$

Question #6: $\dfrac{1}{1+\dfrac{1}{2+\dfrac{1}{2}}}$

Question #7: $1+\dfrac{1}{1+\dfrac{1}{1-\dfrac{1}{7}}}$

Question #8:   What is the value of $\left(\dfrac{1}{2}\right)^{-6}\left(\dfrac{1}{4}\right)^{-5}\left(\dfrac{1}{8}\right)^{-4}\left(\dfrac{1}{16}\right)^{-3}\left(\dfrac{1}{32}\right)^{-2}\left(\dfrac{1}{64}\right)^{-1}$?

Question #9:   Simplify $\dfrac{1}{5^6}+\dfrac{1}{5^7}+\dfrac{1}{5^7}+\dfrac{1}{5^7}+\dfrac{1}{5^7}+\dfrac{1}{5^7}$

Question #10:   If $x = 0.777$, $y = \sqrt{0.777}$, and $z = (0.777)^2$, then what is the correct order of x, y, and z?

PRACTICE EXERCISE – QUESTIONS & ANSWERS WITH EXPLANATIONS:

Question #1:   What is the value of $\dfrac{7.00007}{8.00008}$?

Solution: $\Rightarrow \dfrac{7(1.00001)}{8(1.00001)}$ [Factor out the integer part in the numerator and denominator]

$\Rightarrow \dfrac{7}{8}$ [Cancel out the common factors]

$\Rightarrow 0.875$ [Do the division]

Question #2:   What is the value of $\dfrac{5.0505}{2.0202}$?

Solution: $\Rightarrow \dfrac{5(1.0101)}{2(1.0101)}$ [Factor out the integer part in the numerator and denominator]

$\Rightarrow \dfrac{5}{2}$ [Cancel out the common factors]

$\Rightarrow 2.5$ [Do the division]

Question #3: $\dfrac{\frac{1}{2}+\frac{3}{4}}{\frac{1}{2}+\frac{5}{6}}$

Solution: $\Rightarrow \dfrac{\frac{2}{4}+\frac{3}{4}}{\frac{3}{6}+\frac{5}{6}}$ [In the numerator & denominator, scale-up the fractions to the LCD]

$\Rightarrow \dfrac{\frac{5}{4}}{\frac{8}{6}}$ [Add the fractions in the numerator and the denominator]

$\Rightarrow \dfrac{5}{4} \div \dfrac{8}{6}$ [Divide the fraction in numerator by the fraction in denominator]

$\Rightarrow \dfrac{5}{4} \times \dfrac{6}{8}$ [Switch the division to multiplication sign and flip the second fraction]

$\Rightarrow \dfrac{30}{32}$ [Multiply the two fractions straight across]

$\Rightarrow \dfrac{15}{16}$ [Reduce the fraction to its lowest terms by cancelling by 2]

Question #4: $\dfrac{\left[\frac{\frac{9}{7}}{\frac{8}{7}}\right]\left[\frac{\frac{5}{2}}{\frac{9}{2}}\right]}{\left[\frac{\frac{7}{9}}{\frac{7}{8}}\right]\left[\frac{\frac{2}{5}}{\frac{2}{9}}\right]}$

Solution: $\Rightarrow \dfrac{\left(\dfrac{9}{7} \div \dfrac{8}{7}\right) \bullet \left(\dfrac{5}{2} \div \dfrac{9}{2}\right)}{\left(\dfrac{7}{9} \div \dfrac{7}{8}\right) \bullet \left(\dfrac{2}{5} \div \dfrac{2}{9}\right)}$ [Rewrite fractions in numerator and denominator with division signs]

$\Rightarrow \dfrac{\left(\dfrac{9}{\cancel{7}} \times \dfrac{\cancel{7}}{8}\right) \bullet \left(\dfrac{5}{\cancel{2}} \times \dfrac{\cancel{2}}{9}\right)}{\left(\dfrac{\cancel{7}}{9} \times \dfrac{8}{\cancel{7}}\right) \bullet \left(\dfrac{\cancel{2}}{5} \times \dfrac{9}{\cancel{2}}\right)}$ [Switch the division to multiplication sign and flip the second fraction]

$\Rightarrow \dfrac{\left(\dfrac{\cancel{9}}{8}\right) \bullet \left(\dfrac{5}{\cancel{9}}\right)}{\left(\dfrac{8}{\cancel{9}}\right) \bullet \left(\dfrac{\cancel{9}}{5}\right)}$ [Reduce the fractions in the numerator and denominator]

$\Rightarrow \dfrac{\dfrac{5}{8}}{\dfrac{8}{5}}$ [Again, reduce the fractions in the numerator and denominator]

$\Rightarrow \dfrac{5}{8} \div \dfrac{8}{5}$ [Divide the fraction in numerator by the fraction in denominator]

$\Rightarrow \dfrac{5}{8} \times \dfrac{5}{8}$ [Switch the division to multiplication sign and flip the second fraction]

$\Rightarrow \dfrac{25}{64}$ [Multiply the two fractions straight across]

Question #5: $\dfrac{1}{2 + \dfrac{3}{4 + \dfrac{5}{6}}}$

Solution: $\Rightarrow \dfrac{1}{2 + \dfrac{3}{\dfrac{24}{6} + \dfrac{5}{6}}}$ [In the denominator of the denominator, scale-up the fractions]

$\Rightarrow \dfrac{1}{2 + \dfrac{3}{\dfrac{29}{6}}}$ [In the denominator of the denominator, add the fractions]

$\Rightarrow \dfrac{1}{2 + \dfrac{18}{29}}$ [In the denominator, divide the fractions]

$\Rightarrow \dfrac{1}{\dfrac{58}{29} + \dfrac{18}{29}}$ [In the denominator, scale-up the fractions to their LCD]

$\Rightarrow \dfrac{1}{\dfrac{76}{29}}$ [Add the fractions in the denominator]

$\Rightarrow \dfrac{29}{76}$ [Divide the fraction in the denominator by 1 by flipping it]

Question #6:
$$\cfrac{1}{1+\cfrac{1}{2+\cfrac{1}{2}}}$$

Solution:

$\Rightarrow \cfrac{1}{1+\cfrac{1}{\cfrac{4}{2}+\cfrac{1}{2}}}$ [In the denominator of the denominator, scale-up the fractions]

$\Rightarrow \cfrac{1}{1+\cfrac{1}{\cfrac{5}{2}}}$ [In the denominator of the denominator, add the fractions]

$\Rightarrow \cfrac{1}{1+\cfrac{2}{5}}$ [In the denominator, divide the fractions]

$\Rightarrow \cfrac{1}{\cfrac{5}{5}+\cfrac{2}{5}}$ [In the denominator, scale-up the fractions to their LCD]

$\Rightarrow \cfrac{1}{\cfrac{7}{5}}$ [Add the fractions in the denominator]

$\Rightarrow \cfrac{5}{7}$ [Divide the fraction in the denominator by 1 by flipping it]

Question #7:
$$1+\cfrac{1}{1+\cfrac{1}{1-\cfrac{1}{7}}}$$

Solution:

$\Rightarrow 1+\cfrac{1}{1+\cfrac{1}{\cfrac{7}{7}-\cfrac{1}{7}}}$ [In the bottom most level, scale-up the fractions]

$\Rightarrow 1+\cfrac{1}{1+\cfrac{1}{\cfrac{6}{7}}}$ [In the bottom most level, subtract the fractions]

$\Rightarrow 1+\cfrac{1}{1+\cfrac{7}{6}}$ [In the bottom most level, divide the fraction by 1]

$\Rightarrow 1+\cfrac{1}{\cfrac{6}{6}+\cfrac{7}{6}}$ [In the bottom most level, scale-up the fractions]

$\Rightarrow 1+\cfrac{1}{\cfrac{13}{6}}$ [In the bottom most level, add the fractions]

$\Rightarrow \dfrac{6}{6} + \dfrac{13}{6}$ [In the bottom most level, divide the fractions by 1]

$\Rightarrow \dfrac{19}{6}$ [Add the fractions]

Question #8:   What is the value of $\left(\dfrac{1}{2}\right)^{-6}\left(\dfrac{1}{4}\right)^{-5}\left(\dfrac{1}{8}\right)^{-4}\left(\dfrac{1}{16}\right)^{-3}\left(\dfrac{1}{32}\right)^{-2}\left(\dfrac{1}{64}\right)^{-1}$?

Solution: First, simplify each fraction with a common denominator (½):

$\Rightarrow \left(\dfrac{1}{2}\right)^{-6} = \left[\left(\dfrac{1}{2}\right)^{1}\right]^{-6} = \left(\dfrac{1}{2}\right)^{-6}$ [Rewrite the first term of the expression with a base of ½]

$\Rightarrow \left(\dfrac{1}{4}\right)^{-5} = \left[\left(\dfrac{1}{2}\right)^{2}\right]^{-5} = \left(\dfrac{1}{2}\right)^{-10}$ [Rewrite the second term of the expression with a base of ½]

$\Rightarrow \left(\dfrac{1}{8}\right)^{-4} = \left[\left(\dfrac{1}{2}\right)^{3}\right]^{-4} = \left(\dfrac{1}{2}\right)^{-12}$ [Rewrite the third term of the expression with a base of ½]

$\Rightarrow \left(\dfrac{1}{16}\right)^{-3} = \left[\left(\dfrac{1}{2}\right)^{4}\right]^{-3} = \left(\dfrac{1}{2}\right)^{-12}$ [Rewrite the fourth term of the expression with a base of ½]

$\Rightarrow \left(\dfrac{1}{32}\right)^{-2} = \left[\left(\dfrac{1}{2}\right)^{5}\right]^{-2} = \left(\dfrac{1}{2}\right)^{-10}$ [Rewrite the fifth term of the expression with a base of ½]

$\Rightarrow \left(\dfrac{1}{64}\right)^{-1} = \left[\left(\dfrac{1}{2}\right)^{6}\right]^{-1} = \left(\dfrac{1}{2}\right)^{-6}$ [Rewrite the sixth term of the expression with a base of ½]

Next, find the value of the expression:

$\Rightarrow \left(\dfrac{1}{2}\right)^{-6}\left(\dfrac{1}{2}\right)^{-10}\left(\dfrac{1}{2}\right)^{-12}\left(\dfrac{1}{2}\right)^{-12}\left(\dfrac{1}{2}\right)^{-10}\left(\dfrac{1}{2}\right)^{-6}$ [Substitute the newly formed equivalent fractions]

$\Rightarrow \left(\dfrac{1}{2}\right)^{-6-10-12-12-10-6}$ [Multiply the fractions by using the laws of exponents]

$\Rightarrow \left(\dfrac{1}{2}\right)^{-56}$ [Simplify the value of the exponent]

Question #9:   Simplify $\dfrac{1}{5^6} + \dfrac{1}{5^7} + \dfrac{1}{5^7} + \dfrac{1}{5^7} + \dfrac{1}{5^7} + \dfrac{1}{5^7}$

Solution: $\Rightarrow \dfrac{1\times 5}{5^6 \times 5} + \dfrac{1}{5^7} + \dfrac{1}{5^7} + \dfrac{1}{5^7} + \dfrac{1}{5^7} + \dfrac{1}{5^7}$ [Multiply the numerator and denominator of first fraction by 5]

$\Rightarrow \dfrac{5}{5^7} + \dfrac{1}{5^7} + \dfrac{1}{5^7} + \dfrac{1}{5^7} + \dfrac{1}{5^7} + \dfrac{1}{5^7}$ [Simplify the first fraction so that it has the same denominator]

$\Rightarrow \dfrac{5+1+1+1+1+1}{5^7}$ [Add all the fractions with the common denominator]

$\Rightarrow \dfrac{10}{5^7}$ [Simplify the numerator]

$\Rightarrow \dfrac{5\times 2}{5 \times 5^6}$ [Factor the numerator and denominator]

$\Rightarrow \dfrac{2}{5^6}$ [Simplify the fraction]

Question #10:   If $x = 0.777$, $y = \sqrt{0.777}$, and $z = (0.777)^2$, then what is the correct order of x, y, and z?

Solution: The important thing to note is: when a number between 0 and 1 is squared, it becomes smaller; and when the square root of a number between 0 and 1 taken, it becomes bigger.

$\Rightarrow x = 0.777$ $\quad\Rightarrow$ this will remain the same $\quad\Rightarrow 0.777$

$\Rightarrow y = \sqrt{0.777}$ $\quad\Rightarrow$ this will become bigger $\quad\Rightarrow 0.881$ (approx)

$\Rightarrow z = (0.777)^2$ $\quad\Rightarrow$ this will become smaller $\quad\Rightarrow 0.6$ (approx)

Therefore, the correct order is $z < x < y$.

THIS PAGE HAS BEEN INTENTIONALLY LEFT BLANK

PART 2.0: ALGEBRA:

TOPICS COVERED:

- Algebraic Expressions

- Algebraic Factoring

- Linear Equations

- Unsolvable Equations

- Multiple Equations

- Quadratic Equations

- Inequalities

- Functions

PRACTICE EXERCISE:

ALGEBRAIC EXPRESSIONS:

Question #1: If $p \neq q$ and $n = \dfrac{p-q}{p+q}$, then what is the value of $n + 1$?

Question #2: Simplify $\dfrac{xy + yz + xz}{\dfrac{1}{x} + \dfrac{1}{y} + \dfrac{1}{z}}$

ALGEBRAIC FACTORING:

Question #3: Simplify: $\left(1+\sqrt{2}\right)\left(1-\sqrt{2}\right)\left(\sqrt{9}+1\right)\left(\sqrt{9}-1\right)$

Question #4: Simplify: $\left(\dfrac{1}{n}+n\right)^2 - \left(\dfrac{1}{n}-n\right)^2$

Question #5: If $x > 49$, simplify $\dfrac{x - 5\sqrt{x} - 14}{\sqrt{x} - 7}$

Question #6: Simplify: $\dfrac{x^2 - y^2}{y^2 - x^2} + \dfrac{x-y}{y-x}$

LINEAR EQUATIONS:

Question #7: If $x > 0$ and $\dfrac{1}{x} - \dfrac{1}{x+1} = \dfrac{1}{x+25}$, then what is the value of x?

Question #8: If $\dfrac{pq}{r} = z$, $\dfrac{st}{u} = z$, $s = 5p$, $r = 2u$, and $t = nq$, then what is the value of n?

Question #9: If $2^n + 2^n + 2^n + 2^n = 2^8$, then what is the value of n?

Question #10: If $2^n + 2^n + 2^n + 2^n + 2^n + 2^n + 2^n + 2^n = 2^8$, then what is the value of n?

Question #11: What is the value of n if $3^{10} \times 27^2 = 9^2 \times 3^n$?

Question #12: If $50^{100} = p(100^{50})$, then what is the value of p?

Question #13: If $5^{7x} + 5^{7x} + 5^{7x} + 5^{7x} + 5^{7x} = \left(\dfrac{1}{5}\right)^{2x}$, then what is the value of x?

Question #14: If $\left(\dfrac{1}{2}\right)^x = (128)^{x-1}$, , then what is the value of x?

Question #15: If $(64^x)(2^5) = \left(\dfrac{1}{2}\right)^x$, , then what is the value of x?

Question #16:   If $\left(\dfrac{2}{5}\right)^n = \sqrt{\left(\dfrac{5}{2}\right)^3}$, then what is the value of n?

Question #17:   If $x^{-\frac{2}{3}} = 25$, then what is the value of x?

Question #18:   If $\dfrac{125^{\frac{2}{3}}}{x^5} = 200x^{-6}$, then what is the value of x?

Question #19:   If $x = 7y + 9z - 11$, what will happen to the value of x, if the value of y increases by 2 and the value of z decreases by 1?

Question #20:   If $x = 10 + (y - 5)^2$, then what is the value of y when x has the smallest possible value?

UNSOLVABLE EQUATIONS:

Question #21:   If $x + \dfrac{1}{x} = 10$, then what is the value of $x^2 + \dfrac{1}{x^2}$?

Question #22:   If $(x + y)^{\frac{1}{2}} = (x - y)^{-\frac{1}{2}}$, then what is the value of $x^2 - y^2$?

Question #23:   If $x + 5y = p$ and $x - 5y = q$, then what is the value of xy?

Question #24:   If $\dfrac{0.0018 \times 10^m}{0.02 \times 10^n} = 9 \times 10^9$, then what is the value of $(m - n)^2$?

Question #25:   If $\dfrac{x - 2}{x - 5} = x$, then what is the value of $x^2 - 6x + 10$?

Question #26:   If $n \neq 0$ and $n - \dfrac{2 - 5n^2}{n} = \dfrac{x}{n}$, then what is the value of x in terms of n?

Question #27:   If $x = 2a + 6$ and $y = 20a^2$, then what is the value of y in terms of x?

Question #28:   If $z > 0$ and $\dfrac{m}{n} = x - \dfrac{y}{z}$, then what is the value of $\dfrac{n}{m}$?

Question #29:   If the sum of x, y, and z is twice the sum of x minus y and x minus z, than what is the value of x in terms of y and z?

Question #30:   If $s = \dfrac{r - q}{p - q}$, then what is the value of q in terms of p, r, and s?

MULTIPLE LINEAR EQUATIONS:

Question #31:   If $p + q = r$ and $p - q = s$, then, in terms of r and s, what is the value of $4pq$?

Question #32:   If $x(5x + 1) = 0$ and $\left(x + \dfrac{1}{5}\right)(5x - 10) = 0$, then what is value of x?

Question #33:   If $x = \dfrac{10}{5z+7}$ and $xy = \dfrac{2}{5z+7}$, then what is the value of y?

Question #34:   If $(5^x)(5^y) = 625$ and $(2^x)(4^y) = 64$, then what is the value of (x, y)?

Question #35:   If x, y, and z are positive numbers such that $2x = 5y = 9z$, and if $x + y = kz$, what is the value of k?

QUADRATIC EQUATIONS:

Question #36:   If $(x - 12)$ is a factor of $x^2 - kx - 60$, then what is the value of k?

Question #37:   If 2 is one solution of the equation $x^2 + 5x + k = 20$, where k is a constant, what is the other solution?

INEQUALITIES:

Question #38:   What is the largest integer, n, that satisfies the inequality $n^2 + 8n - 2 < n^2 + 7n + 9$?

Question #39:   What is the solution to $\dfrac{x-9}{x+7} < -1$?

FUNCTIONS:

Question #40:   If $f(x) = \dfrac{1}{x+1}$, then what is the value of $f\left(\dfrac{1}{x+1}\right)$?

Question #41:   If $f(x) = \dfrac{7}{x^2}$, then what is the value of $f\left(\dfrac{1}{2}\right) \times f\left(\dfrac{1}{x}\right)$?

Question #42:   If $f(x) = \dfrac{n}{2}$, then what is the value of $f(x^2) \div \left(f(x)\right)^2$?

Question #43:   If $f(x) = x + 1$, then what is the value of $\dfrac{1}{f(x)} \times f\left(\dfrac{1}{x}\right)$?

Question #44:   If $f(x)$ is defined as the greatest integer less than $\dfrac{x}{7}$, and $g(x)$ is defined as the least integer greater than $\dfrac{x}{7}$, then what is the value of $f(115) + g(60)$?

Question #45:   If $f(x) = x^2 - 7x - 10$ and $g(x) = f(x - 7)$, what is the positive root of the equation $f(x) = g(2)$?

Question #46:   If $f(n) = 2x + 12$, then for what value of n is it true that $5f(n) = f(2n)$?

Question #47:   Statistical and research analysis of a certain pharmaceutical company finds out that the company can expect to generate a revenue of n dollars per month if the average price of all its products, in dollars, is given by the following function: $r(n) = \dfrac{1050}{k+n}$, where k is a constant. If, according to the given function, the company's revenues are \$12 million in a month when the average price of its products was \$75, how much revenue can the company expect to generate, in millions of dollars, in a month, when it sets the average price of all its products to \$50?

Question #48:   The values of function $f(x)$ are shown below in the table. What is the value of $f(10)$?

x	−2	−1	0	1	2

| y | −17 | −9 | −1 | 7 | 15 |

Question #49: For a certain sports car, b feet, the braking distance for the car to come to a complete standstill is given by the function $b = \dfrac{(s^2 + 10s)}{150} + \dfrac{s}{10}$, where s is the speed of the car in miles per hour. According to this function, if the speed of the car is 90 miles per hour, what would be the braking distance?

Question #50: For a certain sports car, b feet, the braking distance for the car to come to a complete standstill is given by the function $b = \dfrac{(s^2 + 10s)}{150}$, where s is the speed of the car in miles per hour. According to this function, if the braking distance of the car is 60 feet, what would be its speed?

PRACTICE EXERCISE – QUESTIONS & ANSWERS WITH EXPLANATIONS:

ALGEBRAIC EXPRESSIONS:

Question #1: If $p \neq q$ and $n = \dfrac{p-q}{p+q}$, then what is the value of $n + 1$?

Solution:

$\Rightarrow n = \dfrac{p-q}{p+q}$ [Given]

$\Rightarrow n + 1 = \dfrac{p-q}{p+q} + 1$ [Add 1 to both sides]

$\Rightarrow n + 1 = \dfrac{p-q}{p+q} + \dfrac{p+q}{p+q}$ [Scale up the fraction on right side to the LCD]

$\Rightarrow n + 1 = \dfrac{(p-q)+(p+q)}{p+q}$ [Add the fractions with the common denominator]

$\Rightarrow n + 1 = \dfrac{2p}{p+q}$ [Combine like-terms]

Question #2: Simplify $\dfrac{xy + yz + xz}{\dfrac{1}{x} + \dfrac{1}{y} + \dfrac{1}{z}}$

Solution:

$\Rightarrow \dfrac{xy + yz + xz}{\dfrac{yz}{xyz} + \dfrac{xz}{xyz} + \dfrac{xy}{xyz}}$ [Scale-Up the fractions in the denominator by using xyz as the LCD]

$\Rightarrow \dfrac{xy + yz + xz}{\dfrac{yz + xz + xy}{xyz}}$ [Combine the fractions in the denominator]

$\Rightarrow (xy + yz + xz) \div \dfrac{yz + xz + xy}{xyz}$ [Divide the numerator by the fraction in the denominator]

$\Rightarrow (xy + yz + xz) \dfrac{xyz}{yz + xz + xy}$ [Change the division sign to multiplication and invert the fraction]

$\Rightarrow xyz$ [Cancel-out the common terms]

ALGEBRAIC FACTORING:

Question #3: Simplify: $\left(1 + \sqrt{2}\right)\left(1 - \sqrt{2}\right)\left(\sqrt{9} + 1\right)\left(\sqrt{9} - 1\right)$

Solution:

$\Rightarrow \left(1 + \sqrt{2}\right)\left(1 - \sqrt{2}\right)\left(\sqrt{9} + 1\right)\left(\sqrt{9} - 1\right)$ [Given]

$\Rightarrow \left[\left(1 + \sqrt{2}\right)\left(1 - \sqrt{2}\right)\right]\left[\left(\sqrt{9} + 1\right)\left(\sqrt{9} - 1\right)\right]$ [Rewrite the terms separated in two brackets]

$\Rightarrow \left[1^2 - \left(\sqrt{2}\right)^2\right]\left[\left(\sqrt{9}\right)^2 - 1^2\right]$ [Factor $(a + b)(a - b) = a^2 - b^2$]

$\Rightarrow (1 - 2)(9 - 1)$ [Apply the rules of exponents]

$\Rightarrow (-1)(8)$ [Combine like-terms within parentheses]

$\Rightarrow -8$ [Apply distributive property]

Question #4: Simplify: $\left(\dfrac{1}{n} + n\right)^2 - \left(\dfrac{1}{n} - n\right)^2$

Solution: $\Rightarrow \left(\dfrac{1}{n}+n\right)^2 - \left(\dfrac{1}{n}-n\right)^2$ [Given]

$\Rightarrow \left[\left(\dfrac{1}{n}+n\right)+\left(\dfrac{1}{n}-n\right)\right]\left[\left(\dfrac{1}{n}+n\right)-\left(\dfrac{1}{n}-n\right)\right]$ [Expand $a^2 - b^2 = (a+b)(a-b)$]

$\Rightarrow \left(\dfrac{2}{n}\right)(2n)$ [Factor $(a+b)(a-b) = a^2 - b^2$]

$\Rightarrow 4$ [Cancel-out common terms]

Question #5: If $x > 49$, simplify $\dfrac{x - 5\sqrt{x} - 14}{\sqrt{x} - 7}$

Solution: $\Rightarrow \dfrac{x - 5\sqrt{x} - 14}{\sqrt{x} - 7}$ [Given]

$\Rightarrow \dfrac{\left(\sqrt{x}+2\right)\left(\sqrt{x}-7\right)}{\sqrt{x}-7}$ [Factor out the trinomial in the numerator into two binomials]

$\Rightarrow \sqrt{x} + 2$ [Cancel-out the common terms in the numerator and denominator]

Question #6: Simplify: $\dfrac{x^2 - y^2}{y^2 - x^2} + \dfrac{x - y}{y - x}$

Solution: $\Rightarrow \dfrac{x^2 - y^2}{y^2 - x^2} + \dfrac{x - y}{y - x}$ [Given]

$\Rightarrow \dfrac{(x+y)(x-y)}{(y+x)(y-x)} + \dfrac{x-y}{y-x}$ [Expand $a^2 - b^2 = (a+b)(a-b)$]

$\Rightarrow \dfrac{x-y}{y-x} + \dfrac{x-y}{y-x}$ [Cancel-out the common terms in the numerator and denominator]

$\Rightarrow \dfrac{x-y+x-y}{y-x}$ [Combine like-denominator fractions]

$\Rightarrow \dfrac{2x-2y}{y-x}$ [Combine like-terms]

$\Rightarrow \dfrac{2(x-y)}{(y-x)}$ [Factor out common terms in the numerator and denominator]

$\Rightarrow \dfrac{-2(x-y)}{(x-y)}$ [Multiply the numerator and denominator by –1]

$\Rightarrow -2$ [Cancel-out the common terms in the numerator and denominator]

LINEAR EQUATIONS:

Question #7: If $x > 0$ and $\dfrac{1}{x} - \dfrac{1}{x+1} = \dfrac{1}{x+25}$, then what is the value of x?

Solution: $\Rightarrow \dfrac{1}{x} - \dfrac{1}{x+1} = \dfrac{1}{x+25}$

$\Rightarrow \dfrac{(x)(x+1)(x+25)}{x} - \dfrac{(x)(x+1)(x+25)}{x+1} = \dfrac{(x)(x+1)(x+25)}{x+25}$ [Multiply all fractions by $(x+1)(x+25)$]

$\Rightarrow (x+1)(x+25) - (x)(x+25) = (x)(x+1)$ [Cancel-out the common factors]

$\Rightarrow (x+25)(x+1-x) = (x)(x+1)$ [Combine common factors]

$\Rightarrow (x+25)(1) = (x)(x+1)$ [Combine like terms]

$\Rightarrow x+25 = x^2 + x$ [Apply distributive property]

$\Rightarrow x^2 = 25$ [Subtract x from both sides]

$\Rightarrow x = \pm 5$ [Square root both sides]
Since $x > 0$, $x = +5$

Question #8: If $\dfrac{pq}{r} = z$, $\dfrac{st}{u} = z$, $s = 5p$, $r = 2u$, and $t = nq$, then what is the value of n?

Solution: Since $\dfrac{pq}{r} = z$ and $\dfrac{st}{u} = z \Rightarrow \dfrac{pq}{r} = \dfrac{st}{u}$

$\Rightarrow pqu = rst$ [Cross-multiply]
$\Rightarrow pqu = (2u)(5p)(nq)$ [Substitute $s = 5p$, $r = 2u$, and $t = nq$]
$\Rightarrow pqu = 10pqun$ [Combine terms]
$\Rightarrow 10n = 1$ [Cancel-out common terms, p, q, and u]
$\Rightarrow n = 1 \div 10 = 0.10$ [Divide both sides by 10]

Question #9: If $2^n + 2^n + 2^n + 2^n = 2^8$, then what is the value of n?
Solution: $\Rightarrow 2^n + 2^n + 2^n + 2^n = 2^8$ [Given]
$\Rightarrow 2^n(1 + 1 + 1 + 1) = 2^8$ [Factor the left side]
$\Rightarrow 2^n(4) = 2^8$ [Combine like-terms]
$\Rightarrow 2^n(4) = 256$ [Expand the exponent on the right side]
$\Rightarrow 2^n = 64$ [Divide both sides by 4]
$\Rightarrow 2^n = 2^6$ [Rewrite the exponents so that they have the same base]
$\Rightarrow n = 6$ [Since both sides have the same base, equate the powers]

Question #10: If $2^n + 2^n + 2^n + 2^n + 2^n + 2^n + 2^n + 2^n = 2^8$, then what is the value of n?
Solution: $\Rightarrow 2^n + 2^n + 2^n + 2^n + 2^n + 2^n + 2^n + 2^n = 2^8$ [Given]
$\Rightarrow 2^n(1 + 1 + 1 + 1 + 1 + 1 + 1 + 1) = 2^8$ [Factor the left side]
$\Rightarrow 2^n(8) = 2^8$ [Combine like-terms]
$\Rightarrow 2^n(8) = 256$ [Expand the exponent on the right side]
$\Rightarrow 2^n = 32$ [Divide both sides by 8]
$\Rightarrow 2^n = 2^5$ [Rewrite the exponents so that they have the same base]
$\Rightarrow n = 5$ [Since both sides have the same base, equate the powers]

Question #11: What is the value of n if $3^{10} \times 27^2 = 9^2 \times 3^n$?
Solution: $\Rightarrow 3^{10} \times (3^3)^2 = (3^2)^2 \times 3^n$ [Write each term so that all terms have the same base]
$\Rightarrow 3^{10} \times 3^6 = 3^4 \times 3^n$ [Apply distributive property in the exponents]
$\Rightarrow 3^{10+6} = 3^{4+n}$ [Combine terms on each side by using laws of exponents]
$\Rightarrow 3^{16} = 3^{4+n}$ [Combine terms in the exponents]
$\Rightarrow 16 = 4 + n$ [Since the bases are same, equate the exponents]
$\Rightarrow n = 12$ [Subtract 4 from both sides]

Question #12: If $50^{100} = p(100^{50})$, then what is the value of p?
Solution: $\Rightarrow 50^{100} = p(100^{50})$ [Given]
$\Rightarrow (50^{50})(50^{50}) = p(2^{50})(50^{50})$ [Spilt the exponential terms on both sides]

$\Rightarrow p = \dfrac{(50^{50})(50^{50})}{(2^{50})(50^{50})}$ [Divide both sides by $(2^{50})(50^{50})$]

$\Rightarrow p = \dfrac{(50^{50})}{(2^{50})}$ [Cancel-out common terms in the numerator/denominator]

$\Rightarrow p = \dfrac{(25^{50})(2^{50})}{(2^{50})}$ [Factor the numerator]

$\Rightarrow p = 25^{50}$ [Cancel-out common terms in the numerator/denominator]

Question #13: If $5^{7x} + 5^{7x} + 5^{7x} + 5^{7x} + 5^{7x} = \left(\dfrac{1}{5}\right)^{2x}$, then what is the value of x?

Solution:

$\Rightarrow 5^{7x} + 5^{7x} + 5^{7x} + 5^{7x} + 5^{7x} = \left(\dfrac{1}{5}\right)^{2x}$ [Given]

$\Rightarrow 5(5^{7x}) = (5^{-1})^{2x}$ [Combine terms on each side by using laws of exponents]

$\Rightarrow 5^1(5^{7x}) = (5^{-1})^{2x}$ [Write each term so that all terms have the same base]

$\Rightarrow 5^{1+7x} = 5^{-2x}$ [Combine terms on each side by using laws of exponents]

$\Rightarrow 1 + 7x = -2x$ [Combine terms in the exponents]

$\Rightarrow 7x = -2x - 1$ [Subtract 1 from both sides]

$\Rightarrow 9x = -1$ [Add 2x to both sides]

$\Rightarrow x = -\dfrac{1}{9}$ [Divide both sides by 9]

Question #14: If $\left(\dfrac{1}{2}\right)^x = (128)^{x-1}$, , then what is the value of x?

Solution:

$\Rightarrow \left(\dfrac{1}{2}\right)^x = (128)^{x-1}$ [Given]

$\Rightarrow (2^{-1})^x = (2^7)^{x-1}$ [Write each term so that all terms have the same base]

$\Rightarrow 2^{-x} = 2^{7x-7}$ [Apply distributive property in the exponents]

$\Rightarrow -x = 7x - 7$ [Since the bases are same, equate the exponents]

$\Rightarrow -8x = -7$ [Subtract 7x from both sides]

$\Rightarrow x = \dfrac{7}{8} = 0.875$ [Divide both sides by –8]

Question #15: If $(64^x)(2^5) = \left(\dfrac{1}{2}\right)^x$, , then what is the value of x?

Solution:

$\Rightarrow (64^x)(2^5) = \left(\dfrac{1}{2}\right)^x$ [Given]

$\Rightarrow (2^6)^x(2^5) = (2^{-1})^x$ [Write each term so that all terms have the same base]

$\Rightarrow (2^{6x})(2^5) = (2^{-x})$ [Apply distributive property in the exponents]

$\Rightarrow (2^{6x+5}) = (2^{-x})$ [Combine terms on each side by using laws of exponents]

$\Rightarrow 6x + 5 = -x$ [Since the bases are same, equate the exponents]

$\Rightarrow 6x = -x - 5$ [Subtract 5 from both sides]

$\Rightarrow 7x = -5$ [Add x to both sides]

$\Rightarrow x = -\dfrac{5}{7}$ [Divide both sides by 7]

Question #16: If $\left(\dfrac{2}{5}\right)^n = \sqrt{\left(\dfrac{5}{2}\right)^3}$, then what is the value of n?

Solution:

$\Rightarrow \left(\dfrac{2}{5}\right)^n = \sqrt{\left(\dfrac{5}{2}\right)^3}$ [Given]

$\Rightarrow \left(\dfrac{2}{5}\right)^n = \left[\left(\dfrac{5}{2}\right)^3\right]^{\frac{1}{2}}$ [Apply laws of radicals]

$\Rightarrow \left(\dfrac{2}{5}\right)^n = \left(\dfrac{5}{2}\right)^{\frac{3}{2}}$ [Apply distributive property of exponents]

$$\Rightarrow \left(\frac{2}{5}\right)^n = \left(\frac{2}{5}\right)^{-\frac{3}{2}}$$ [Rewrite the exponents so that they have the same base]

$$\Rightarrow n = -\frac{3}{2}$$ [Since both sides have the same base, equate the powers]

Question #17:   If $x^{-\frac{2}{3}} = 25$, then what is the value of x?

Solution: $\Rightarrow x^{-\frac{2}{3}} = 25$ [Given]

$$\Rightarrow \frac{1}{x^{\frac{2}{3}}} = 25$$ [Write the left side with a positive exponent]

$$\Rightarrow \frac{1}{\left(\sqrt[3]{x}\right)^2} = \frac{25}{1}$$ [Cube root the denominator in the left side]

$$\Rightarrow \frac{\left(\sqrt[3]{x}\right)^2}{1} = \frac{1}{25}$$ [Invert the fraction on both sides]

$$\Rightarrow \sqrt{\frac{\left(\sqrt[3]{x}\right)^2}{1}} = \sqrt{\frac{1}{25}}$$ [Square root both sides]

$$\Rightarrow \frac{\left(\sqrt[3]{x}\right)}{1} = \frac{1}{5}$$ [Solve the square root on both sides]

$$\Rightarrow \left(\frac{\left(\sqrt[3]{x}\right)}{1}\right)^3 = \left(\frac{1}{5}\right)^3$$ [Cube both sides]

$$\Rightarrow x = \frac{1}{125}$$ [Solve the cube on both sides]

Question #18:   If $\dfrac{125^{\frac{2}{3}}}{x^5} = 200x^{-6}$, then what is the value of x?

Solution: $\Rightarrow \dfrac{125^{\frac{2}{3}}}{x^5} = 200x^{-6}$ [Given]

$$\Rightarrow \frac{\left(\sqrt[3]{125}\right)^2}{x^5} = 200x^{-6}$$ [Cube root the numerator on the left side]

$$\Rightarrow \frac{(5)^2}{x^5} = 200x^{-6}$$ [Solve the cube root on the left side]

$$\Rightarrow \frac{25}{x^5} = 200x^{-6}$$ [Square the numerator on the left side]

$\Rightarrow 25 = 200x^{-6} (x^5)$ [Cross multiply]
$\Rightarrow 25 = 200x^{-1}$ [Apply distributive property of exponents]

$$\Rightarrow 25 = \frac{200}{x^1}$$ [Rewrite the right side with a positive exponent]

$\Rightarrow 25x = 200$ [Cross multiply]
$\Rightarrow x = 8$ [Divide both sides by 25]

Question #19:   If $x = 7y + 9z - 11$, what will happen to the value of x, if the value of y increases by 2 and the value of z decreases by 1?

Solution: Original Equation: $\Rightarrow x = 7y + 9z - 11$

New Value of y $\Rightarrow (y + 2)$
New Value of z $\Rightarrow (z - 1)$
New Equation: $\Rightarrow x = 7(y + 2) + 9(z - 1) - 11$
                          $\Rightarrow x = 7y + 14 + 9z - 9 - 11$ [Apply distributive property]
                          $\Rightarrow x = 7y + 9z - 6$ [Combine like-terms]
Compare the new and old equation:
$\Rightarrow x = 7y + 9z - 6$ and $\Rightarrow x = 7y + 9z - 11$
Change in value of $x \Rightarrow 7y + 9z - 6 - (7y + 9z - 11)$ [Subtract the second one from the first one]
                          $\Rightarrow -6 - (-11) = -6 + 11 = 5$ [Combine like-terms]
Therefore, the value of x will increase by 5.

Question #20: If $x = 10 + (y - 5)^2$, then what is the value of y when x has the smallest possible value?
Solution: In order to have the smallest possible value for x, the value of $(y - 5)^2$ must be the least possible. Since the square of any number or expression is always positive, the least value that $(y - 5)^2$ can have is 0.
$\Rightarrow (y - 5)^2 = 0$
$\Rightarrow y - 5 = 0$ [Square root both sides]
$\Rightarrow y = 5$ [Add 5 to both sides]
The expression $(y - 5)^2$ will have a zero value when $y = 5$.
$\Rightarrow x = 10 + (5 - 5)^2 = 10 + 0 = 10$

UNSOLVABLE EQUATIONS:

Question #21: If $x + \dfrac{1}{x} = 10$, then what is the value of $x^2 + \dfrac{1}{x^2}$?

Solution: $\Rightarrow x + \dfrac{1}{x} = 10$ [Given]

$\Rightarrow \left(x + \dfrac{1}{x}\right)^2 = (10)^2$ [Square both sides]

$\Rightarrow (x)^2 + \left(\dfrac{1}{x}\right)^2 + 2(x)\left(\dfrac{1}{x}\right) = 100$ [Expand $(a + b)^2 = a^2 + b^2 + 2ab$]

$\Rightarrow x^2 + \dfrac{1}{x^2} + 2 = 100$ [Apply distributive property]

$\Rightarrow x^2 + \dfrac{1}{x^2} = 100 - 2 = 98$ [Subtract 2 from both sides]

Question #22: If $\left(x + y\right)^{\frac{1}{2}} = \left(x - y\right)^{-\frac{1}{2}}$, then what is the value of $x^2 - y^2$?

Solution: $\Rightarrow \left(x + y\right)^{\frac{1}{2}} = \left(x - y\right)^{-\frac{1}{2}}$ [Given]

$\Rightarrow \left[\left(x + y\right)^{\frac{1}{2}}\right]^2 = \left[\left(x - y\right)^{-\frac{1}{2}}\right]^2$ [Square both sides]

$\Rightarrow x + y = (x - y)^{-1}$ [Take the square of both sides]

$\Rightarrow x + y = \dfrac{1}{x - y}$ [Write the right side with positive exponent]

$\Rightarrow (x + y)(x - y) = 1$ [Cross multiply]
$\Rightarrow x^2 - y^2 = 1$ [Combine $(a + b)(a - b) = a^2 - b^2$]

Question #23: If $x + 5y = p$ and $x - 5y = q$, then what is the value of xy?
Solution: Add the two given equations:
$\quad\quad x + 5y = p$ $\Rightarrow$ Equation #1
$\underline{+\quad x - 5y = q}$ $\Rightarrow$ Equation #2
$\quad\quad 2x \quad\quad = p + q$ [Add both equations]

$$x = \frac{p+q}{2}$$ [Divide both sides by 2]

Substitute the value of x in Equation #1

$\Rightarrow x + 5y = p$ [Rewrite Equation #1]

$\Rightarrow \dfrac{p+q}{2} + 5y = p$ [Substitute the value of x from above]

$\Rightarrow 5y = p - \dfrac{p+q}{2}$ [Isolate $5y$ on left side]

$\Rightarrow 5y = \dfrac{2p}{2} - \dfrac{p+q}{2}$ [Scale up the fractions to their LCD]

$\Rightarrow 5y = \dfrac{2p - p - q}{2}$ [Combine like-fractions]

$\Rightarrow 5y = \dfrac{p-q}{2}$ [Combine like-terms]

$\Rightarrow y = \dfrac{p-q}{10}$ [Divide both sides by 5]

Value of $xy \Rightarrow \left(\dfrac{p+q}{2}\right)\left(\dfrac{p-q}{10}\right)$ [Substitute the value of x and y from above]

$\Rightarrow \dfrac{(p+q)(p-q)}{(2)(10)}$ [Multiply the numerator and denominator of the fractions]

$\Rightarrow \dfrac{p^2 - q^2}{20}$ [Simplify the fraction by using laws of factoring]

Question #24:   If $\dfrac{0.0018 \times 10^m}{0.02 \times 10^n} = 9 \times 10^9$, then what is the value of $(m-n)^2$?

Solution: $\Rightarrow \dfrac{0.0018 \times 10^m}{0.02 \times 10^n} = 9 \times 10^9$ [Given]

$\Rightarrow \dfrac{0.0018}{0.02} \times \dfrac{10^m}{10^n} = 9 \times 10^9$ [Separate the numerical and variable part on the left side]

$\Rightarrow 0.09 \times 10^{m-n} = 9 \times 10^9$ [Divide the fraction on the left side by using laws of exponents]

$\Rightarrow 9 \times 10^{-2} \times 10^{m-n} = 9 \times 10^9$ [Convert 0.09 into exponential form]

$\Rightarrow 9 \times 10^{m-n-2} = 9 \times 10^9$ [Combine exponents with terms that have the same base]

$\Rightarrow 10^{m-n-2} = 10^9$ [Divide both sides by 9]

$\Rightarrow m - n - 2 = 9$ [Since the base on both sides are the same, equate the exponents]

$\Rightarrow m - n = 11$ [Add 2 to both sides]

$\Rightarrow (m-n)^2 = 121$ [Square both sides]

Question #25:   If $\dfrac{x-2}{x-5} = x$, then what is the value of $x^2 - 6x + 10$?

Solution: $\Rightarrow \dfrac{x-2}{x-5} = x$ [Given]

$\Rightarrow x(x-5) = x - 2$ [Cross multiply]

$\Rightarrow x^2 - 5x = x - 2$ [Apply distributive property]

$\Rightarrow x^2 - 6x = -2$ [Subtract x from both sides]

$\Rightarrow x^2 - 6x + 2 = 0$ [Add 2 to both sides]

Value of $x^2 - 6x + 10 \Rightarrow (x^2 - 6x + 2) + 8$ [Split the algebraic expression]

$\Rightarrow 0 + 8 = 8$ [Substitute $x^2 - 6x + 2 = 0$]

Question #26:   If $n \neq 0$ and $n - \dfrac{2 - 5n^2}{n} = \dfrac{x}{n}$, then what is the value of x in terms of n?

Solution:

$$n - \frac{2 - 5n^2}{n} = \frac{x}{n} \qquad \text{[Given]}$$

$$\Rightarrow (n)n - (n)\frac{2 - 5n^2}{n} = (n)\frac{x}{n} \qquad \text{[Multiply both sides by } n\text{]}$$

$$\Rightarrow n^2 - (2 - 5n^2) = x \qquad \text{[Apply distributive property]}$$

$$\Rightarrow n^2 - 2 + 5n^2 = x \qquad \text{[Remove the parentheses]}$$

$$\Rightarrow x = 6n^2 - 2 \qquad \text{[Combine like-terms]}$$

Question #27: If $x = 2a + 6$ and $y = 20a^2$, then what is the value of y in terms of x?

Solution:

$$\Rightarrow x = 2a + 6 \qquad \text{[Given]}$$

$$\Rightarrow x - 6 = 2a \qquad \text{[Subtract 6 from both sides]}$$

$$\Rightarrow a = \frac{x - 6}{2} \qquad \text{[Divide both sides by 2]}$$

$$\Rightarrow y = 20a^2 \qquad \text{[Given]}$$

$$\Rightarrow y = 20\left(\frac{x - 6}{2}\right)^2 \qquad \text{[Substitute the value of } a\text{]}$$

$$\Rightarrow y = 20\left(\frac{(x - 6)^2}{4}\right) \qquad \text{[Take the square of the fraction on the right side]}$$

$$\Rightarrow y = 5(x - 6)^2 \qquad \text{[Apply distributive property]}$$

Question #28: If $z > 0$ and $\frac{m}{n} = x - \frac{y}{z}$, then what is the value of $\frac{n}{m}$?

Solution:

$$\Rightarrow \frac{m}{n} = x - \frac{y}{z} \qquad \text{[Given]}$$

$$\Rightarrow \frac{m}{n} = \frac{xz}{z} - \frac{y}{z} \qquad \text{[Scale-Up the fraction on the right side by using } z \text{ as the LCD]}$$

$$\Rightarrow \frac{m}{n} = \frac{xz - y}{z} \qquad \text{[Combine the fractions on the right side]}$$

$$\Rightarrow \frac{n}{m} = \frac{z}{xz - y} \qquad \text{[Invert both fractions to find their reciprocals]}$$

Question #29: If the sum of x, y, and z is twice the sum of x minus y and x minus z, than what is the value of x in terms of y and z?

Solution:

$$\Rightarrow x + y + z = 2[(x - y) + (x - z)]$$

$$\Rightarrow x + y + z = 2[2x - y - z] \qquad \text{[Combine like-terms]}$$

$$\Rightarrow x + y + z = 4x - 2y - 2z \qquad \text{[Apply distributive property]}$$

$$\Rightarrow x = 4x - 3y - 3z \qquad \text{[Subtract } y + z \text{ from both sides]}$$

$$\Rightarrow -3x = -3y - 3z \qquad \text{[Subtract } 4x \text{ from both sides]}$$

$$\Rightarrow 3x = 3y + 3z \qquad \text{[Multiply both sides by } -1\text{]}$$

$$\Rightarrow 3x = 3(y + z) \qquad \text{[Factor out 3 from the right side]}$$

$$\Rightarrow x = y + z \qquad \text{[Divide both sides by 3]}$$

Question #30: If $s = \frac{r - q}{p - q}$, then what is the value of q in terms of p, r, and s?

Solution:

$$\Rightarrow \frac{s}{1} = \frac{r - q}{p - q} \qquad \text{[Given]}$$

$$\Rightarrow s(p - q) = r - q \qquad \text{[Cross multiply]}$$

$$\Rightarrow ps - qs = r - q \qquad \text{[Apply distributive property]}$$

$$\Rightarrow ps - qs - r = -q \qquad \text{[Subtract } r \text{ from both sides]}$$

$$\Rightarrow ps - r = qs - q \qquad \text{[Add } qs \text{ to both sides]}$$

$$\Rightarrow ps - r = q(s - 1) \qquad \text{[Factor out } q \text{ on the right side]}$$

$$\Rightarrow q = \frac{ps - r}{s - 1} \qquad\qquad \text{[Divide both sides by } (s - 1)\text{]}$$

MULTIPLE LINEAR EQUATIONS:

Question #31:   If $p + q = r$ and $p - q = s$, then, in terms of r and s, what is the value of $4pq$?

Solution: Solve the two given equation simultaneously by adding them:

$$
\begin{array}{rcll}
p + q & = & r & \Rightarrow \text{Equation \#1} \\
+\quad p - q & = & s & \Rightarrow \text{Equation \#2} \\
\hline
2p & = & r + s & \\
p & = & \dfrac{r + s}{2} & \Rightarrow \text{Equation \#3}
\end{array}
$$

Substitute the value of p from Equation #3 into Equation #1 and solve for q:

$$\Rightarrow p + q = r \qquad\qquad \text{[Equation \#1]}$$

$$\Rightarrow \frac{r + s}{2} + q = r \qquad\qquad \text{[Substitute the value of } p \text{ from Equation \#3]}$$

$$\Rightarrow q = r - \frac{r + s}{2} \qquad\qquad \text{[Subtract } (r + s)/2 \text{ from both sides]}$$

$$\Rightarrow q = \frac{2r}{2} - \frac{r + s}{2} \qquad\qquad \text{[Scale up the fractions on the right to their LCD, which is 2]}$$

$$\Rightarrow q = \frac{2r - r - s}{2} = \frac{r - s}{2} \qquad\qquad \text{[Combine like-terms]} \qquad \Rightarrow \text{Equation \#4}$$

Find the value of $4pq$, by substituting the value of p from Equation #3 and q from Equation #4:

$$\Rightarrow 4pq = 4\left(\frac{r + s}{2}\right)\left(\frac{r - s}{2}\right)$$

$$\Rightarrow 4pq = \frac{4(r + s)(r - s)}{4} \qquad\qquad \text{[Apply distributive property]}$$

$$\Rightarrow 4pq = (r + s)(r - s) \qquad\qquad \text{[Cancel-out common terms]}$$

$$\Rightarrow 4pq = r^2 - s^2 \qquad\qquad \text{[factor out right side]}$$

Question #32:   If $x(5x + 1) = 0$ and $\left(x + \dfrac{1}{5}\right)(5x - 10) = 0$, then what is value of x?

Solution: Simplify the first equation $\Rightarrow x(5x + 1) = 0$
$\Rightarrow 5x^2 + x = 0$ [Apply distributive property] $\Rightarrow$ Equation #1

Simplify the second equation $\Rightarrow \left(x + \dfrac{1}{5}\right)(5x - 10) = 0$

$\Rightarrow 5x^2 - 10x + x - 2 = 0$ [Apply distributive property]
$\Rightarrow 5x^2 - 9x - 2 = 0$ [Combine like-terms] $\Rightarrow$ Equation #2

Subtract Equation #1 from Equation #2:

$$
\begin{array}{rll}
5x^2 - 9x - 2 = 0 & \text{[Rewrite Equation \#2]} \\
-\quad (5x^2 + x \quad\;\; = 0) & \text{[Rewrite Equation \#1]} \\
\hline
\Rightarrow \qquad -10x - 2 = 0 & \\
\end{array}
$$

$$\Rightarrow -10x = 2 \qquad\qquad \text{[Add 2 to both sides]}$$

$$\Rightarrow x = -\frac{2}{10} = -\frac{1}{5} \qquad\qquad \text{[Divide both sides by } -10\text{]}$$

Question #33:   If $x = \dfrac{10}{5z + 7}$ and $xy = \dfrac{2}{5z + 7}$, then what is the value of y?

Solution:

$$\Rightarrow xy = \frac{2}{5z + 7} \qquad\qquad \Rightarrow \text{Equation \#1}$$

$$\Rightarrow x = \frac{10}{5z + 7} \qquad\qquad \Rightarrow \text{Equation \#2}$$

$$\Rightarrow \frac{xy}{x} = \frac{\dfrac{2}{5z+7}}{\dfrac{10}{5z+7}}$$ [Divide Equation #1 by Equation #2]

$$\Rightarrow y = \left(\frac{2}{5z+7}\right) \times \left(\frac{5z+7}{10}\right)$$ [Switch to multiplication & flip the fraction in denominator]

$$\Rightarrow y = \frac{2}{10}$$ [Cancel-out common terms]

$$\Rightarrow y = \frac{1}{5}$$ [Reduce the fraction to its lowest terms]

Question #34: If $(5^x)(5^y) = 625$ and $(2^x)(4^y) = 64$, then what is the value of (x, y)?
Solution: Simplify the first equation:
$\Rightarrow (5^x)(5^y) = 625$ $\Rightarrow$ Equation #1
$\Rightarrow (5^x)(5^y) = (5^4)$ [Convert all terms into exponential form]
$\Rightarrow (5^{x+y}) = (5^4)$ [Combine exponents with terms that have the same base]
$\Rightarrow x + y = 4$ [Since the base on both sides are the same, equate the exponents]
Simplify the second equation:
$\Rightarrow (2^x)(4^y) = 64$ $\Rightarrow$ Equation #2
$\Rightarrow (2^x)(2^{2y}) = (2^6)$ [Convert all terms into exponential form]
$\Rightarrow (2^{x+2y}) = (2^6)$ [Combine exponents with terms that have the same base]
$\Rightarrow x + 2y = 6$ [Since the base on both sides are the same, equate the exponents]
Subtract first equation from the second equation:

$$\begin{array}{r} x + 2y = 6 \\ -\underline{(x + y = 4)} \\ y = 2 \end{array}$$

Substitute the value of $y = 2$ in the first equation to solve for x:
$\Rightarrow x + y = 4$
$\Rightarrow x + 2 = 4$
$\Rightarrow x = 2$
Therefore, the value of $(x, y) = (2, 2)$

Question #35: If x, y, and z are positive numbers such that $2x = 5y = 9z$, and if $x + y = kz$, what is the value of k?
Solution: Solve for x $\Rightarrow 2x = 9z$ [Given]

$$\Rightarrow x = \frac{9}{2}z$$ [Divide both sides by 2]

Solve for y $\Rightarrow 5y = 9z$ [Given]

$$\Rightarrow y = \frac{9}{5}z$$ [Divide both sides by 5]

Solve for k $\Rightarrow x + y = kz$ [Given]

$$\Rightarrow \frac{9}{2}z + \frac{9}{5}z = kz$$ [Substitute the value of x and y from above]

$$\Rightarrow \frac{45}{10}z + \frac{18}{10}z = kz$$ [Scale up the fraction on left side to their LCD]

$$\Rightarrow \frac{63}{10}z = kz$$ [Combine like-fractions]

$$\Rightarrow k = \frac{63}{10}$$ [Divide both sides by z]

QUADRATIC EQUATIONS:

Question #36: If $(x - 12)$ is a factor of $x^2 - kx - 60$, then what is the value of k?
Solution: Since $(x - 12)$ is a factor of the given trinomial $x^2 - kx - 60$, the given trinomial expression $x^2 - kx - 60$ can be written as the product of two binomials $(x - 12)$ and $(x + a)$:

Note: since the sign of the middle term of the trinomial is negative, the sign of the last term is negative, and the sign between one of the binomial factor is negative, the sign between the other binomial factor must be positive.

$\Rightarrow x^2 - kx - 60 \quad = (x - 12)(x + a)$ [Given]
$\Rightarrow x^2 - kx - 60 \quad = x^2 + ax - 12x - 12a$ [Apply distributive property]
$\Rightarrow x^2 - kx - 60 \quad = x^2 - (12 - a)x - 12a$ [Combine the x terms]

Compare the last terms of the above expressions:

$\Rightarrow -12a = -60$
$\Rightarrow a = 5$ [Divide both sides by -12]

Now, substitute the value of a in the binomial above:

$\Rightarrow x^2 - kx - 60 \quad = (x - 12)(x + 5)$ [Given]
$\Rightarrow x^2 - kx - 60 \quad = x^2 + 5x - 12x - 60$ [Apply distributive property]
$\Rightarrow x^2 - kx - 60 \quad = x^2 - 7x - 60$ [Combine the x terms]

Now again compare the middle terms of the above expressions:

$\Rightarrow -kx = -7x$
$\Rightarrow k = 7$ [Divide both sides by $-x$]

Question #37: If 2 is one solution of the equation $x^2 + 5x + k = 20$, where k is a constant, what is the other solution?
Solution: Since 2 is one solution of the equation, substitute $x = 2$ and solve for k:

$\Rightarrow x^2 + 5x + k = 20$ [Given]
$\Rightarrow (2)^2 + 5(2) + k = 20$ [Substitute $x = 2$]
$\Rightarrow 4 + 10 + k = 20$ [Apply distributive property]
$\Rightarrow 14 + k = 20$ [Combine the like-terms]
$\Rightarrow k = 6$ [Subtract 14 from both sides]

Now substitute $k = 6$ in the given equation and solve for x:

$\Rightarrow x^2 + 5x + k = 20$ [Given]
$\Rightarrow x^2 + 5x + 6 = 20$ [Substitute $k = 6$]
$\Rightarrow x^2 + 5x - 14 = 0$ [Subtract 20 from both sides]
$\Rightarrow (x + 7)(x - 2) = 0$ [Factor out the quadratic into two binomials]
$\Rightarrow x = -7$ or 2 [solve for x]

Therefore, the other solution is -7.

INEQUALITIES:

Question #38: What is the largest integer, n, that satisfies the inequality $n^2 + 8n - 2 < n^2 + 7n + 9$?
Solution:
$\Rightarrow n^2 + 8n - 2 < n^2 + 7n + 9$
$\Rightarrow 8n - 2 < 7n + 9$ [Subtract n^2 from both sides]
$\Rightarrow n - 2 < 9$ [Subtract $7n$ from both sides]
$\Rightarrow n < 11$ [Add 2 to both sides]

Therefore, the largest integer, n, that satisfies the given inequality is 10.

Question #39: What is the solution to $\dfrac{x - 9}{x + 7} < -1$?

Solution:
$\Rightarrow \dfrac{x - 9}{x + 7} < -1$ [Given]

$\Rightarrow \dfrac{x - 9}{x + 7} + 1 < -1 + 1$ [Add 1 to both sides]

$\Rightarrow \dfrac{x - 9}{x + 7} + 1 < 0$ [Combine like-terms]

$\Rightarrow \dfrac{x - 9}{x + 7} + \dfrac{x + 7}{x + 7} < 0$ [Scale-Up the fraction on the left side to get the LCD]

$\Rightarrow \dfrac{x - 9 + x + 7}{x + 7} < 0$ [Add the fractions on the left side]

$$\Rightarrow \frac{2x-2}{x+7} < 0 \qquad\qquad \text{[Combine like-terms]}$$

$$\Rightarrow \frac{2(x-1)}{x+7} < 0 \qquad\qquad \text{[Factor the numerator on the left side]}$$

$$\Rightarrow \frac{x-1}{x+7} < 0 \qquad\qquad \text{[Divide both sides by 2]}$$

For the above expression to be less than zero or negative, x must be greater than –7 and less than 1; any value outside this range will make the above inequality false by making the expression positive.

$$\Rightarrow -7 < x < 1$$

FUNCTIONS:

Question #40: If $f(x) = \dfrac{1}{x+1}$, then what is the value of $f\left(\dfrac{1}{x+1}\right)$?

Solution:

$$f(x) \qquad\qquad \Rightarrow \frac{1}{x+1} \qquad\qquad \text{[Given function]}$$

$$f\left(\frac{1}{x+1}\right) \qquad \Rightarrow \frac{1}{\dfrac{1}{x+1}+1} \qquad\qquad \text{[Find the value of the function when } x = 1/(x+1)]$$

$$\Rightarrow \frac{1}{\dfrac{1}{x+1}+\dfrac{x+1}{x+1}} \qquad\qquad \text{[Scale up the fractions in the denominator to LCD]}$$

$$\Rightarrow \frac{1}{\dfrac{1+(x+1)}{x+1}} \qquad\qquad \text{[Combine the like-fractions in the denominator]}$$

$$\Rightarrow \frac{1}{\dfrac{x+2}{x+1}} \qquad\qquad \text{[Combine like-terms]}$$

$$\Rightarrow \frac{x+1}{x+2} \qquad\qquad \text{[Divide the fraction in the denominator by 1]}$$

Question #41: If $f(x) = \dfrac{7}{x^2}$, then what is the value of $f\left(\dfrac{1}{2}\right) \times f\left(\dfrac{1}{x}\right)$?

Solution:

$$f(x) \qquad\qquad\qquad \Rightarrow \frac{7}{x^2} \qquad\qquad\qquad\qquad \text{[Given function]}$$

$$f\left(\frac{1}{2}\right) \qquad\qquad \Rightarrow \frac{7}{\left(\dfrac{1}{2}\right)^2} = \frac{7}{\dfrac{1}{4}} = 7 \div \frac{1}{4} = 7 \times 4 = 28 \qquad \text{[Find the value of the function when } x = \tfrac{1}{2}]$$

$$f\left(\frac{1}{x}\right) \qquad\qquad \Rightarrow \frac{7}{\left(\dfrac{1}{x}\right)^2} = \frac{7}{\dfrac{1}{x^2}} = 7 \div \frac{1}{x^2} = (7) \times (x^2) = 7x^2 \quad \text{[Find the value of the function when } x=1/x]$$

$$f\left(\frac{1}{2}\right) \times f\left(\frac{1}{x}\right) \quad \Rightarrow 28 \times 7x^2 = 196x^2 \qquad\qquad \text{[Find the product of the two functions]}$$

Question #42: If $f(x) = \dfrac{n}{2}$, then what is the value of $f(x^2) \div \left(f(x)\right)^2$?

Solution:

$$f(x) \qquad\qquad\qquad \Rightarrow \frac{n}{2} \qquad\qquad\qquad \text{[Given function]}$$

$f(x^2)$ $\Rightarrow \dfrac{n^2}{2}$ [Find the value of the function when $x = x^2$]

$(f(x))^2$ $\Rightarrow \left(\dfrac{n}{2}\right)^2 = \dfrac{n^2}{4}$ [Find the value of square of the function]

$f(x^2) \div (f(x))^2$ $\Rightarrow \dfrac{n^2}{2} \div \dfrac{n^2}{4} = \dfrac{n^2}{2} \times \dfrac{4}{n^2} = \dfrac{4}{2} = 2$ [Find the quotient of the two functions]

Question #43: If $f(x) = x + 1$, then what is the value of $\dfrac{1}{f(x)} \times f\left(\dfrac{1}{x}\right)$?

Solution:

$f(x)$ $\Rightarrow x + 1$ [Given function]

$\dfrac{1}{f(x)}$ $\Rightarrow \dfrac{1}{x+1}$ [Find the value of the reciprocal of the function]

$f\left(\dfrac{1}{x}\right)$ $\Rightarrow \dfrac{1}{x} + 1 = \dfrac{1+x}{x}$ [Find the value of the function when $x = 1/x$]

$\dfrac{1}{f(x)} \times f\left(\dfrac{1}{x}\right)$ $\Rightarrow \dfrac{1}{x+1} \times \dfrac{1+x}{x} = \dfrac{1}{x}$ [Find the product of the two functions]

Question #44: If $f(x)$ is defined as the greatest integer less than $\dfrac{x}{7}$, and $g(x)$ is defined as the least integer greater than $\dfrac{x}{7}$, then what is the value of $f(115) + g(60)$?

Solution: $f(x)$ is defined as the greatest integer less than $\dfrac{x}{7}$ $\Rightarrow f(115) < \dfrac{115}{7} < 16.5$ (approx) $\Rightarrow 16$

$g(x)$ is defined as the least integer greater than $\dfrac{x}{7}$ $\Rightarrow g(60) > \dfrac{60}{7} > 8.5$ (approx) $\Rightarrow 9$

$f(115) + g(60) = 16 + 9 = 25$

Question #45: If $f(x) = x^2 - 7x - 10$ and $g(x) = f(x - 7)$, what is the positive root of the equation $f(x) = g(2)$?
Solution:
$f(x)$ $\Rightarrow x^2 - 7x - 10$ [Given function]
$f(2 - 7) \Rightarrow f(-5)$
$\Rightarrow (-5)^2 - 7(-5) - 10 = 25 + 35 - 10 = 50$ [Find the value of the function]
$g(x) \Rightarrow f(x - 7)$ [Given function]
$g(2) \Rightarrow f(2 - 7) = f(-5) = 50$ [Find the value of the function]
EZ Problem Set-Up $\Rightarrow f(x) = g(2)$
$\Rightarrow x^2 - 7x - 10 = 50$ [Set up the equation]
$\Rightarrow x^2 - 7x - 60 = 0$ [Subtract 50 from both sides]
$\Rightarrow (x + 5)(x - 12)$ [Factor the trinomial into two binomials]
$\Rightarrow x = -5$ or 12 [Solve for the two values of x]
The positive root is 12

Question #46: If $f(n) = 2x + 12$, then for what value of n is it true that $5f(n) = f(2n)$?
Solution:
$f(n)$ $\Rightarrow 2x + 12$ [Given function]
$5f(n)$ $\Rightarrow 5(2n + 12) = 10n + 60$ [Find five times the value of the function]
$f(2n)$ $\Rightarrow 2(2n) + 12 = 4n + 12$ [Find the value of the function when $x = 2n$]
EZ Problem Set-Up $\Rightarrow 5f(n) = f(2n)$
$\Rightarrow 10n + 60 = 4n + 12$ [Set up the equation]
$\Rightarrow 6n + 60 = 12$ [Subtract $4n$ from both sides]
$\Rightarrow 6n = -48$ [Subtract 60 from both sides]
$\Rightarrow n = -8$ [Divide both sides by 6]

Question #47: Statistical and research analysis of a certain pharmaceutical company finds out that the company can expect to generate a revenue of n dollars per month if the average price of all its products, in dollars, is given by the following function: $r(n) = \dfrac{1050}{k+n}$, where k is a constant. If, according to the given function, the company's revenues are \$12 million in a month when the average price of its products was \$75, how much revenue can the company expect to generate, in millions of dollars, in a month, when it sets the average price of all its products to \$50?

Solution: Find the value of constant k, when profit = \$12 million and average price or $r(n)$ = \$75:

$\Rightarrow r(n) = \dfrac{1050}{k+n}$ [Given function]

$\Rightarrow 75 = \dfrac{1050}{k+12}$ [Substitute $r(n)$ = 75 and n = 12]

$\Rightarrow 75(k + 12) = 1050$ [Cross multiply]
$\Rightarrow 75K + 900 = 1050$ [Apply distributive property]
$\Rightarrow 75k = 150$ [Subtract 900 from both sides]
$\Rightarrow k = 2$ [Divide both sides by 75]

Now, the functions is $r(n) = \dfrac{1050}{2+n}$

Find the revenues, n, when the average price or $r(n)$ = \$50:

$\Rightarrow 50 = \dfrac{1050}{2+n}$ [Substitute $r(n)$ = 50 and k = 2]

$\Rightarrow 50(2 + n) = 1050$ [Cross multiply]
$\Rightarrow 100 + 50n = 1050$ [Apply distributive property]
$\Rightarrow 50n = 950$ [Subtract 100 from both sides]
$\Rightarrow n = \$19$ million   [Divide both sides by 50]

Question #48: The values of function $f(x)$ are shown below in the table. What is the value of $f(10)$?

x	−2	−1	0	1	2
y	−17	−9	−1	7	15

Solution: The y-intercept can be found when x = 0.
Since (0, −1) is a point on the graph, the y-intercept $\Rightarrow b$ = −1
The slope can be found by dividing the difference between the y-coordinates and x-coordinates.
Since the y-value goes up 8 units for every 1 unit that x-value goes up, the slope $\Rightarrow m$ = 8
Equation of $f(x)$ $\Rightarrow y = mx + b$
                    $\Rightarrow y = 8x − 1$
Value of $f(10)$ $\Rightarrow y = 8(10) − 1 = 80 − 1 = 79$

Question #49: For a certain sports car, b feet, the braking distance for the car to come to a complete standstill is given by the function $b = \dfrac{(s^2 + 10s)}{150} + \dfrac{s}{10}$, where s is the speed of the car in miles per hour. According to this function, if the speed of the car is 90 miles per hour, what would be the braking distance?

Solution: Substitute the value of s, the speed of the car, to find b, the breaking distance:

$\Rightarrow b = \dfrac{(s^2 + 10s)}{150} + \dfrac{s}{10}$ [Given function]

$\Rightarrow b = \dfrac{(90^2 + 10 \times 90)}{150} + \dfrac{90}{10}$ [Substitute s = 90]

$\Rightarrow b = \dfrac{(8100 + 900)}{150} + \dfrac{90}{10}$ [Simplify within parentheses]

$\Rightarrow b = \dfrac{9000}{150} + \dfrac{90}{10}$ [Combine like-terms]

$\Rightarrow b = 60 + 9$ [Reduce each fraction to their lowest terms]
$\Rightarrow b = 69$ [Do the addition]
Therefore, according to this function, if the speed of the car is 90 mph., then the braking distance would be 69 feet.

Question #50: For a certain sports car, b feet, the braking distance for the car to come to a complete standstill is given by the function $b = \dfrac{(s^2 + 10s)}{150}$, where s is the speed of the car in miles per hour. According to this function, if the braking distance of the car is 60 feet, what would be its speed?

Solution: Substitute the value of b, the breaking distance, to find s, the speed of the car:

$\Rightarrow b = \dfrac{(s^2 + 10s)}{150}$ [Given function]

$\Rightarrow 60 = \dfrac{(s^2 + 10s)}{150}$ [Substitute $b = 60$]

$\Rightarrow s^2 + 10s = 9000$ [Cross multiply]

$\Rightarrow s^2 + 10s - 9000 = 0$ [Subtract 9000 from both sides]

$\Rightarrow (s + 100)(s - 90)$ [Factor the trinomial into two binomials]

$\Rightarrow s = -100$ or 90 [Solve for the two value of s]

Therefore, according to this function, if the braking distance of the car is 60 feet, its speed would be 90 mph.

PART 3.0: APPLICATIONS:

TOPICS COVERED:

- Percent Calculations

- Percent Changes

- Percent Discounts

- Percent Mark-Ups/Mark-Downs

- Percent Interests

- Percent Taxes & Commissions

- Ratios

- Proportions

PRACTICE EXERCISE:

PERCENT CALCULATION:

Question #1:   If x% of y is 12, then what is y% of x?

Question #2:   If x% of x% of y equals z and x^2% of y equals nz, such that x and y are positive numbers, what is the value of n?

Question #3:   If Jar Y has 10% more marbles than Jar X, what percent of the marbles in Jar Y have to be moved to Jar X, so that the number of marbles in each jar will be the same?

Question #4:   In a truckload of 9,600 pieces of fruits, ¼ are apples. If ¼ of the apples were thrown because they were spoiled, what percent of the total number of the remaining fruits would then be apples?

Question #5:   In a certain writing club, 60 percent of all male members and 90 percent of all female members are left handed. If 20 percent of the members are male, what percent of all the members are not left handed?

Question #6:   A fruit basket contains 15 peaches and 22 mangoes. How many mangoes must be removed from the basket so that 75 percent of the pieces of fruit in the basket will be peaches?

Question #7:   Of the 180 members in a club, 25 percent are to be allocated to Group X and the remaining 75 percent to Group Y. However according to a survey conducted, 80 percent of the members prefer Group X and the remaining 20 percent prefer Group Y. What is the least possible number of members who will not be allocated to the group of their preference?

Question #8:   In a certain bookstore, 90 percent of the books cost less than $75, and a total of 162 books cost less than $25. If 80 percent of the books cost at least $25, how many of the books cost at least $25 but less than $75?

Question #9:   In a recent anonymous poll of a certain private community, 22 percent of its 2,500 residents reported that they were suffering from depression. Of this group of depressed people, 20 percent were at least sixty years old. If 25 percent of all the people are at least sixty years old, how many people over the age of sixty did not report that they were suffering from depression?

Question #10: A certain conference room consists of 180 delegates, 15 percent of whom are men. A group of delegates, 25 percent of whom are men, quits the conference room. Of the delegates that are still in the conference room, 10 percent are men. How many delegates quit the conference room?

PERCENT CHANGES:

Question #11: Ever since 1950, EZ corporation has been awarded 5 credit rating points every year for its outstanding performance. In 1975, the companies' average rating points were 25 percent greater than in 1950. What percent of its 2000 rating was its 1950 rating?

Question #12: In a certain factory, a stock of packing material lasts for 120 days. If the production in the factory goes up and the consumption of the packing material is increased by 50%, how many days would the same stock of packing material last?

Question #13: If a certain type of bacteria doubles every 5 hours, then the population in hour (n + 25) will be how many times the population in hour (n + 5)?

Question #14: In a certain high school, there are 750 students, 10 percent of whom are girls. If 150 additional students are to be admitted and all of the present students remain, how many of the additional students must be girls in order to raise the percent of girls to 15 percent?

Question #15:   A manager decided to raise a workers hourly wage rate by 25 percent but reduced the number of hours worked per week so that the workers weekly paycheck would remain unchanged. By what percent should the number of hours worked be reduced?

Question #16:   A manager decided to reduce a workers hourly wage rate by 20 percent but raised the number of hours worked per week so that the workers weekly paycheck would remain unchanged. By what percent should the number of hours worked be raised?

Question #17:   The number that is 500 percent greater than 15 is what percent greater than 150% of 50?

Question #18:   If increasing 20 by P percent gives the same result as decreasing 60 by P percent, what is P percent of 110?

Question #19:   In a certain factory that produces sockets, in the 1960's, the rate of defective sockets manufactured was 9.6 per hundred sockets manufactured. By 1980's, the rate of defective sockets manufactured had declined to 5.76 per 100 sockets manufactured. If the rate declined by 20 percent from 1970's to 1980's, by what percent did it decline from 1960's to 1970's?

Question #20:   A bookstore charges a flat price for each book that it sells. If the current flat price of each book were to be increased by $1, then 10 fewer books could be bought for $720, not considering the sales tax. With the current flat rate for each book, how many books can be bought for $720?

PERCENT DISCOUNT:

Question #21:   During a special sale, sales clerk accidentally marked-up the price of an item by 10% instead of lowering it by 10%. As a result, the price on the tag was $22 too high. What was the original price of that item?

PERCENT PROFIT:

Question #22:   If a trader had sold an antique for $900, he would have made a 20 percent profit. Instead, the trader had to sell it for a 80 percent loss. At what price did the traders sell the antique?

Question #23:   If a retailer had sold an item for $900, he would have made a 20 percent profit. Instead, the retailer sold that same item for a 20 percent loss. At what price was the item sold?

Question #24:   At a certain bookstore, the total profit from sales increased by 25 percent over the previous month, while the number of books sold decreased by 25 percent over the previous month. What was the average percent increase in profit per book over the previous month?

PERCENT INTEREST

Question #25:   If a man invests $25,000 for 1 year at the rate of 10% per annum, compounded semi-annually, how much will be the value of his investment after 1 year?

Question #26:   An amount of money was invested at 10% a year. Five times that amount was invested at 15%. How much was invested at 15% if the total annual return was $1,615?
Amount invested at 15% $\Rightarrow$ 5 × 1,900 = $9,500

PERCENT TAXES & COMMISSION:

Question #27:   A certain company offers its entry-level sales employees two options for their weekly pay. They can either opt to take a weekly salary of $570 plus a commission of 7 percent of the total sales above $1,000 for that week or no weekly salary with a 9 percent commission of the total sales for that week. What must be the total weekly sales of an employee to give them the same weekly pay with either option?

Question #28:   A certain company offers its entry-level sales employees two options for their annual pay. They can either opt to take an annual salary of $25,000 with no commission or an annual salary of $10,000 plus a 20 percent commission on their total annual sales. What must be the total annual sales of an employee to give them the same annual pay with either option?

RATIOS:

Question #29:   John played a game several times. He received $12 every time he won and had to pay $10 every time he lost. If the ratio of the number of times he won to the number of times he lost was 5:2, and if he won a total of $600, what is the total number of times he played this game?

Question #30:   An artist, who is trying to develop a new shade for his oil painting, mixed red, blue, and green color pigments in the ratio of 1:25:50. After looking at the result, he decided to double the ratio of red to blue and halve the ratio of red to green. If the final mixture contains 125 liters of blue, how many liters of red would it have?

Question #31:   In a certain auto dealership, if one-half of the number of vans is one-tenth of the total number of vehicles, and one-third of the number of jeeps is one-eighteenth of the total number of vehicles, then what is the ratio of vans to jeeps?

Question #32:   In a certain company, the ratio of managers to supervisors is 2 to 5. If one-third of the managers are females and one-fourth of the supervisors are females, what fraction of the combined managers and supervisors are males?

PROPORTIONS:

Question #33:   If two numbers are in the ratio 9 to 8 and their difference is 10, what is the larger number?

Question #34:   In a certain manufacturing facility, the ratio of the number of nuts produced to the number of bolts produced on a certain day was 2 to 3. If the factory produced 8 more nuts, the ratio of the number of nuts produced to the number of bolts produced would have been 3 to 4. How many bolts did the factory produce?

Question #35:   During a one day sale at a certain bookstore, the ratio of the number of hardcover books sold to the number of soft cover books sold was 6 to 7. If the store had sold 12 more hardcover books, the ratio of the number of hardcover books sold to the number of soft cover books sold would have been 7 to 8. How many soft cover books did the store sell?

Question #36:   In a certain club, there is an equal number of male members and female members. If 1 male and 2 females quit the club, the ratio of male members to female members would be 6:5. How many female members are in the club before anyone quits?

Question #37:   In a certain company, the ratio of managers to supervisors is 5:1. If 225 new employees were hired as managers and supervisors in the ratio of 1:2, the new ratio of managers to supervisors would be 9:2. What was the original number of supervisors?

Question #38:   In a certain school, the ratio of the number of teachers to the number of assistants is 7 to 56. If 6 additional assistants were to be hired, the ratio of the number of teachers to the number of assistants would become 7 to 58. How many staff members does the school have before hiring any new staff?

Question #39:   In a certain school, the ratio of the number of teachers to the number of assistants is 1 to 5. If 5 additional teachers and 75 additional assistants were to be hired, the ratio of the number of teachers to the number of assistants would become 1 to 7. How many staff members does the school have before hiring any new staff?

Question #40:   The force with which a hammer is hit on a nail against a wall is directly proportional to the length of the nail that goes inside the wall. The length of the nail is 20 millimeters and 2 millimeters are already inside the wall. If a force of 20 pounds pushes the nail 7 millimeters inside the wall, then, what magnitude of force, in pounds must be applied so that the nail is 7 millimeters further inside the wall?

PRACTICE EXERCISE – QUESTIONS & ANSWERS WITH EXPLANATIONS:

PERCENT CALCULATION:

Question #1: If $x\%$ of y is 12, then what is $y\%$ of x?

Solution: $x\%$ of y is $12 \Rightarrow \dfrac{x}{100} \bullet y = 12$ [Convert the statement into an equation]

$\Rightarrow \dfrac{xy}{100} = 12$ [Rewrite the expressions with combined terms]

$\Rightarrow xy = 1,200$ [Multiply both sides by 100]

$y\%$ of x? $\Rightarrow \dfrac{y}{100} \bullet x$ [Convert the statement into an expression]

$\Rightarrow \dfrac{xy}{100}$ [Rewrite the expression with combined terms]

$\Rightarrow \dfrac{1,200}{100} = 12$ [Substitute $xy = 1,200$]

Question #2: If $x\%$ of $x\%$ of y equals z and $x^2\%$ of y equals nz, such that x and y are positive numbers, what is the value of n?

Solution: $x\%$ of $x\%$ of y equals z $\Rightarrow \dfrac{x}{100} \bullet \dfrac{x}{100} \bullet y = z$ [Convert the statement into an equation]

$\Rightarrow \dfrac{x^2 y}{10000} = z$ [Rewrite the expressions with combined terms]

$\Rightarrow x^2 y = 10,000z$ [Multiply both sides by 10,000] $\Rightarrow$ Equation #1

$x^2\%$ of y equals nz $\Rightarrow \dfrac{x^2}{100} \bullet y = nz$ [Convert the statement into an equation]

$\Rightarrow \dfrac{x^2 y}{100} = nz$ [Rewrite the expressions with combined terms]

$\Rightarrow x^2 y = 100nz$ [Multiply both sides by 100] $\Rightarrow$ Equation #2

Equate Equation #1 & #2 $\Rightarrow x^2 y = 10000z = 100nz$

$\Rightarrow n = 100$ [Divide both sides by 100z]

Question #3: If Jar Y has 10% more marbles than Jar X, what percent of the marbles in Jar Y have to be moved to Jar X, so that the number of marbles in each jar will be the same?

Solution: Assume there are 100 marbles in Jar X and 110 (10% more) in Jar Y

EZ Problem Set-Up $\Rightarrow$ If n marbles are moved from Jar Y to Jar X, both jars will have same marbles

$\Rightarrow 110 - n = 100 + n$ [Set up the equation]

$\Rightarrow 2n = 10$ [Isolate n on the left side]

$\Rightarrow n = 5$ [Divide both sides by 2]

5 is what percent of 110? $\Rightarrow \dfrac{5}{110} \times 100 = 4.54\%$

Question #4: In a truckload of 9,600 pieces of fruits, ¼ are apples. If ¼ of the apples were thrown because they were spoiled, what percent of the total number of the remaining fruits would then be apples?

Solution: Total No. of Fruits in Truck $\Rightarrow$ 9,600

Total No. of Apples in Truck $\Rightarrow$ ¼ of 9,600 = 2,400

Total No. of Apples Thrown Away $\Rightarrow$ ¼ of 2,400 = 600

Remaining No. of Fruits in Truck $\Rightarrow$ 9,600 – 600 = 9,000

Remaining No. of Apples in Truck $\Rightarrow$ 2,400 – 600 = 1,800

EZ Problem Set-Up $\Rightarrow$ Remaining Apples is what percent of Remaining Fruits?

$\Rightarrow$ 1,800 is what percent of 9,000?   [Substitute the values]

$$\Rightarrow \frac{1,800}{9,000} \times 100 \qquad\qquad \text{[Set up the equation]}$$

$$\Rightarrow 20\% \qquad\qquad \text{[Simplify the expression]}$$

Question #5: In a certain writing club, 60 percent of all male members and 90 percent of all female members are left handed. If 20 percent of the members are male, what percent of all the members are not left handed?

Solution:

Let the total No. of members	$\Rightarrow$ 100
No. of male members	$\Rightarrow$ 20% of 100 = 20
No. of female members	$\Rightarrow$ 100 − 20 = 80
No. of left-handed male members	$\Rightarrow$ 60% of 20 = 12
No. of left-handed female members	$\Rightarrow$ 90% of 80 = 72
Total No. of left-handed members	$\Rightarrow$ 12 + 72 = 84
Total No. of non left-handed members	$\Rightarrow$ 100 − 84 = 16
Percent of non left-handed members	$\Rightarrow$ 16%

Question #6: A fruit basket contains 15 peaches and 22 mangoes. How many mangoes must be removed from the basket so that 75 percent of the pieces of fruit in the basket will be peaches?

Solution: No. of fruits in the basket initially = 15 peaches + 22 mangoes = 37
Let the No. of mangoes removed = x
EZ Problem Set-Up $\Rightarrow$ After the removal, peaches should account for 75% of all fruits in basket

$$\Rightarrow \frac{original\ no\ of\ peaches}{original\ total - removal} = 75\% \qquad \text{[Set up the equation]}$$

$$\Rightarrow \frac{15}{37 - x} = \frac{75}{100} \qquad \text{[Substitute the known values]}$$

$$\Rightarrow 75(37 - x) = 1,500 \qquad \text{[Cross multiply]}$$

$$\Rightarrow 2,775 - 75x = 1,500 \qquad \text{[Apply distributive property]}$$

$$\Rightarrow -75x = -1,275 \qquad \text{[Subtract 2,775 from both sides]}$$

$$\Rightarrow x = 17 \qquad \text{[Divide both sides by −75]}$$

Therefore, 17 mangoes must be removed from the basket so that 75 percent of the pieces of fruit in the basket will be peaches

Alternately: To calculate the total number of fruits required for 15 peaches to be 75% of the total fruits in the basket, take 15/75%, which gives a total of 20 fruits in the basket. We already have 15 peaches. For the total number of fruits to be 20, there should be only 5 mangoes. Since we originally had 22 mangoes, in order to have 5 mangoes, we must remove (22 − 5), or 17 mangoes. Now we'll have 15 peaches out of a total of 20, which is exactly 75% of total number of fruits in the basket.

Question #7: Of the 180 members in a club, 25 percent are to be allocated to Group X and the remaining 75 percent to Group Y. However according to a survey conducted, 80 percent of the members prefer Group X and the remaining 20 percent prefer Group Y. What is the least possible number of members who will not be allocated to the group of their preference?

Solution:

Total No. of Members in the Club	$\Rightarrow$ 180
No. of Members Assigned to Group X	$\Rightarrow$ 25% of 180 = (0.25) 180 = 45
No. of Members Assigned to Group Y	$\Rightarrow$ 75% of 180 = (0.75) 180 = 135
No. of Members who Prefer Group X	$\Rightarrow$ 80% of 180 = (0.80) 180 = 144
No. of Members who Prefer Group Y	$\Rightarrow$ 20% of 180 = (0.20) 180 = 36

Let's assume if all 36 members who prefer Group Y are allocated to Groups Y, then the remaining (135 − 36) 99 members allocated to Group Y, actually preferred Group X.
Likewise, Group X can only take 45 members, but since 144 members prefer Group X, the remaining (144 − 45) 99 members allocated to Group Y, actually preferred Group X.
Therefore, the least possible number of members who will not be allocated to the group of their preference is 99.

Question #8: In a certain bookstore, 90 percent of the books cost less than $75, and a total of 162 books cost less than $25. If 80 percent of the books cost at least $25, how many of the books cost at least $25 but less than $75?

Solution: 20% of Total No. of Books $\Rightarrow$ 162

Total No. of Books $\rightarrow 162 \times \dfrac{100}{20} = 810$

	⇒ Percent	⇒ Number
Books that cost less than $75	⇒ 90%	⇒ 0.90 × 810 = 729
Books that cost more than $75	⇒ 100% – 90% = 10%	⇒ 0.10 × 810 = 81
Books that cost more than $25	⇒ 80%	⇒ 0.80 × 810 = 648
Books that cost less than $25	⇒ 100% – 80% = 20%	⇒ 0.20 × 810 = 162

EZ Problem Set-Up ⇒ No. of Books that cost at least $25 but less than $75
⇒ No. of Books that cost less than $75 – No. of Books that cost less than $25
⇒ 729 – 162   [Substitute the known values]
⇒ 567   [Simplify the expression]

Question #9: In a recent anonymous poll of a certain private community, 22 percent of its 2,500 residents reported that they were suffering from depression. Of this group of depressed people, 20 percent were at least sixty years old. If 25 percent of all the people are at least sixty years old, how many people over the age of sixty did not report that they were suffering from depression?

Solution:
No. of Residents in the private community ⇒ 2,500
No. of residents who reported depression ⇒ 22% of 2,500 = 550
No. of residents who reported depression and were at least sixty ⇒ 20% of 550 = 110
No. of residents who are at least sixty years old ⇒ 25% of 2,500 = 625
No. of residents who didn't reported depression & are at least sixty years old ⇒ 625 – 110 = 515

Question #10: A certain conference room consists of 180 delegates, 15 percent of whom are men. A group of delegates, 25 percent of whom are men, quits the conference room. Of the delegates that are still in the conference room, 10 percent are men. How many delegates quit the conference room?

Solution:
Total No. of delegates in the room ⇒ 180
No. of men in the room ⇒ 15% of 180 = 27
Let, the No. of delegates who leaves the room ⇒ x
Then, the No. of men who leaves the room ⇒ 25% of x = $0.25x$
Remaining No. of delegates in the room ⇒ $180 - x$
No. of men remaining in the room ⇒ 10% of $(180 - x)$
⇒ $0.10(180 - x)$

EZ Problem Set-Up ⇒ Original No. of men in the room – No. of men who leaves the room = Remaining No. of men in the room:
⇒ $27 - 0.25x = 0.10(180 - x)$ [Set up the equation]
⇒ $27 - 0.25x = 18 - 0.10x$ [Apply distributive property]
⇒ $0.15x = 9$ [Isolate x on one side]
⇒ $x = 60$ [Divide both sides by 0.15]

PERCENT CHANGES:

Question #11: Ever since 1950, EZ corporation has been awarded 5 credit rating points every year for its outstanding performance. In 1975, the companies' average rating points were 25 percent greater than in 1950. What percent of its 2000 rating was its 1950 rating?

Solution:
Let the No. of rating points in 1950 ⇒ x
Then, the No. of rating points in 1975 ⇒ $x + (5 \times 25) = x + 125$
And, the No. of rating points in 2000 ⇒ $x + (5 \times 50) = x + 250$
Rating in 1975 was 25% greater than in 1950 ⇒ $x + 125 = 1.25x$
⇒ $0.25x = 125$
⇒ $x = 500$

No. of rating points in 1950 ⇒ $x = 500$
No. of rating points in 2000 ⇒ $x + 250 = 500 + 250 = 750$

What percent of its 2000 rating was its 1950 rating? ⇒ $\dfrac{500}{750} \times 100 = 66\dfrac{2}{3}\%$

Question #12: In a certain factory, a stock of packing material lasts for 120 days. If the production in the factory goes up and the consumption of the packing material is increased by 50%, how many days would the same stock of packing material last?

Solution: Let the original consumption of the packing material before any increase = 100
Then, the new consumption of the packing material after the 50% increase = 100 + (50% of 100) = 150
No. of days that the stock of packing material lasts before any increase = 120
Let the No. of days that the stock of packing material lasts after the 50% increase = x
EZ Problem Set-Up $\Rightarrow$ Set up an inverse proportion and solve for x

$$\Rightarrow \frac{100}{150} \quad \frac{120\,days}{x\,days} \qquad \text{[Set up the proportion]}$$

$$\Rightarrow \frac{100}{150} = \frac{x}{120} \qquad \text{[In inverse proportion, flip the second fraction]}$$

$\Rightarrow 150x = 12,000$ [Cross multiply]
$\Rightarrow x = 80$ [Divide both sides by 150]

Therefore, if consumption of the packing material is increased by 50%, the same stock of packing material would last 80 days.

Question #13: If a certain type of bacteria doubles every 5 hours, then the population in hour $(n + 25)$ will be how many times the population in hour $(n + 5)$?

Solution:
Let the population in hour n $\Rightarrow 1x$
Then, the population in hour $n + 5$ $\Rightarrow 2x$
Then, the population in hour $n + 10$ $\Rightarrow 4x$
Then, the population in hour $n + 15$ $\Rightarrow 8x$
Then, the population in hour $n + 20$ $\Rightarrow 16x$
Then, the population in hour $n + 25$ $\Rightarrow 32x$
The population in hour $(n + 25)$ will be how many times the population in hour $(n + 5)$?

$$\Rightarrow \frac{32x}{2x} = 16 \text{ times}$$

Question #14: In a certain high school, there are 750 students, 10 percent of whom are girls. If 150 additional students are to be admitted and all of the present students remain, how many of the additional students must be girls in order to raise the percent of girls to 15 percent?

Solution:
Originally: Original Total No. of Students $\Rightarrow 750$
            Original Total No. of Girls $\Rightarrow$ 10% of 750 = (0.10) 750 = 75
            Original Total No. of Boys $\Rightarrow 750 - 75 = 675$
New: New No. of Students Admitted $\Rightarrow 150$
            New Total No. of Students $\Rightarrow 750 + 150 = 900$
            Let, No. of New Girls Admitted $\Rightarrow g$
            New Total No. of Girls $\Rightarrow 75 + g$
EZ Problem Set-Up $\Rightarrow$ 15% of the total number of new students = Total number of girls

$\Rightarrow$ 15% of 900 = 75 + g [Set up the equation]
$\Rightarrow 135 = 75 + g$ [Calculate the percent]
$\Rightarrow g = 60$ [Subtract 75 from both sides]

Question #15: A manager decided to raise a workers hourly wage rate by 25 percent but reduced the number of hours worked per week so that the workers weekly paycheck would remain unchanged. By what percent should the number of hours worked be reduced?

Solution:
Let the Original Hourly Wage Rate $\Rightarrow r$
And, the Original No. of Hours Worked per week $\Rightarrow w$
Then, the Original Weekly Paycheck $\Rightarrow rw$
New Hourly Wage Rate $\Rightarrow r + 25\% \text{ of } r = r + 0.25r = 1.25r$
Let, the New No. of Hours Worked per week $\Rightarrow n$
Then, the New Weekly Paycheck $\Rightarrow 1.25rn$
EZ Problem Set-Up $\Rightarrow$ Original Weekly Paycheck = New Weekly Paycheck

$\Rightarrow rw = 1.25rn$ [Set up the equation]
$\Rightarrow n = 0.80w$ [Divide both sides by 1.25r]

Since the new number of hours (n) is equal to 80% of the original number of hours worked (w), the new number of hours worked should be reduced by 20%.
Note: This problem can also be worked by picking numbers.

Question #16: A manager decided to reduce a workers hourly wage rate by 20 percent but raised the number of hours worked per week so that the workers weekly paycheck would remain unchanged. By what percent should the number of hours worked be raised?

Solution:
Let the Original Hourly Wage Rate $\Rightarrow r$
And, the Original No. of Hours Worked per week $\Rightarrow w$
Then, the Original Weekly Paycheck $\Rightarrow rw$
New Hourly Wage Rate $\Rightarrow r - 20\%$ of $r = r - 0.20r = 0.80r$
Let, the New No. of Hours Worked per week $\Rightarrow n$
The, the New Weekly Paycheck $\Rightarrow 0.80rn$
EZ Problem Set-Up $\Rightarrow$ Original Weekly Paycheck = New Weekly Paycheck
$\Rightarrow rw = 0.80rn$ [Set up the equation]
$\Rightarrow n = 1.25w$ [Divide both sides by 0.80r]
Since the new number of hours (n) is equal to 125% of the original number of hours worked (w), the new number of hours worked should be raised by 25%.

Question #17: The number that is 500 percent greater than 15 is what percent greater than 150% of 50?
Solution:
Value of 500% greater than 15 $\Rightarrow 15 + (500\%$ of $15) = 15 + 75 = 90$
Value of 150% of 50 $\Rightarrow 1.5 \times 50 = 75$

Percent Change $\Rightarrow \dfrac{\text{Actual Change}}{\text{Original Amount}} \times 100 = \dfrac{90 - 75}{90} \times 100 = \dfrac{15}{90} \times 100 = 16.67\%$

Question #18: If increasing 20 by P percent gives the same result as decreasing 60 by P percent, what is P percent of 110?
Solution:
EZ Problem Set-Up $\Rightarrow$ Increasing 20 by P percent = Decreasing 60 by P percent

$\Rightarrow 20\left(1 + \dfrac{P}{100}\right) = 60\left(1 - \dfrac{P}{100}\right)$ [Set up the equation]

$\Rightarrow 20 + \dfrac{20P}{100} = 60 - \dfrac{60P}{100}$ [Apply distributive property]

$\Rightarrow \dfrac{20P}{100} = 40 - \dfrac{60P}{100}$ [Subtract 20 from both sides]

$\Rightarrow \dfrac{20P}{100} + \dfrac{60P}{100} = 40$ [Add 60P/100 to both sides]

$\Rightarrow \dfrac{80P}{100} = 40$ [Combine like-terms]

$\Rightarrow \dfrac{4P}{5} = 40$ [Reduce the fraction to its lowest terms]

$\Rightarrow 4P = 200$ [Multiply both sides by 5]
$\Rightarrow P = 50$ [Divide both sides by 4]
P percent of 110 = 50% of 110 = 0.5(110) = 55

Question #19: In a certain factory that produces sockets, in the 1960's, the rate of defective sockets manufactured was 9.6 per hundred sockets manufactured. By 1980's, the rate of defective sockets manufactured had declined to 5.76 per 100 sockets manufactured. If the rate declined by 20 percent from 1970's to 1980's, by what percent did it decline from 1960's to 1970's?
Solution:
Defective rate in 1960's $\Rightarrow$ 9.6 per hundred
Defective rate in 1980's $\Rightarrow$ 5.76 per hundred
Defective rate in 1970's $\Rightarrow x$ per hundred
EZ Problem Set-Up $\Rightarrow$ Defective rate declined by 20% from 1970's to 1980's
$\Rightarrow \dfrac{x - 5.76}{x}(100) = 20$ [Set up the equation]

$$\Rightarrow 100(x - 5.76) = 20x \qquad \text{[Multiply both sides by } x\text{]}$$
$$\Rightarrow 100x - 576 = 20x \qquad \text{[Apply distributive property]}$$
$$\Rightarrow 80x = 576 \qquad \text{[Subtract } 20x \text{ from both sides]}$$
$$\Rightarrow x = 7.2 \qquad \text{[Divide both sides by 80]}$$

Defective rate in 1970's $\Rightarrow$ 7.2 per hundred

Percent decline in defective rate $\Rightarrow \dfrac{change}{original}(100)$ [Write the appropriate formula]

(from 60's to 70's) $\qquad\qquad \Rightarrow \dfrac{9.6 - 7.2}{9.6}(100)$ [Substitute the known values]

$$\Rightarrow \dfrac{2.4}{9.6}(100) \qquad \text{[Simplify the numerator]}$$

$$\Rightarrow 25\% \qquad \text{[Simplify the expression]}$$

Question #20: A bookstore charges a flat price for each book that it sells. If the current flat price of each book were to be increased by $1, then 10 fewer books could be bought for $720, not considering the sales tax. With the current flat rate for each book, how many books can be bought for $720?

Solution: Let the current price per book = b
And the number of book that can be bought for $720 = n
With the Original Pricing $\Rightarrow bn = 720$

$$\Rightarrow n = \dfrac{720}{b} \qquad\qquad\qquad \Rightarrow \text{Equation \#1}$$

With the Changed Pricing $\Rightarrow (b + 1)(n - 10) = 720 \qquad \Rightarrow$ Equation #2

$\Rightarrow (b + 1)\left(\dfrac{720}{b} - 10\right) = 720$ [Substitute the value of n from Equation #1 into Equation #]

$\Rightarrow (b + 1)\left(\dfrac{720 - 10b}{b}\right) = 720$ [Simplify within parentheses]

$\Rightarrow (b + 1)\left(\dfrac{720 - 10b}{b}\right)b = 720b$ [Multiply both sides by b]

$\Rightarrow (b + 1)(720 - 10b) = 720b$ [Simplify the left sides]
$\Rightarrow 720b - 10b^2 + 720 - 10b = 720b$ [Apply distributive property]
$\Rightarrow 10b^2 + 10b - 720 = 0$ [Combine like terms]
$\Rightarrow b^2 + b - 72 = 0$ [Divide the whole equation by 10]
$\Rightarrow (b + 9)(b - 8) = 0$ [Factor out the trinomial into two binomials]
Either $\Rightarrow b + 9 = 0$ OR $\qquad \Rightarrow b - 8 = 0$ [Equate each factor equal to zero]
$\qquad\qquad \Rightarrow b = -9$ OR $\qquad \Rightarrow b = 8$ [Solve for both values of b]
Since price of anything can't be negative, the current price of each book $\Rightarrow b = \$8$
Therefore, the number of books that can be bought with $720 \Rightarrow \$720 \div 8 = 90$

PERCENT DISCOUNT:

Question #21: During a special sale, sales clerk accidentally marked-up the price of an item by 10% instead of lowering it by 10%. As a result, the price on the tag was $22 too high. What was the original price of that item?

Solution: Let the original price of the item $\qquad \Rightarrow p$
Wrong Price of the item $\qquad\qquad \Rightarrow 1.1p$
Right Price of the item $\qquad\qquad \Rightarrow 0.9p$
Price Difference due to wrong marking $\Rightarrow \$22$
EZ Problem Set-Up $\Rightarrow$ Wrong Price of the item – Right Price of the item = Price Difference due to wrong marking
$\qquad\qquad \Rightarrow 1.1p - 0.9p = 22$ [Set up the equation]
$\qquad\qquad \Rightarrow 0.2p = 22$ [Combine like terms]
$\qquad\qquad \Rightarrow p = \$110$ [Divide both sides by 0.20]

PERCENT PROFIT:

Question #22: If a trader had sold an antique for $900, he would have made a 20 percent profit. Instead, the trader had to sell it for a 80 percent loss. At what price did the traders sell the antique?

Solution: Let the trader's Cost Price = x

EZ Problem Set-Up ⇒ If the trader had sold the antique for $900, he would have made a 20% profit

⇒ 900 = x + 20% of x	[Set up the equation]
⇒ 900 = 120% of x	[Combine the percents on right side]
⇒ 900 = 1.20x	[Convert the percent to decimal]
⇒ x = 750	[Divide both sides by 1.20]
Trader's Cost Price ⇒ $750	[From above]
Actual Selling Price ⇒ $750 − (80% of $750)	[Selling price is cost price minus loss]
⇒ $750 − $600 = $150	[Simplify the expression]

Question #23: If a retailer had sold an item for $900, he would have made a 20 percent profit. Instead, the retailer sold that same item for a 20 percent loss. At what price was the item sold?

Solution: Let the Cost Price = x

Then, the Selling Price at a 20% Profit = $900

EZ Problem Set-Up ⇒ Cost Price + 20% Profit = Selling Price

⇒ x + (20% of x) = $900	[Set up the equation]
⇒ x + 0.20x = $900	[Calculate the percent]
⇒ 1.20x = $900	[Combine like terms]
⇒ x = 750	[Divide both sides by 1.20]

Cost Price ⇒ $750

Selling Price at a 20% Loss ⇒ $750 − (20% of $750) = $750 − $150 = $600

Question #24: At a certain bookstore, the total profit from sales increased by 25 percent over the previous month, while the number of books sold decreased by 25 percent over the previous month. What was the average percent increase in profit per book over the previous month?

Solution:

Let	⇒ Previous Months Profit from Books	⇒ $100
	⇒ Previous Months No. of Books Sold	⇒ 100
	⇒ Previous Months Profit per Book	⇒ $\frac{\$100}{100}$ = $1
Then	⇒ This Months Profit from Books	⇒ $100 + (25% of 100) = $100 + $25 = $125
	⇒ This Months No. of Books Sold	⇒ 100 − (25% of 100) = 100 − 25 = 75
	⇒ This Months Profit per Book	⇒ $125 ÷ 75 = $$\frac{\$125}{75}$ = $1\frac{2}{3}$

Average Percent Increase in Profit per Books ⇒ $\dfrac{1\frac{2}{3} - 1}{1} \times 100 = \dfrac{2}{3} \times 100 = 66\frac{2}{3}\%$

PERCENT INTEREST

Question #25: If a man invests $25,000 for 1 year at the rate of 10% per annum, compounded semi-annually, how much will be the value of his investment after 1 year?

Solution:

Principal for the First Half Year ⇒ P_1 = $25,000

Interest for the First Half Year ⇒ $I_1 = PRT = 25,000 \times \dfrac{10}{100} \times \dfrac{1}{2}$ = $1,250

Principal for the Second Half Year ⇒ $P_2 = P_1 + I_1$ = $25,000 + $1,250 = $26,250

Interest for the Second Half Year ⇒ $I_2 = PRT = 26,250 \times \dfrac{10}{100} \times \dfrac{1}{2}$ = $1,312.50

Total Value of the invest after 2 years = Initial Investment + Interest Earned
⇒ $25,000 + ($1,250 + $1,312.50) = $25,000 + $2,562.50 = $27,562.50

Alternate Method: Calculate the compound interest using the formula:

$$\text{Final Balance} = (25,000) \times \left(1 + \frac{0.10}{2}\right)^{(1)(2)} = 25,000 \times 1.05^2 = 25,000 \times 1.1025 = \$27,562.50$$

Question #26: An amount of money was invested at 10% a year. Five times that amount was invested at 15%. How much was invested at 15% if the total annual return was $1,615?

Solution: Let the amount invested at 10% $\Rightarrow x$
Annual return on the amount invested at 10% $\Rightarrow$ 10% of $x = 0.10x$
Then, the amount invested at 15% $\Rightarrow 5x$
Annual return on the amount invested at 15% $\Rightarrow$ 15% of $5x = 0.15(5x) = 0.75x$
EZ Problem Set-Up $\Rightarrow$ Total Annual Return on both Investments = Return on 10% Investment + Return on 15% Investment
$\Rightarrow 1,615 = 0.10x + 0.75x$ [Set up the equation]
$\Rightarrow 1,615 = 0.85x$ [Combine like-terms]
$\Rightarrow x = 1,900$ [Divide both sides by 0.85]
Amount invested at 10% $\Rightarrow$ $1,900
Amount invested at 15% $\Rightarrow 5 \times 1,900 = \$9,500$

PERCENT TAXES & COMMISSION:

Question #27: A certain company offers its entry-level sales employees two options for their weekly pay. They can either opt to take a weekly salary of $570 plus a commission of 7 percent of the total sales above $1,000 for that week or no weekly salary with a 9 percent commission of the total sales for that week. What must be the total weekly sales of an employee to give them the same weekly pay with either option?

Solution: Let the total weekly sales of the employee at which they earn the same pay $\Rightarrow x$
Weekly Pay with salary of $570 and 7% commission of sales over $1,000 $\Rightarrow \$570 + 7\%$ of $(x–1000)$
Weekly Pay with no salary and 9% commission of total sales $\Rightarrow 9\%$ of x
Now, find the amount of total weekly sales for an employee to get the same pay:
EZ Problem Set-Up $\Rightarrow$ Weekly Pay with salary of $570 and 7% commission of sales over $1,000 = Weekly Pay with no salary and 9% commission of total sales
$\Rightarrow \$570 + 0.07(x–1000) = 0.09x$ [Set up the equation]
$\Rightarrow \$570 + 0.07x – 70 = 0.09x$ [Apply distributive property]
$\Rightarrow 0.02x = \$500$ [Isolate x on left side]
$\Rightarrow x = \$25,000$ [Divide both sides by 0.02]
Therefore, the total weekly sales of an employee to give them the same weekly pay with either option should be $25,000.

Question #28: A certain company offers its entry-level sales employees two options for their annual pay. They can either opt to take an annual salary of $25,000 with no commission or an annual salary of $10,000 plus a 20 percent commission on their total annual sales. What must be the total annual sales of an employee to give them the same annual pay with either option?

Solution: Let the total annual sales of an employee at which they earn the same pay $\Rightarrow x$
Annual Pay with salary of $25,000 and no commission of sales $\Rightarrow \$25,000$
Annual Pay with salary of $10,000 and 20% commission of total annual sales$\Rightarrow \$10,000 + 20\%$ of x
Now, find the amount of total annual sales for an employee to get the same pay:
EZ Problem Set-Up $\Rightarrow$ Annual Pay with salary of $25,000 and no commission = Annual Pay with salary of $10,000 and 20% commission
$\Rightarrow \$25,000 = \$10,000 + 0.2x$ [Set up the equation]
$\Rightarrow \$15,000 = 0.2x$ [Subtract 10,000 from both sides]
$\Rightarrow x = 75,000$ [Divide both sides by 0.2]
Therefore, the total annual sales of an employee to give them the same annual pay with either option should be $75,000.

RATIOS:

Question #29: John played a game several times. He received $12 every time he won and had to pay $10 every time he lost. If the ratio of the number of times he won to the number of times he lost was 5:2, and if he won a total of $600, what is the total number of times he played this game?

Solution: Ratio of games won to games lost = 5:2

Total Games Played $\Rightarrow 7x$

Games Won = $5x$ $\Rightarrow$ Money received = $12(5x) = $60x$

Games Lost = $2x$ $\Rightarrow$ Money paid out = $10(2x) = $20x$

Net Earnings $\Rightarrow$ Money Received – Money Paid

$\Rightarrow $60x – $20x = 40x = 600

$\Rightarrow x = $600 \div 40 = 15$

Total Games Played $\Rightarrow 7x = 7 \times 15 = 105$

Question #30: An artist, who is trying to develop a new shade for his oil painting, mixed red, blue, and green color pigments in the ratio of 1:25:50. After looking at the result, he decided to double the ratio of red to blue and halve the ratio of red to green. If the final mixture contains 125 liters of blue, how many liters of red would it have?

Solution: Original Ratio of Red, Blue, and Green $\Rightarrow$ 1:25:50

First Alteration: Double the Ratio of Red to Blue $\Rightarrow$ from 1:25 to 2:25
            (When a ratio is doubled, the first part of the ratio is doubled)

Second Alteration: Halve the Ratio of Red to Green $\Rightarrow$ from 1:50 to 0.5:50 or 2:200
            (When a ratio is halved, the first part of the ratio is halved)

New Ratio of Red, Blue, and Green $\Rightarrow$ 2:25:200

Amount of Blue Color in Final Mixture $\Rightarrow$ 125 liters, which is 25 parts × 5

Amount of Red Color in Final Mixture $\Rightarrow$ 2 parts × 5 = 10 liters

Question #31: In a certain auto dealership, if one-half of the number of vans is one-tenth of the total number of vehicles, and one-third of the number of jeeps is one-eighteenth of the total number of vehicles, then what is the ratio of vans to jeeps?

Solution: 1/2 the No. of vans is 1/10 the total No. of vehicles $\Rightarrow \dfrac{1}{2}V = \dfrac{1}{10}T$

$\Rightarrow 2T = 10V$ [Cross-multiply]

$\Rightarrow T = 5V$ [Divide both side sides 2]

1/3 the No. of jeeps is 1/18 the total No. of vehicles $\Rightarrow \dfrac{1}{3}J = \dfrac{1}{18}T$

$\Rightarrow 3T = 18J$ [Cross-multiply]

$\Rightarrow T = 6J$ [Divide both side sides 3]

EZ Problem Set-Up $\Rightarrow$ Equate the two values of T to find the ratio of vans to jeeps

$\Rightarrow 5V = 6J$ [Set up the equation]

$\Rightarrow \dfrac{V}{J} = \dfrac{6}{5}$ [Divide both sides by 5J]

Question #32: In a certain company, the ratio of managers to supervisors is 2 to 5. If one-third of the managers are females and one-fourth of the supervisors are females, what fraction of the combined managers and supervisors are males?

Solution: Ratio of Managers to Supervisors $\Rightarrow$ 2:5

Let, the No. of Managers = 2 $\Rightarrow$ Then, the No. of Female Managers = $\dfrac{1}{3} \times 2 = \dfrac{2}{3}$

$\Rightarrow$ And, the No. of Male Managers = $\dfrac{2}{3} \times 2 = \dfrac{4}{3}$

And, the No. of Supervisors = 5 $\Rightarrow$ Then the No. of Female Supervisors = $\dfrac{1}{4} \times 5 = \dfrac{5}{4}$

$\Rightarrow$ And, the No. of Male Supervisors = $\dfrac{3}{4} \times 5 = \dfrac{15}{4}$

Total No. of Managers and Supervisors = 2 + 5 = 7

Total No. of Male Managers and Male Supervisors $\Rightarrow \dfrac{4}{3} + \dfrac{15}{4} = \dfrac{16}{12} + \dfrac{45}{12} = \dfrac{61}{12}$

Fraction of the combined Managers and Supervisors who are Males $\Rightarrow \dfrac{61}{12} \div 7 = \dfrac{61}{12} \times \dfrac{1}{7} = \dfrac{61}{84}$

PROPORTIONS:

Question #33: If two numbers are in the ratio 9 to 8 and their difference is 10, what is the larger number?
Solution: Let the two number be, a and b.

The difference between a and b is 10	$\Rightarrow a - b = 10$	$\Rightarrow$ Equation #1
	$\Rightarrow a = b + 10$	[Subtract b from both sides]
The ratio of a and b is 9 to 8	$\Rightarrow a : b = 9 : 8$	[Given]
	$\Rightarrow \dfrac{a}{b} = \dfrac{9}{8}$	[Set up the proportion]
	$\Rightarrow 8a = 9b$	[Cross multiply]
	$\Rightarrow a = \dfrac{9}{8}b$	[Divide both sides by 8]
	$\Rightarrow b + 10 = \dfrac{9}{8}b$	[Substitute $a = b + 10$]
	$\Rightarrow \dfrac{9}{8}b - b = 10$	[Subtract b from both sides]
	$\Rightarrow \dfrac{1}{8}b = 10$	[Combine like-terms]
	$\Rightarrow b = 80$	[Multiply both sides by 8]
Substitute the value of b in Equation #1	$\Rightarrow a - b = 10$	[Rewrite Equation #1]
	$\Rightarrow a - 80 = 10$	[Substitute $b = 80$]
	$\Rightarrow a = 90$	[Add 80 to both sides]

Therefore, the smaller number is 10 and the larger number is 90

Question #34: In a certain manufacturing facility, the ratio of the number of nuts produced to the number of bolts produced on a certain day was 2 to 3. If the factory produced 8 more nuts, the ratio of the number of nuts produced to the number of bolts produced would have been 3 to 4. How many bolts did the factory produce?
Solution: Let, the No. of nuts produced $= n$
And, the No. of bolts produced $= b$

Ratio without additional production	$\Rightarrow \dfrac{n}{b} = \dfrac{2}{3}$	[Given]
	$\Rightarrow 3n = 2b$	[Cross-multiply]
	$\Rightarrow 3n - 2b = 0$	[Subtract $2b$ from both sides] $\Rightarrow$ Equation #1
Ratio with additional production	$\Rightarrow \dfrac{n+8}{b} = \dfrac{3}{4}$	[Given]
	$\Rightarrow 4(n + 8) = 3b$	[Cross-multiply]
	$\Rightarrow 4n + 32 = 3b$	[Apply distributive property]
	$\Rightarrow 4n - 3b = -32$	[Subtract $3b + 32$ from both sides]
		$\Rightarrow$ Equation #2
Multiply Equation #1 by 3	$\Rightarrow 9n - 6b = 0$	$\Rightarrow$ Equation #3
Multiply Equation #2 by -2	$\Rightarrow \underline{-8n + 6b = 64}$	$\Rightarrow$ Equation #4
Add Equation #3 and #4	$\Rightarrow \quad n \quad\;\; = 64$	
Original No. of nuts produced	$\Rightarrow n = 64$	
Original No. of screws produced	$\Rightarrow 3n - 2b = 0$	[Rewrite Equation #1]
	$\Rightarrow 3(64) = 2b$	[Substitute $n = 64$]
	$\Rightarrow 192 = 2b$	[Apply distributive property]
	$\Rightarrow b = 96$	[Divide both sides by 2]

Therefore, the total number of screws produced = 96

Question #35: During a one day sale at a certain bookstore, the ratio of the number of hardcover books sold to the number of soft cover books sold was 6 to 7. If the store had sold 12 more hardcover books, the ratio of the number of hardcover books sold to the number of soft cover books sold would have been 7 to 8. How many soft cover books did the store sell?

Solution: Let, the No. of hardcover books sold $= h$
And, the No. of soft cover books sold $= s$

Ratio without additional sale $\Rightarrow \dfrac{h}{s} = \dfrac{6}{7}$ [Given]

$\Rightarrow 7h = 6s$ [Cross-multiply]

$\Rightarrow 7h - 6s = 0$ [Subtract $6s$ from both sides] $\Rightarrow$ Equation #1

Ratio with additional sale $\Rightarrow \dfrac{h+12}{s} = \dfrac{7}{8}$ [Given]

$\Rightarrow 8(h + 12) = 7s$ [Cross-multiply]

$\Rightarrow 8h + 96 = 7s$ [Apply distributive property]

$\Rightarrow 8h - 7s = -96$ [Subtract $7s + 96$ from both sides] $\Rightarrow$ Equation #2

Multiply Equation #1 by -7 $\Rightarrow -49h + 42s = 0$ $\Rightarrow$ Equation #3

Multiply Equation #2 by 6 $\Rightarrow \underline{\;\;48h - 42s = -576\;\;}$ $\Rightarrow$ Equation #4

Add Equation #3 and #4 $\Rightarrow \quad h \qquad\quad = 576$

Original No. of hardcover books sold $\Rightarrow h = 576$

Original No. of soft cover books sold $\Rightarrow 7h - 6s = 0$ [Rewrite Equation #1]

$\Rightarrow 7(576) = 6s$ [Substitute $h = 576$]

$\Rightarrow 4032 = 6s$ [Apply distributive property]

$\Rightarrow s = 672$ [Divide both sides by 6]

Therefore, the total number of books sold = 576 + 672 = 1,248

Question #36: In a certain club, there is an equal number of male members and female members. If 1 male and 2 females quit the club, the ratio of male members to female members would be 6:5. How many female members are in the club before anyone quits?

Solution: Ratio of Males to Females before anyone quits $\Rightarrow$ 1:1   [Given]

$\Rightarrow \dfrac{M}{F} = \dfrac{1}{1}$ [Set up the proportion]

$\Rightarrow M = F$ [Cross-multiply]
                          $\Rightarrow$ Equation #1

Ratio of Males to Females after $1M$ & $2F$ quits $\Rightarrow$ 6:5   [Given]

$\Rightarrow \dfrac{M-1}{F-2} = \dfrac{6}{5}$ [Set up the proportion]

$\Rightarrow 5(M - 1) = 6(F - 2)$ [Cross-multiply]

$\Rightarrow 5M - 5 = 6F - 12$ [Apply distributive property]

$\Rightarrow 6F - 5M - 12 = -5$ [Subtract $5M$ from both sides]

$\Rightarrow 6F - 5M = 7$ [Add 12 to both sides]
                          $\Rightarrow$ Equation #2

Substitute the value of M from #1 into #2 $\Rightarrow 6F - 5F = 7$ [Substitute $M = F$]

$\Rightarrow F = 7$ [Combine like-terms]

Therefore, there are 7 female members in the club before anyone quits.

Question #37: In a certain company, the ratio of managers to supervisors is 5:1. If 225 new employees were hired as managers and supervisors in the ratio of 1:2, the new ratio of managers to supervisors would be 9:2. What was the original number of supervisors?

Solution: Ratio before hiring $\Rightarrow M{:}S = 5{:}1$ [Given]

$\Rightarrow \dfrac{M}{S} = \dfrac{5}{1}$ [Set up the proportion]

$\Rightarrow M = 5S$ [Cross-multiply]

No. of new hires $\Rightarrow$ 225 manager and supervisors in the ratio of 1:2

$$\Rightarrow \text{Managers} = \frac{1}{3} \times 225 = 75$$

$$\Rightarrow \text{Supervisors} = \frac{2}{3} \times 225 = 150$$

Ratio after hiring $\Rightarrow M:S = 9:2$ [Given]

$\Rightarrow \dfrac{M+75}{S+150} = \dfrac{9}{2}$ [Set up the proportion]

$\Rightarrow 2(M + 75) = 9(S + 150)$ [Cross-multiply]

$\Rightarrow 2M + 150 = 9S + 1{,}350$ [Apply distributive property]

$\Rightarrow 2M - 9S + 150 = 1{,}350$ [Subtract 9S from both sides]

$\Rightarrow 2M - 9S = 1{,}200$ [Subtract 150 from both sides]

$\Rightarrow 2(5S) - 9S = 1{,}200$ [Substitute $M = 5S$]

$\Rightarrow 10S - 9S = 1{,}200$ [Apply distributive property]

$\Rightarrow S = 1{,}200$ [Combine like-terms]

Therefore, originally there were 1,200 supervisors.

Question #38: In a certain school, the ratio of the number of teachers to the number of assistants is 7 to 56. If 6 additional assistants were to be hired, the ratio of the number of teachers to the number of assistants would become 7 to 58. How many staff members does the school have before hiring any new staff?

Solution: Let, the No. of teachers $= t$

And, the No. of assistants $= a$

Ratio before hiring new staff $\Rightarrow \dfrac{t}{a} = \dfrac{7}{56}$ [Set up the proportion]

$\Rightarrow 56t = 7a$ [Cross-multiply] $\Rightarrow$ Equation #1

Ratio after hiring new staff $\Rightarrow \dfrac{t}{a+6} = \dfrac{7}{58}$ [Set up the proportion]

$\Rightarrow 58t = 7(a + 6)$ [Cross-multiply]

$\Rightarrow 58t = 7a + 42$ [Apply distributive property] $\Rightarrow$ Equation #2

Subtract Equation #1 from #2 $\Rightarrow 58t = 7a + 42$ [Rewrite Equation #2]

$\underline{\Rightarrow -(56t = 7a)}$ [Rewrite Equation #1]

$\Rightarrow 2t = 42$ [Subtract the two equations]

$\Rightarrow t = 21$ [Divide both sides by 2]

Original No. of teachers $\Rightarrow t = 21$

Original No. of assistants $\Rightarrow 56t = 7a$ [Rewrite Equation #1]

$\Rightarrow 56(21) = 7a$ [Substitute $t = 21$]

$\Rightarrow 1176 = 7a$ [Apply distributive property]

$\Rightarrow a = 168$ [Divide both sides by 7]

Therefore, the total number of staff members in the school = $t + a$ = 21 + 168 = 189

Question #39: In a certain school, the ratio of the number of teachers to the number of assistants is 1 to 5. If 5 additional teachers and 75 additional assistants were to be hired, the ratio of the number of teachers to the number of assistants would become 1 to 7. How many staff members does the school have before hiring any new staff?

Solution: Let, the No. of teachers $= t$

And, the No. of assistants $= a$

Ratio before hiring new staff $\Rightarrow \dfrac{t}{a} = \dfrac{1}{5}$ [Set up the proportion]

$\Rightarrow 5t = a$ [Cross-multiply] $\Rightarrow$ Equation #1

Ratio after hiring new staff $\Rightarrow \dfrac{t+5}{a+75} = \dfrac{1}{7}$ [Set up the proportion]

$\Rightarrow 7(t + 5) = (a + 75)$ [Cross-multiply]

$\Rightarrow 7t + 35 = a + 75$ [Apply distributive property]

$\Rightarrow 7t = a + 40$ [Subtract 35 from both sides] $\Rightarrow$ Equation #2

Subtract Equation #1 from #2 $\Rightarrow 7t \quad = a + 40$ [Rewrite Equation #2]

$\underline{\Rightarrow -(5t \quad = a)}$ [Rewrite Equation #1]

$$\Rightarrow 2t \quad = 40 \qquad \text{[Subtract the two equations]}$$
$$\Rightarrow t \quad\ = 20 \qquad \text{[Divide both sides by 2]}$$

Original No. of teachers $\Rightarrow t = 20$

Original No. of assistants $\Rightarrow 5t = a$ [Rewrite Equation #1]
$$\Rightarrow 5(20) = a \qquad \text{[Substitute } t = 20]$$
$$\Rightarrow a = 100 \qquad \text{[Do the multiplication]}$$

Therefore, the total number of staff members in the school = $t + a$ = 20 + 100 = 120

Question #40: The force with which a hammer is hit on a nail against a wall is directly proportional to the length of the nail that goes inside the wall. The length of the nail is 20 millimeters and 2 millimeters are already inside the wall. If a force of 20 pounds pushes the nail 7 millimeters inside the wall, then, what magnitude of force, in pounds must be applied so that the nail is 7 millimeters further inside the wall?

Solution: The nail is already 2 mm inside the wall, with a force of 20 pounds, the nail goes inside 7 mm inside the wall, so, the nail goes inside an additional 7 − 2 = 5 mm $\Rightarrow f_1 = 20$ pounds and $p_1 = 5$ millimeters

We are asked to find the magnitude of force that must be applied so that the nail is 7 mm further inside the wall $\Rightarrow f_2 = ?$ pounds and $p_2 = 7$ millimeters

Note: Don't forget to find the changes in the length of the nail.

Set Up a Direct Proportion $\Rightarrow$ Force is directly proportional to the push

$$\Rightarrow \frac{force_1}{push_1} = \frac{force_2}{push_2} \qquad \text{[Set up the proportion]}$$

$$\Rightarrow \frac{20}{5} = \frac{f_2}{7} \qquad \text{[Substitute the known values]}$$

$$\Rightarrow 5f_2 = 140 \qquad \text{[Cross-multiply]}$$

$$\Rightarrow f_2 = 28 \qquad \text{[Divide both sides by 5]}$$

PART 4.0: GEOMETRY:

TOPICS COVERED:

- Lines & Angles

- Polygons

- Triangles

- Quadrilaterals

- Circles

- Solid Geometry

- Coordinate Geometry

- Multiple Figures

PRACTICE EXERCISE:

LINES & ANGLES:

Question #1: In the figure given below, the ratio of *AB* to *BC* is 1:1, and the ratio of *CD* to *DE* is 3:4. If the length of *AE* is 28 and the length of *BD* is 13, what is the ratio of *AD* to *BE*?

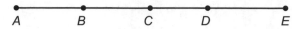

Note: Figure not drawn to scale.

Question #2: In the figure given below, all lines are straight lines and angle measures are as marked. What is the measure of ∠*F*?

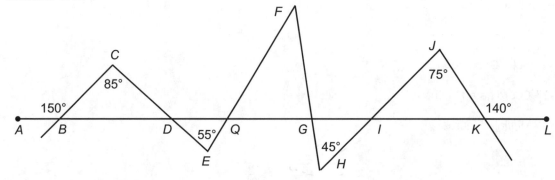

POLYGONS:

Question #3: In the figure given below, what is the total number of degrees of the internal angles?

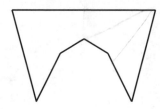

Question #4: In a quadrilateral, the measure of one angle is 25 more than twice the average of the measures of the other three angles. What is the measure of that one angle?

Question #5: If the side of a regular pentagon is 18 units and radius is 15 units, what is its area?

Question #6: If the side of a regular hexagon is 8 units, what is its area?

TRIANGLES:

Question #7: In the figure given below, what is the value of *x*?

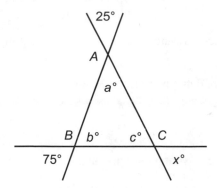

Question #8: In the figure given below, if △PQR is an equilateral triangle and △SQR is an isosceles triangle. If x = 33°, what is the value of y?

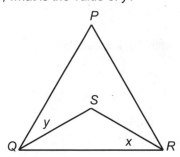

Note: Figure not drawn to scale.

Question #9: In the figure given below, in △ABC, what is the length of AB?

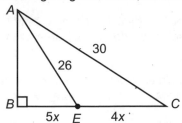

Question #10: In the figure given below, what is the value of x?

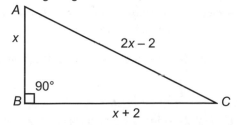

Question #11: If the sides of a triangle are in the ratio of 2:5:7 and the perimeter is 168 units, what is the positive difference between the length of the largest and smallest side?

Question #12: If P is the perimeter of an equilateral triangle, then, in terms of P, what is the height of the triangle?

Question #13: If A is the area of an equilateral triangle, then, in terms of A, what is the side of the triangle?

Question #14: If s is the side and h is the height of an equilateral triangle, then, in terms of h, what is the side of the triangle?

QUADRILATERALS:

Question #15:   The length of a rectangle is 8 units less than twice its width. If the area of the rectangle is 192 unit^2, what is the perimeter of the rectangle?

Question #16:   If the area of a rectangular plot is 84 square feet and its perimeter is 38 feet, what is the length of each of the longer sides?

CIRCLES:

Question #17:   If A is the area and C is the circumference of a circle, what is A expressed in terms of C?

Question #18:   If the circumference of circle A is equal to the diameter of circle B, what is the ratio of the area of circle A to the area of circle B?

SOLID GEOMETRY:

Question #19:   In the figure shown below, the cube has edge of length 10 units, and X and Y are midpoints of two of the edges. What is the shortest distance from X to Y?

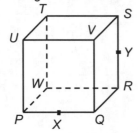

Question #20:   A cube made of white wood is painted black on all sides. If the cube is then cut into two parts such that two identical rectangular solids are formed, what fraction of the surface area of the each of the new solids is not painted black?

Question #21:   A solid white cube with an edge of 9 inches is first painted black and then it is sliced into 729 1-inch cubes. What is the ratio of the cubes with two black faces to cubes with three black faces?

Question #22:   A solid white cube with an edge of 10 inches is first painted black and then it is sliced into 1,000 1-inch cubes. How many of these cubes have no black faces?

Question #23:   A cylindrical pipe is 5 units long with an inner diameter of 12 units and outer diameter of 16 units. What is the total surface area of the pipe (inside, outside, and including the ends)?

Question #24:   If the height of a cylinder is twice its circumference, C, what is the volume of the cylinder in terms of C?

COORDINATE GEOMETRY:

Question #25:   A rectangle lies in the xy-coordinate plane so that its sides are not parallel to either axis. What is the product of the slopes of all four sides of the rectangle?

Question #26:   A rectangle lies in the xy-coordinate plane so that one of its sides is parallel to one of the axis. What is the product of the slopes of all four sides of the rectangle?

Question #27:   In the xy-coordinate system, if (p, q) and $(p + 5, q + k)$ are two points on the line defined by the equation $x = 2y - 7$, then what is the value of k?

Question #28:   If $m \neq n$ and the slope of the line passing through $(-m, m)$ and $(5m, n)$ is 1, what is the value of n in terms of m?

Question #29:   What value of k will make the line containing points $(k, 7)$ and $(-2, 5)$ perpendicular to the line containing $(9, k)$ and $(1, 0)$?

Question #30:   If the figure given below, the coordinates of the $\triangle ABC$ are $A(p, q)$, $B(r, 0)$, and $C(s, 0)$, what is the area of $\triangle ABC$?

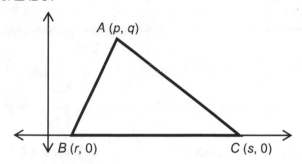

Question #31:   In the figure given below, point P has coordinates $(-5, 0)$ and $\angle QOR = 150°$. What is the slope of line QO?

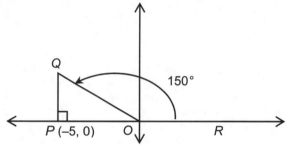

Question #32:   In the figure given below, point P has coordinates $(-1, 0)$ and $\angle QOR = 120°$. What is the slope of line QO?

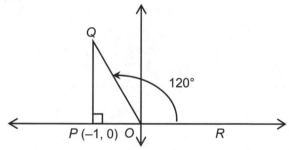

Question #33:   In the figure given below, point P has coordinates $(-7, 0)$ and $\angle QOR = 135°$. What is the slope of line QO?

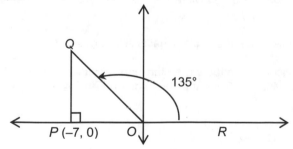

Question #34:   In the figure given below, if the area of the circle with center P at $(5, 5)$ is $n\pi$, what is the value of n?

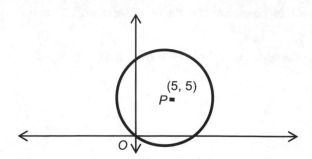

Question #35: In a *xy*-coordinate plane, a circle with center (8, 0) is tangent to the line *y* = *x*. What is the diameter of the circle?

Question #36: In the figure given below, *PQRST* is a regular hexagon. What is the slope of line *QR*?

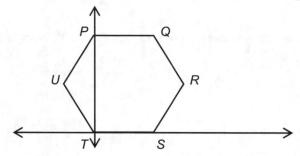

MULTIPLE FIGURES:

Question #37: In the figure given below, the smaller circle is inscribed in the square and the square is inscribed in the larger circle. If the length of each side of the square is *n*, what is the ratio of the area of the larger circle to the area of the smaller circle?

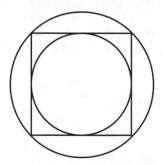

Question #38: If the area of a rectangle *A* with length *x* + 8 and width *x* + 1 is 100, what is the area of rectangle *B* with length *x* + 7 and width *x* + 2?

Question #39: If *A* is the area and *C* is the circumference of a circle, what is *A* in terms of *C*?

Question #40: In the figure given below, a semicircle is attached to the narrow sides of the two rectangles. If the length of the rectangle is 100 and width is 50, what is the total area enclosed by the figure?

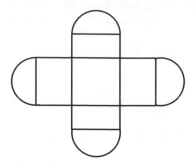

Question #41: In the figure given below, all the circles are tangent to one another, and the total area of four equal circles is 100π. What is the diameter of the small circle in the center?

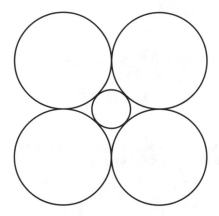

Question #42: A certain recipe makes enough batter for identical 8 large circular cookies that are each 20 inches in diameter. How many circular identical small cookies, each with ¼ the diameter of large cookie and of the same thickness as the large cookie, can be made with the same batter?

Question #43: The internal dimensions of a rectangular cargo container are 16 meters by 18 meters by 20 meters. A cylindrical oil tank is to be packed inside the box so that it's placed straight up when the closed box stands on one of its six sides. What should be the radius of the cylindrical tank so that it can contain the maximum amount of oil?

Question #44: Three identical balls fit snuggly into a cylindrical can, meaning, the radius of the spheres equals the radius of the can, and the balls just touch the bottom and the top of the can. What fraction of the volume of the can is taken up by the balls?

Question #45: There are five small circles, all of which are of exactly same size, lie inside a large circle as shown below. The diameter of the large circle passes through the centers of the small circles. If each of the smaller circles has a circumference of 10π, what is the area of the shaded region?

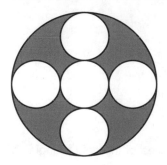

Question #46:   In the figure given below, the rectangular plot, which is *x* units by *y* units, is surrounded by a walkway, which is 2.5 units wide. What is the area of the shaded walkway in terms of *x* and *y*?

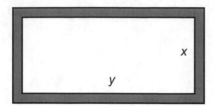

Question #47:   In the figure given below, trapezoid *ABCDEF* is divided into rectangle *ABDE*, Δ*AEF*, and Δ*BDC*. What is the combined area of the two shaded triangles?

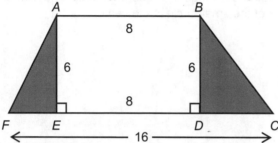

Question #48:   The figure given below consists of four semicircles in a large semicircle. If the small semicircles have radii of 1, 2, 3, and 4, what is the perimeter and area of the shaded region?

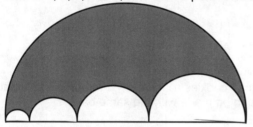

Question #49:   The figure given below consists of four shaded semicircles. If *AB* = 2, *BC* = 2*AB*, *CD* = 2*BC*, and *DE* = 2*CD*. what is the area of the shaded region?

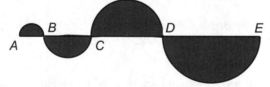

Question #50:   In the figure given below, ∠*POQ* = 60°, and *OP* is 12. What is the area and perimeter of the shaded region?

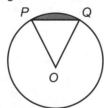

Question #51:   In the figure given below, if the radius *OP* is 16 and the area of the right triangle *OPQ* is 128, what is the area of the shaded region?

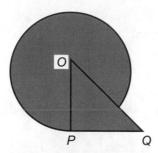

Question #52: In the figure given below, if the radius *OP* is 12 and the area of the square *OPXQ* is 144, what is the area of the shaded region?

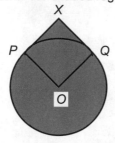

Question #53: In the figure given below, an equilateral triangle with side 18 is inscribed in a circle. What is the area of the shaded region?

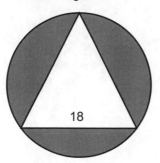

Question #54: In the figure given below, a right circular cylinder is inscribed in a cone with height 25 and radius 15. The radius of the base of the cylinder is 6. What is the volume of the white region?

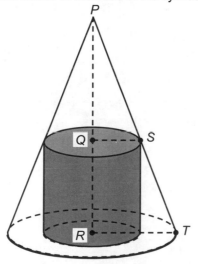

Note: Figure not drawn to scale.

Question #55: If the figure given below, what is the area of the shaded region?

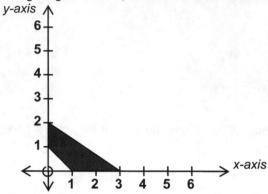

PRACTICE EXERCISE – QUESTIONS & ANSWERS WITH EXPLANATIONS:

LINES & ANGLES:

Question #1: In the figure given below, the ratio of AB to BC is 1:1, and the ratio of CD to DE is 3:4. If the length of AE is 28 and the length of BD is 13, what is the ratio of AD to BE?

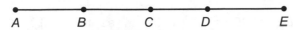

    A   B   C   D   E

Note: Figure not drawn to scale.

Solution: Label the segments on the number line:

      x x $3y$ $4y$

    A   B   C   D   E

Measure of AE	$\Rightarrow AB + BC + CD + DE = 28$	[Add all the segments of AE]
	$\Rightarrow x + x + 3y + 4y = 28$	[Substitute the known values]
	$\Rightarrow 2x + 7y = 28$	[Combine like-terms] $\Rightarrow$ Equation #1
Measure of BD	$\Rightarrow BC + CD = 13$	[Add all the segments of BD]
	$\Rightarrow x + 3y = 13$	[Substitute the known values]
	$\Rightarrow -2x -6y = -26$	[Multiply both sides by –2] $\Rightarrow$ Equation #2
Add #1 & #2	$\Rightarrow \quad 2x +7y = \quad 28$	[Rewrite Equation #1]
	$\Rightarrow \underline{-2x -6y = -26}$	[Rewrite Equation #2]
	$\Rightarrow \qquad +1y = \quad 2$	[Add the two equations]
Solve for x	$\Rightarrow 2x + 7y = 28$	[Rewrite Equation #1]
	$\Rightarrow 2x + 7(2) = 28$	[Substitute $y = 2$]
	$\Rightarrow 2x + 14 = 28$	[Do the multiplication]
	$\Rightarrow 2x = 14$	[Subtract 14 from both sides]
	$\Rightarrow x = 7$	[Divide both sides by 2]
Measure of AD	$\Rightarrow AB + BC + CD$	[AD is made up of AB, BC, and CD]
	$\Rightarrow x + x + 3y$	[Substitute the values of AB, BC, and CD]
	$\Rightarrow 2x + 3y$	[Combine like-terms]
	$\Rightarrow 2(7) + 3(2)$	[Substitute $x = 7$ and $y = 2$]
	$\Rightarrow 14 + 6$	[Do the multiplication]
	$\Rightarrow 20$	[Do the addition]
Measure of BE	$\Rightarrow BC + CD + DE$	[BE is made up of BC, CD, and DE]
	$\Rightarrow x + 3y + 4y$	[Substitute the values of BC, CD, and DE]
	$\Rightarrow x + 7y$	[Combine like-terms]
	$\Rightarrow 1(7) + 7(2)$	[Substitute $x = 7$ and $y = 2$]
	$\Rightarrow 7 + 14$	[Do the multiplication]
	$\Rightarrow 21$	[Do the addition]
Ratio of AD to BE	$\Rightarrow 20:21$	[Substitute the values of AD and BE]

Question #2: In the figure given below, all lines are straight lines and angle measures are as marked. What is the measure of $\angle F$?

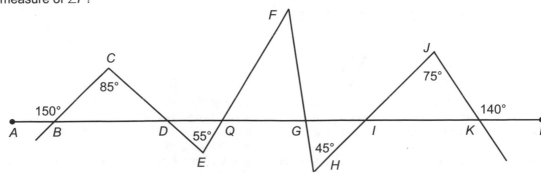

Solution: Start from one end and keep finding the measures of angles until the problem is solved.

In Extreme Left $\Rightarrow \angle ABC + \angle CBD = 180°$ [Sum of supplementary angles equal 180°]

$\Rightarrow 150° + \angle CBD = 180°$ [Substitute $\angle CBD = 150°$]

$\Rightarrow \angle CBD = 30°$ [Subtract 150° from both sides]

In $\triangle CBD$ $\Rightarrow \angle CBD + \angle BCD + \angle CDB = 180°$ [Sum of angles in triangle equals 180°]

$\Rightarrow 30° + 85° + \angle CDB = 180°$ [Substitute $\angle CBD = 30°$ and $\angle BCD = 85°$]

$\Rightarrow 115° + \angle CDB = 180°$ [Combine like-terms]

$\Rightarrow \angle CDB = 65°$ [Subtract 115° from both sides]

Intersection of CE & BQ $\Rightarrow \angle CDB = \angle QDE = 65°$ [vertical angles are equal]

In $\triangle DEQ$ $\Rightarrow \angle QDE + \angle DEQ + \angle DQE = 180°$ [Sum of angles in triangle equals 180°]

$\Rightarrow 65° + 55° + \angle DQE = 180°$ [Substitute $\angle QDE = 65°$ and $\angle DEQ = 55°$]

$\Rightarrow 120° + \angle DQE = 180°$ [Combine like-terms]

$\Rightarrow \angle DQE = 60°$ [Subtract 120° from both sides]

Intersection of FE & DG $\Rightarrow \angle DQE = \angle FQG = 60°$ [Vertical angles are equal]

In Extreme Right $\Rightarrow \angle LKJ + \angle JKI = 180°$ [Sum of supplementary angles equal 180°]

$\Rightarrow 140° + \angle JKI = 180°$ [Substitute $\angle LKJ = 140°$]

$\Rightarrow \angle JKI = 40°$ [Subtract 140° from both sides]

In $\triangle JIK$ $\Rightarrow \angle JKI + \angle IJK + \angle JIK = 180°$ [Sum of angles in triangle equals 180°]

$\Rightarrow 40° + 75° + \angle JIK = 180°$ [Substitute $\angle JKI = 40°$ and $\angle IJK = 75°$]

$\Rightarrow 115° + \angle JIK = 180°$ [Combine like-terms]

$\Rightarrow \angle JIK = 65°$ [Subtract 115° from both sides]

Intersection of JH & GK $\Rightarrow \angle JIK = \angle GIH = 65°$ [Vertical angles are equal]

In $\triangle GHI$ $\Rightarrow \angle GIH + \angle GHI + \angle IGH = 180°$ [Sum of angles in triangle equals 180°]

$\Rightarrow 65° + 45° + \angle IGH = 180°$ [Substitute $\angle GIH = 65°$ and $\angle GHI = 45°$]

$\Rightarrow 110° + \angle IGH = 180°$ [Combine like-terms]

$\Rightarrow \angle IGH = 70°$ [Subtract 110° from both sides]

Intersection of FH & IQ $\Rightarrow \angle IGH = \angle FGQ = 70°$ [Vertical angles are equal]

In $\triangle QFG$ $\Rightarrow \angle FQG + \angle FGQ + \angle QFG = 180°$ [Sum of angles in triangle equals 180°]

$\Rightarrow 60° + 70° + \angle QFG = 180°$ [Substitute $\angle FQG = 60°$ and $\angle FGQ = 70°$]

$\Rightarrow 130° + \angle QFG = 180°$ [Combine like-terms]

$\Rightarrow \angle QFG = 50°$ [Subtract 130° from both sides]

POLYGONS:

Question #3:   In the figure given below, what is the total number of degrees of the internal angles?

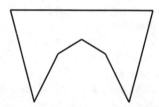

Solution: Divide the given figure into five triangles by connecting its vertices as shown below:

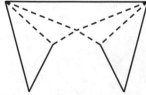

Sum of Number of Degrees of the Internal Angle of 1 Triangle $\Rightarrow 180°$

Sum of Number of Degrees of the Internal Angle of 5 Triangles $\Rightarrow 180° \times 5 = 900°$

Alternately, apply the formula: $(n - 2) \times 180° = (7 - 2) \times 180° = 5 \times 180° = 900°$

Question #4:   In a quadrilateral, the measure of one angle is 25 more than twice the average of the measures of the other three angles. What is the measure of that one angle?

Solution: Let the measure of that angle = n
Sum of all 4 angles in a quadrilateral = $360°$
Sum of those other three angles in the quadrilateral in this question = $360° - n$

Average of those other three angles in the quadrilateral in this question = $\dfrac{360 - n}{3}$

EZ problem Set-Up $\Rightarrow$ Measure of one angle is 25 more than twice the average of the measures of the other three angles

$$\Rightarrow n = 25 + 2\left(\frac{360 - n}{3}\right)$$ [Set up the equation]

$$\Rightarrow n = 25 + \frac{2}{3}(360) - \frac{2}{3}(n)$$ [Apply distributive property]

$$\Rightarrow n = 25 + 240 - \frac{2}{3}n$$ [Simplify the fractions]

$$\Rightarrow n = 265 - \frac{2}{3}n$$ [Combine like-terms]

$$\Rightarrow n + \frac{2}{3}n = 265$$ [Add 2/3n to both sides]

$$\Rightarrow \frac{5}{3}n = 265$$ [Combine like-terms]

$$\Rightarrow n = 159°$$ [Multiply both sides by 3/5]

Question #5:   If the side of a regular pentagon is 18 units and radius is 15 units, what is its area?
Solution: Let's first draw a figure:

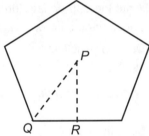

Perimeter of Polygon $\Rightarrow$ Length of Side × No. of Sides   [Write the appropriate formula]
$\Rightarrow$ 18 × 5 = 90 units   [Substitute the known values and simplify]
$\Rightarrow$ 90 units   [Do the multiplication]
In ΔPQR $\Rightarrow PR^2 + QR^2 = PQ^2$ [Apply Pythagorean Theorem]
$\Rightarrow apothem^2 + (\frac{1}{2}base)^2 = radius^2$ [Write the quantities of pentagon]
$\Rightarrow a^2 + (18/2)^2 = 15^2$ [Substitute the values of the known sides]
$\Rightarrow a^2 = 15^2 - 9^2$ [Subtract 9^2 from both side]
$\Rightarrow a^2 = 225 - 81$ [Solve the exponents]
$\Rightarrow a^2 = 144$ [Do the subtraction]
$\Rightarrow a = 12$ units   [Square root both sides]
Area of Regular Polygon $\Rightarrow \frac{1}{2}ap$ [Write the appropriate formula]
$\Rightarrow \frac{1}{2}(12)(90)$ [Substitute the known values]
$\Rightarrow 540$ unit^2 [Do the multiplication]

Question #6:   If the side of a regular hexagon is 8 units, what is its area?
Solution: Let's first draw a figure:

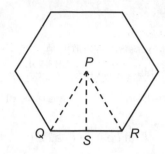

Perimeter of Polygon ⇒ Length of Side × No. of Sides   [Write the appropriate formula]
⇒ 8 × 6 = 48 units   [Substitute the known values and simplify]
In ΔPQS   ⇒ $PS^2 + QS^2 = PQ^2$ [Apply Pythagorean Theorem]
⇒ $apothem^2 + (½base)^2 = radius^2$ [Write the quantities of hexagon]
⇒ $a^2 + (8/2)^2 = 8^2$ [In regular hexagon, side = base = radius]
⇒ $a^2 = 8^2 - 4^2$ [Subtract 4^2 from both side]
⇒ $a^2 = 64 - 14$ [Solve the exponents]
⇒ $a^2 = 48$ [Do the subtraction]
⇒ $a = 4\sqrt{3}$ units   [Square root both sides]

You can also find the apothem by using the 30°-60°-90° triangle concept:

In ΔPQS   ⇒ It's a 30°-60°-90° triangle whose sides are in the ratio of $x : x\sqrt{3} : 2x$
Side Opposite 30° ⇒ x   = QS = ½(8) = 4
Side Opposite 60° ⇒ $x\sqrt{3}$ = PS = $4\sqrt{3}$
Side Opposite 90° ⇒ 2x   = PQ = 8

Area of Regular Polygon ⇒ ½ap   [Write the appropriate formula]
⇒ ½($4\sqrt{3}$)(48)   [Substitute the known values]
⇒ $96\sqrt{3}$ unit²   [Do the multiplication]

Alternate Method: This problem can also be solved by dividing the hexagon into equilateral triangles

Area of Equilateral Triangle PQR ⇒ $\dfrac{s^2\sqrt{3}}{4}$ [Write the appropriate formula]

⇒ $\dfrac{8^2\sqrt{3}}{4}$ [Substitute s = 8]

⇒ $16\sqrt{3}$ unit²   [Simplify the fraction]

Area of Regular Hexagon   ⇒ 6 × Area of ΔPQR   [Write the appropriate formula]
⇒ $6 \times 16\sqrt{3}$ [Substitute the known values]
⇒ $96\sqrt{3}$ unit²   [Do the multiplication]

TRIANGLES:

Question #7:   In the figure given below, what is the value of x?

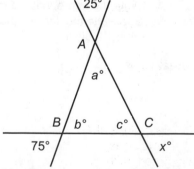

Solution: Measure of ∠a = 25°   [Vertical angles are equal to each other]

Measure of $\angle b = 75°$ [Vertical angles are equal to each other]
Measure of $\angle c = \angle x$ [Vertical angles are equal to each other]
EZ Problems Set-Up $\Rightarrow$ Sum of all the interior angles of any type of triangle equals 180°
        $\Rightarrow \angle a + \angle b + \angle c = 180°$ [Set up the equation]
        $\Rightarrow 25° + 75° + x = 180°$ [Substitute the values of the angles]
        $\Rightarrow 100° + x = 180°$ [Combine like-terms]
        $\Rightarrow x = 80°$ [Subtract 100° from both sides]

Question #8:   In the figure given below, if ΔPQR is an equilateral triangle and ΔSQR is an isosceles triangle. If $x = 33°$, what is the value of y?

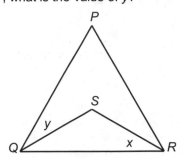

Note: Figure not drawn to scale.

Solution: Measure of $\Rightarrow \angle QPR = \angle PQR = \angle PRQ = 60°$ [In equilateral triangles, all three angles are equal]
In ΔPQR $\Rightarrow \angle QPR + \angle PQR + \angle PRQ = 180°$ [Sum of angles in a triangle equals 180°]
        $\Rightarrow \angle QPR + (\angle PQS + \angle SQR) + (\angle PRS + \angle SRQ) = 180°$ [Split the bottom two angles]
        $\Rightarrow 60° + (y + \angle SQR) + (\angle PRS + \angle x) = 180°$ [Substitute $\angle QPR = 60°$]
        $\Rightarrow 60° + (y + x) + (y + x) = 180°$ [Opposite angles are equal in isosceles triangle: $\angle SQR = x$ and $\angle PRS = y$]
        $\Rightarrow 60° + 2x + 2y = 180°$ [Combine like-terms]
        $\Rightarrow 2x + 2y = 120°$ [Subtract 60° from both sides]
        $\Rightarrow 2(x + y) = 120°$ [Factor out 2 on the left side]
        $\Rightarrow (x + y) = 60°$ [Divide both sides by 2]
        $\Rightarrow 33° + y = 60°$ [Substitute $x = 33°$]
        $\Rightarrow y = 27°$ [Subtract 33° from both sides]

Question #9:   In the figure given below, in ΔABC, what is the length of AB?

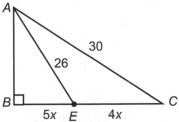

Solution: In ΔABC $\Rightarrow AC^2 = AB^2 + BC^2$ [Apply Pythagorean Theorem]
        $\Rightarrow 30^2 = AB^2 + (9x)^2$ [Substitute the values of the known sides]
        $\Rightarrow AB^2 = 30^2 - (9x)^2$ [Subtract $(9x)^2$ from both sides]
        $\Rightarrow AB^2 = 900 - 81x^2$ [Solver the exponents]
In ΔABE $\Rightarrow AE^2 = AB^2 + BE^2$ [Apply Pythagorean Theorem]
        $\Rightarrow 26^2 = AB^2 + (5x)^2$ [Substitute the values of the given sides]
        $\Rightarrow AB^2 = 26^2 - (5x)^2$ [Subtract $(5x)^2$ from both sides]
        $\Rightarrow AB^2 = 676 - 25x^2$ [Solve the exponents]
Equate the two value of AB^2:
        $\Rightarrow AB^2 \Rightarrow 900 - 81x^2 = 676 - 25x^2$ [Equate the two values of AB^2 from above]
        $\Rightarrow 900 = 81x^2 + 676 - 25x^2$ [Add $81x^2$ to both sides]
        $\Rightarrow 900 - 676 = 81x^2 - 25x^2$ [Subtract 676 from both sides]
        $\Rightarrow 56x^2 = 224$ [Combine like-terms]

$$\Rightarrow x^2 = 4 \qquad\qquad \text{[Divide both sides by 56]}$$
$$\Rightarrow x = 2 \text{ units} \qquad\qquad \text{[Square root both sides]}$$

Measure of BC $\Rightarrow 5x + 4x = 9x$ [Add BE and EC to find BC]
$\Rightarrow 9(2) = 18$ units [Substitute $x = 2$]
In $\triangle ABC$ $\Rightarrow AC^2 = AB^2 + BC^2$ [Apply Pythagorean Theorem]
$\Rightarrow 30^2 = AB^2 + (18)^2$ [Substitute the values of the known sides]
$\Rightarrow AB^2 = 30^2 - 18^2$ [Subtract 18^2 from both sides]
$\Rightarrow AB^2 = 900 - 324$ [Solve the exponents]
$\Rightarrow AB^2 = 576$ [Do the subtraction]
$\Rightarrow AB = 24$ units [Square root both sides]

Question #10: In the figure given below, what is the value of x?

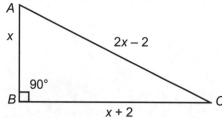

Solution: Apply Pythagorean Theorem $\Rightarrow a^2 + b^2 = c^2$ [Write the Pythagorean Theorem]
$\Rightarrow (x)^2 + (x + 2)^2 = (2x - 2)^2$ [Substitute the values of known sides]
$\Rightarrow x^2 + x^2 + 4x + 4 = 4x^2 - 8x + 4$ [Apply distributive property]
$\Rightarrow 2x^2 + 4x + 4 = 4x^2 - 8x + 4$ [Combine like-terms]
$\Rightarrow 4x + 4 = 2x^2 - 8x + 4$ [Subtract $2x^2$ from both sides]
$\Rightarrow 4 = 2x^2 - 12x + 4$ [Subtract $4x$ from both sides]
$\Rightarrow 2x^2 - 12x = 0$ [Subtract 4 from both sides]
$\Rightarrow 2x(x - 6) = 0$ [Factor out $2x$ from the polynomial]
Either: $2x = 0$ $\Rightarrow x = 0$
Or: $x - 6 = 0$ $\Rightarrow x = 6$

Since lengths can never be zero or negative, the only value of x is 6 units.

Question #11: If the sides of a triangle are in the ratio of 2:5:7 and the perimeter is 168 units, what is the positive difference between the length of the largest and smallest side?

Solution: Ratio of Sides of Triangle $\Rightarrow$ 2:5:7
Perimeter of Triangle $\Rightarrow$ 168 units

Length of Smallest Side $\Rightarrow \dfrac{2}{14} \times 168 = 24$ units

Length of Largest Side $\Rightarrow \dfrac{7}{14} \times 168 = 84$ units

Difference between the Length of Largest and Smallest Side $\Rightarrow 84 - 24 = 60$ units

Question #12: If P is the perimeter of an equilateral triangle, then, in terms of P, what is the height of the triangle?

Solution: Area of Equilateral Triangle $\Rightarrow \dfrac{1}{2} \times b \times h = \dfrac{s^2\sqrt{3}}{4}$ [Equate both area formulas of triangle]

$\Rightarrow \dfrac{1}{2} \times s \times h = \dfrac{s^2\sqrt{3}}{4}$ [In equilateral triangles, base = side]

$\Rightarrow 2sh = s^2\sqrt{3}$ [Multiply both sides by 4]

$\Rightarrow h = \dfrac{s\sqrt{3}}{2}$ [Divide both sides by $2s$]

$\Rightarrow h = \left(\dfrac{3}{3}\right)\dfrac{s\sqrt{3}}{2}$ [Multiply the right side by 3/3]

$$\Rightarrow h = \frac{3s\sqrt{3}}{6}$$ [Combine fractions]

$$\Rightarrow h = \frac{P\sqrt{3}}{6}$$ [Since $P = 3s$, replace $3s$ with P]

Question #13: If A is the area of an equilateral triangle, then, in terms of A, what is the side of the triangle?

Solution: Area of Equilateral Triangle $\Rightarrow \dfrac{s^2\sqrt{3}}{4} = A$ [Equate area formula with given area]

$$\Rightarrow s^2\sqrt{3} = 4A$$ [Multiply both sides by 4]

$$\Rightarrow s^2 = \frac{4A}{\sqrt{3}}$$ [Divide both sides by $\sqrt{3}$]

$$\Rightarrow s = \sqrt{\frac{4A}{\sqrt{3}}}$$ [Square root both sides]

$$\Rightarrow s = 2\sqrt{\frac{A}{\sqrt{3}}}$$ [Simplify the expression]

Question #14: If s is the side and h is the height of an equilateral triangle, then, in terms of h, what is the side of the triangle?

Solution: Area of Equilateral Triangle $\Rightarrow \dfrac{1}{2} \times b \times h = \dfrac{s^2\sqrt{3}}{4}$ [Equate both area formulas of triangle]

$$\Rightarrow \frac{1}{2} \times s \times h = \frac{s^2\sqrt{3}}{4}$$ [In equilateral triangles, base = side]

$$\Rightarrow 2sh = s^2\sqrt{3}$$ [Multiply both sides by 4]

$$\Rightarrow s = \frac{2h}{\sqrt{3}}$$ [Divide both sides by $s\sqrt{3}$]

QUADRILATERALS:

Question #15: The length of a rectangle is 8 units less than twice its width. If the area of the rectangle is 192 unit^2, what is the perimeter of the rectangle?

Solution:
Let, the width of the rectangle $\Rightarrow W$ units   [Assumption]
Then, the length of the rectangle $\Rightarrow 2W - 8$ units   [Length is 8 less than twice its width]
Area of Rectangle $\Rightarrow LW = 192$ [Equate the area formula with given area]
$\Rightarrow W(2W - 8) = 192$ [Substitute the values of the sides]
$\Rightarrow 2W^2 - 8W = 192$ [Apply distributive property]
$\Rightarrow 2W^2 - 8W - 192 = 0$ [Subtract 192 from both sides]
$\Rightarrow W^2 - 4W - 96 = 0$ [Divide both sides by 2]
$\Rightarrow (W - 12)(W + 8) = 0$ [Factor the trinomial into two binomials]
$\Rightarrow W = +12$ and -8 [Solve for the two value of W]
Measure of Width $\Rightarrow W = 12$ units   [Take the positive value of W]
Measure of Length $\Rightarrow L = 2W - 8 = 2(12) - 8 = 16$ units   [Substitute $W = 12$]
Perimeter of Rectangle $\Rightarrow 2(L + W)$ [Write the appropriate formula]
$\Rightarrow 2(12 + 16) = 2(28) = 56$ units   [Substitute the known values and simplify]

Question #16: If the area of a rectangular plot is 84 square feet and its perimeter is 38 feet, what is the length of each of the longer sides?

Solution:
Area $\Rightarrow LW = 84$ unit^2 [Given] $\Rightarrow$ Equation #1
Perimeter $\Rightarrow 2(L + W) = 38$ [Equate perimeter formula with given perimeter]
$\Rightarrow L + W = 19$ [Divide both sides by 2]
$\Rightarrow L = 19 - W$ units   [Subtract W from both sides] $\Rightarrow$ Equation #2
Substitute the value of L from Equation #2 into Equation #1:

$\Rightarrow LW = 84$ [Rewrite Equation #1]

$\Rightarrow (19 - W)W = 84$ [Substitute $L = 19 - W$ from Equation #2]

$\Rightarrow 19W - W^2 = 84$ [Apply distributive property]

$\Rightarrow 19W - W^2 - 84 = 0$ [Subtract 84 from both sides]

$\Rightarrow W^2 - 19W + 84 = 0$ [Multiply the equation by −1]

$\Rightarrow (W - 12)\,(W - 7)$ [Factor the trinomial into two binomials]

$\Rightarrow W - 12 = 0$ or $W - 7 = 0$ [Equate each factor equal to zero]

$\Rightarrow W = 12$ or $W = 7$ [Solve for W]

Substitute the value of W's in Equation #2:

$\Rightarrow L = 19 - W$ [Rewrite Equation #2]

$\Rightarrow L = 19 - 12 = 7$ or $L = 19 - 7 = 12$ [Solve for both values of L]

Therefore, the length of the each of the longer sides is 12 units & the length of each of the shorter sides is 7 units.

Alternately: You can also solve this problem by using common sense.

You know that ($LW = 84$) and ($L + W = 19$). This means you need to find a set of two numbers, whose product is 84 and sum is 19. There is only one possibility for this combination. The two numbers must be 12 and 7.

CIRCLES:

Question #17: If A is the area and C is the circumference of a circle, what is A expressed in terms of C?

Solution: Circumference of Circle $\Rightarrow C = 2\pi r$ [Write the formula of circumference of a circle]

$$\Rightarrow \frac{C}{2\pi} = \frac{2\pi r}{2\pi}$$ [Divide both sides by 2π]

$$\Rightarrow \frac{C}{2\pi} = r$$ [Cancel-out common terms]

Area of Circle $\Rightarrow A = \pi r^2$ [Write the formula of area of circle]

$$\Rightarrow A = \pi \left(\frac{C}{2\pi}\right)^2$$ [Substitute $r = C/2\pi$]

$$\Rightarrow A = \frac{\pi C^2}{4\pi^2}$$ [Solve the exponent]

$$\Rightarrow A = \frac{C^2}{4\pi}$$ [Cancel-out common terms]

Question #18: If the circumference of circle A is equal to the diameter of circle B, what is the ratio of the area of circle A to the area of circle B?

Solution: Let, the radius of Circle A $\Rightarrow r$

Then, the circumference of Circle A $\Rightarrow 2\pi r$

And, the area of Circle A $\Rightarrow \pi r^2$

Let, the radius of Circle B $\Rightarrow R$

Then, the diameter of Circle B $\Rightarrow 2R$

And, the area of Circle B $\Rightarrow \pi R^2$

EZ Problem Set-Up $\Rightarrow$ Circumference of Circle A = Diameter of Circle B

                       $\Rightarrow 2\pi r = 2R$ [Set up the equation]

                       $\Rightarrow R = \pi r$ [Divide both sides by 2]

Ratio of Area of Circle A to B $\Rightarrow \dfrac{Area\ of\ Circle\ A}{Area\ of\ Circle\ B}$

$$\Rightarrow \frac{\pi R^2}{\pi r^2}$$ [Substitute the areas of two circles]

$$\Rightarrow \frac{\pi(\pi r)^2}{\pi r^2}$$ [Substitute $R = \pi r$]

$$\Rightarrow \frac{\pi(\pi^2 r^2)}{\pi r^2}$$ [Distribute the exponent in the numerator]

$$\Rightarrow \frac{\pi^3 r^2}{\pi r^2}$$ [Apply distributive property]

$$\Rightarrow \pi^2$$ [Simplify the expression]

SOLID GEOMETRY:

Question #19:   In the figure shown below, the cube has edge of length 10 units, and *X* and *Y* are midpoints of two of the edges. What is the shortest distance from *X* to *Y*?

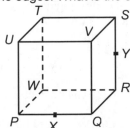

Solution: In $\triangle XQR$ $\Rightarrow XQ^2 + QR^2 = XR^2$ [Apply Pythagorean Theorem]
   $\Rightarrow 5^2 + 10^2 = XR^2$ [Since *X* is the midpoint of *PQ*, XQ = ½(10)]
   $\Rightarrow 25 + 100 = XR^2$ [Solve the exponents]
   $\Rightarrow XR^2 = 125$ [Combine like-terms]
   $\Rightarrow XR = \sqrt{125} = 5\sqrt{5}$ units   [Square root both sides]

   In $\triangle XRY$ $\Rightarrow XR^2 + YR^2 = XY^2$ [Apply Pythagorean Theorem]

   $\Rightarrow \left(5\sqrt{5}\right)^2 + 5^2 = XY^2$ [Since *Y* is the midpoint of *SR*, YR = ½(10)]

   $\Rightarrow 125 + 25 = XY^2$ [Solve the exponents]
   $\Rightarrow XY^2 = 150$ [Combine like-terms]
   $\Rightarrow XY = \sqrt{150} = 5\sqrt{6}$ units   [Square root both sides]

Question #20:   A cube made of white wood is painted black on all sides. If the cube is then cut into two parts such that two identical rectangular solids are formed, what fraction of the surface area of the each of the new solids is not painted black?

Solution: Let the dimension of the original cube be $\Rightarrow 2 \times 2 \times 2$
   For the cube to be cut into two identical rectangular solids, it must be cut parallel to one of the parallel sides.
   The dimensions of each of the two cut rectangular solid $\Rightarrow 2 \times 2 \times 1$
   SA of 1 Rectangular Solid $\Rightarrow 2[LW + WH + LH] = 2[(2 \times 1) + (2 \times 2) + (2 \times 1)] = 2[2+4+2] = 2[8] = 16$ unit^2
   The dimension of the rectangular side of the rectangular solid that is still not painted black $\Rightarrow 2 \times 2$
   SA of white/un-painted side $\Rightarrow L \times W = 2 \times 2 = 4$ unit^2

   Fraction of the surface area of the each of the two new solids that is not painted black $\Rightarrow \dfrac{4}{16} = \dfrac{1}{4}$

Question #21:   A solid white cube with an edge of 9 inches is first painted black and then it is sliced into 729 1-inch cubes. What is the ratio of the cubes with two black faces to cubes with three black faces?

Solution: Since it's difficult to draw an exact picture, this problem requires your imaginative skills.
   Imagine in your mind that there is a white cube and you paint it black on all sides.
   Next, imagine that you slice this big 9-inch cube into little 1-inch cubes.
   Since the volume of the big cube is $9 \times 9 \times 9 = 729$, and we have to slice it into 729 cubes, the big cube will be completely divided into 729 identical cubes, each one of which is 1 by 1 by 1.
   First, find the 1-inch cubes that are painted black on exactly three faces $\Rightarrow$ only the corner cubes will be painted black on three faces. Since cubes have 8 corners, there will be 8 cubes with exactly three black faces.

Next, find the 1-inch cubes that are painted black on exactly two faces ⇒ only the cubes on the edges except the corner cubes will be painted black on two sides. Since cubes have 12 edges and each edge has 9 cubes lined up, but 2 of these are corner cubes with three black faces, there are only 7 cubes on each edge that has two black faces. So, the total number of cubes with exactly two black faces are 12 × 7 = 84.

Note that all the other cubes on the faces have exactly one back face and all other cubes from the inside have no black faces.

Ratio of cubes with two black faces to cubes with three black faces ⇒ 84: 8 = 21:2

Question #22:   A solid white cube with an edge of 10 inches is first painted black and then it is sliced into 1,000 1-inch cubes. How many of these cubes have no black faces?

Solution: Since it's difficult to draw an exact picture, this problem requires your imaginative skills.

Imagine in your mind that there is a white cube and you paint it black on all sides.

Next, imagine that you slice this big 10-inch cube into little 1-inch cubes.

Since the volume of the big cube is 10 × 10 × 10 = 1,000, and we have to slice it into 1,000 cubes, the big cube will be completely divided into 1,000 identical cubes, each one of which is 1 by 1 by 1.

First, find the 1-inch cubes that are painted black on exactly three faces ⇒ only the corner cubes will be painted black on three sides. Since cubes have 8 corners, there will be 8 cubes with exactly three black faces.

Next, find the 1-inch cubes that are painted black on exactly two faces ⇒ only the cubes on the edges except the corner cubes will be painted black on two sides. Since each edge has 10 cubes lined up, but 2 of these are corner cubes with three black faces, there are only 8 cubes on each edge that has two black faces. Since cubes have 12 edges, the total number of cubes with exactly two black faces are 12 × 8 = 96.

Finally, find the 1-inch cubes that are painted on exactly one face ⇒ only the middle cubes of the faces of the big cube will be painted black on one side. Since each face of the big cube has 10 × 10 = 100 cubes, but all the corner ones are already counted, there are only 8 × 8 = 64 cubes on each face that has one black face. Since a cube has 6 faces, the total number of cubes with exactly one black face are 64 × 6 = 384.

Note that there will be no cubes, which will be painted on more than three faces.

Number of non-black faces ⇒ Total No of Cubes − Three Black Faced Cubes − Two black Faced Cubes − One Black Faced Cubes ⇒ 1,000 − 8 − 96 − 384 = 512 cubes.

Question #23:   A cylindrical pipe is 5 units long with an inner diameter of 12 units and outer diameter of 16 units. What is the total surface area of the pipe (inside, outside, and including the ends)?

Solution: Draw a diagram, it will help you envision the problem better.

Height of Cylinder   ⇒ 5 units
Inner Diameter   ⇒ 12   &   Inner Radius   ⇒ ½(12) = 6 units
Outer Diameter   ⇒ 16   &   Outer Radius   ⇒ ½(16) = 8 units
SA of Outside Surface ⇒ $2\pi rh = 2\pi(8)(5) = 80\pi$ units^2 [Apply appropriate formula and simplify]
SA of Inside Surface ⇒ $2\pi rh = 2\pi(6)(5) = 60\pi$ units^2 [Apply appropriate formula and simplify]
SA of Outer Circle   ⇒ $\pi r^2 = \pi(8)^2 = 64\pi$ units^2 [Apply appropriate formula and simplify]
SA of Inner Circle   ⇒ $\pi r^2 = \pi(6)^2 = 36\pi$ units^2 [Apply appropriate formula and simplify]
SA of Two Ends   ⇒ Area of Outer Circle − Area of Inner Circle
                   ⇒ $2(64\pi-36\pi) = 2(28\pi) = 56\pi$ units^2 [Substitute the values and simplify]
Total SA of the Pipe ⇒ Surface Area of (Outside Surface + Inside Surface + Two Ends)
                   ⇒ $80\pi + 60\pi + 56\pi = 196\pi$ units^2 [Substitute the values and simplify]

Question #24:   If the height of a cylinder is twice its circumference, C, what is the volume of the cylinder in terms of C?

Solution:

Height of Cylinder	$\Rightarrow 2C$	[Height is twice its circumference]
Circumference	$\Rightarrow C = 2\pi r$	[Write the appropriate formula]
	$\Rightarrow r = \dfrac{C}{2\pi}$	[Divide both sides by 2π]
Volume of Cylinder	$\Rightarrow \pi r^2 h$	[Write the appropriate formula]
	$\Rightarrow \pi \left(\dfrac{C}{2\pi}\right)^2 (2C)$	[Substitute the values from above]
	$\Rightarrow \pi \left(\dfrac{C^2}{4\pi^2}\right)(2C)$	[Solve the exponent]
	$\Rightarrow \dfrac{2C^3 \pi}{4\pi^2}$	[Do the multiplication]
	$\Rightarrow \dfrac{C^3}{2\pi}$	[Simplify the fraction]

COORDINATE GEOMETRY:

Question #25: A rectangle lies in the xy-coordinate plane so that its sides are not parallel to either axis. What is the product of the slopes of all four sides of the rectangle?

Solution: Notice that since the length and width of any rectangle are perpendicular to each other, the product of the slope of length and the slope of width is -1.

Product of Slopes $\Rightarrow$ (Slope of Length × Slope of Width) × (Slope of Length × Slope of Width)
                             $\Rightarrow (-1) \times (-1) = 1$

Question #26: A rectangle lies in the xy-coordinate plane so that one of its sides is parallel to one of the axis. What is the product of the slopes of all four sides of the rectangle?

Solution: Notice that since one of the sides of rectangle is parallel to one of the axes, it means that one pair of parallel sides must be parallel to the x-axis and the other pair of parallel sides must be parallel to the y-axis. Since the slope of any line that is parallel to the y-axis is undefined, the product of all the slopes of all the sides of the rectangle will also be undefined.

Question #27: In the xy-coordinate system, if (p, q) and $(p + 5, q + k)$ are two points on the line defined by the equation $x = 2y - 7$, then what is the value of k?

Solution:

Substitute (p, q) in the given equation	$\Rightarrow p = 2q - 7$	$\Rightarrow$ Equation #1
Substitute $(p + 5, q + k)$ in the given equation	$\Rightarrow p + 5 = 2(q + k) - 7$	$\Rightarrow$ Equation #2
Substitute the value of p from Eq #1 into Eq #2	$\Rightarrow 2q - 7 + 5 = 2(q + k) - 7$	
	$\Rightarrow 2q - 2 = 2q + 2k - 7$	[Combine like-terms]
	$\Rightarrow -2 = 2k - 7$	[Subtract $2q$ from both sides]
	$\Rightarrow 2k = 5$	[Add 7 to both sides]
	$\Rightarrow k = 2.5$	[Divide both sides by 2]

Question #28: If $m \neq n$ and the slope of the line passing through $(-m, m)$ and $(5m, n)$ is 1, what is the value of n in terms of m?

Solution: EZ Problem Set Up $\Rightarrow$ Slope of the line passing through $(-m, m)$ and $(5m, n)$ is 1,

	$\Rightarrow \dfrac{y_2 - y_1}{x_2 - x_1} = 1$	[Set up the equation]
	$\Rightarrow \dfrac{n - m}{5m - (-m)} = 1$	[Substitute the given values]
	$\Rightarrow \dfrac{n - m}{5m + m} = 1$	[Simplify the expression on the left side]
	$\Rightarrow n - m = 6m$	[Cross-multiply]
	$\Rightarrow n = 7m$	[Add m to both sides]

Question #29: What value of k will make the line containing points $(k, 7)$ and $(-2, 5)$ perpendicular to the line containing $(9, k)$ and $(1, 0)$?

Solution: EZ Problem Set-Up $\Rightarrow$ For two lines to perpendicular, the product of their slopes must be -1.

$$\Rightarrow \left(\frac{7-5}{k+2}\right)\left(\frac{k-0}{9-1}\right) = -1 \qquad \text{[Set up the equation]}$$

$$\Rightarrow \left(\frac{2}{k+2}\right)\left(\frac{k}{8}\right) = -1 \qquad \text{[Combine like-terms]}$$

$$\Rightarrow \frac{2k}{8(k+2)} = -1 \qquad \text{[Multiply the two fractions]}$$

$$\Rightarrow \frac{2k}{8k+16} = -1 \qquad \text{[Apply distributive property in the denominator]}$$

$\Rightarrow 2k = -1(8k + 16)$ [Cross multiply]
$\Rightarrow 2k = -8k - 16$ [Apply distributive property on right side]
$\Rightarrow 10k = -16$ [Add $8k$ to both sides]

$$\Rightarrow k = -\frac{16}{10} = -\frac{8}{5} \qquad \text{[Divide both sides by 10]}$$

Question #30: If the figure given below, the coordinates of the $\triangle ABC$ are $A(p, q)$, $B(r, 0)$, and $C(s, 0)$, what is the area of $\triangle ABC$?

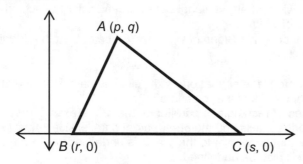

Solution: Base of $\triangle ABC$ $\Rightarrow BC = (s - r)$ [B and C lie on the same horizontal line]
Height of $\triangle ABC$ $\Rightarrow q - 0 = q$ [A and B lie on the same vertical line]

Area of $\triangle ABC$ $\Rightarrow \frac{1}{2}bh = \frac{1}{2} \times (s-r) \times q = \frac{q(s-r)}{2}$ [Apply the appropriate formula and simplify]

Question #31: In the figure given below, point P has coordinates $(-5, 0)$ and $\angle QOR = 150°$. What is the slope of line QO?

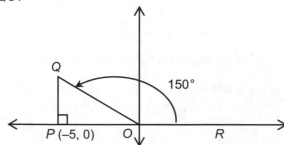

Solution: Linear pairs are supplementary $\Rightarrow \angle QOP + \angle QOR = 180°$
                                             $\Rightarrow \angle QOP + 150° = 180°$ [Substitute $\angle QOR = 150°$]
                                             $\Rightarrow \angle QOP = 30°$ [Subtract 150° from both sides]
Sum of angles in triangle equal 180° $\Rightarrow \angle PQO + \angle QOP + \angle QPO = 180°$
                                             $\Rightarrow \angle PQO + 30° + 90° = 180°$ [Substitute the known values]
                                             $\Rightarrow \angle PQO + 120° = 180°$ [Combine like-terms]
                                             $\Rightarrow \angle PQO = 60°$ [Subtract 120° from both sides]

$\triangle QPO$ is 30°-60°-90° $\Rightarrow$ Sides in the ratio: $1x : \sqrt{3}x : 2x$

$$\text{Side opposite } 60° = PO \;\Rightarrow \sqrt{3}x = 5$$

$$\Rightarrow x = \frac{5}{\sqrt{3}}$$

$$\text{Side opposite } 30° = PQ \;\Rightarrow x = \frac{5}{\sqrt{3}}$$

Coordinates of point $Q \;\Rightarrow \left(-5, \dfrac{5}{\sqrt{3}}\right)$ [Point Q has the same x-coordinate as point P]

Coordinates of point $O \;\Rightarrow (0, 0)$ [Point O is the origin]

Slope of $QO \Rightarrow \dfrac{y_1 - y_2}{x_1 - x_2} = \dfrac{\dfrac{5}{\sqrt{3}} - 0}{-5 - 0} = \dfrac{-1}{\sqrt{3}}$ [Apply the appropriate formula and simplify]

Question #32: In the figure given below, point P has coordinates (–1, 0) and $\angle QOR = 120°$. What is the slope of line QO?

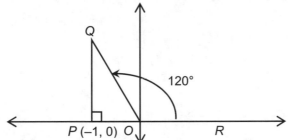

Solution: Linear pairs are supplementary $\Rightarrow \angle QOP + \angle QOR = 180°$

$\Rightarrow \angle QOP + 120° = 180°$ [Substitute $\angle QOR = 120°$]

$\Rightarrow \angle QOP = 60°$ [Subtract 120° from both sides]

Sum of angles in triangle equal 180° $\Rightarrow \angle PQO + \angle QOP + \angle QPO = 180°$

$\Rightarrow \angle PQO + 60° + 90° = 180°$ [Substitute the known values]

$\Rightarrow \angle PQO + 150° = 180°$ [Combine like-terms]

$\Rightarrow \angle PQO = 30°$ [Subtract 150° from both sides]

$\triangle QPO$ is 30°-60°-90° $\Rightarrow$ Sides in the ratio: $1x : \sqrt{3}x : 2x$

$$\Rightarrow \text{Side opposite } 30° = PO = x = 1$$

$$\Rightarrow \text{Side opposite } 60° = PQ = \sqrt{3}x = \sqrt{3}$$

Coordinates of point $Q \;\Rightarrow \left(-1, \sqrt{3}\right)$ [Point Q has the same x-coordinate as point P]

Coordinates of point $O \;\Rightarrow (0, 0)$ [Point O is the origin]

Slope of $QO \Rightarrow \dfrac{y_1 - y_2}{x_1 - x_2} = \dfrac{\sqrt{3} - 0}{-1 - 0} = -\sqrt{3}$ [Apply the appropriate formula and simplify]

Question #33: In the figure given below, point P has coordinates (–7, 0) and $\angle QOR = 135°$. What is the slope of line QO?

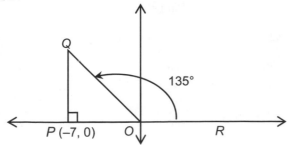

Solution: Linear pairs are supplementary $\Rightarrow \angle QOP + \angle QOR = 180°$
$\Rightarrow \angle QOP + 135° = 180°$ [Substitute $\angle QOR = 135°$]
$\Rightarrow \angle QOP = 45°$ [Subtract 135° from both sides]

Sum of angles in triangle equal 180° $\Rightarrow \angle PQO + \angle QOP + \angle QPO = 180°$
$\Rightarrow \angle PQO + 45° + 90° = 180°$ [Substitute the known values]
$\Rightarrow \angle PQO + 135° = 180°$ [Combine like-terms]
$\Rightarrow \angle PQO = 45°$ [Subtract 135° from both sides]

ΔQPO is 45°-45°-90° $\Rightarrow$ Sides in the ratio: $1x : 1x : \sqrt{2}x$
Side opposite 45° = $PO = x = 7$
Side opposite 45° = $PQ = x = 7$
Coordinates of point Q $\Rightarrow (-7, 7)$ [Point Q has the same x-coordinate as point P]
Coordinates of point O $\Rightarrow (0, 0)$ [Point O is the origin]

Slope of $QO \Rightarrow \dfrac{y_1 - y_2}{x_1 - x_2} = \dfrac{7-0}{-7-0} = -1$ [Apply the appropriate formula and simplify]

Question #34:   In the figure given below, if the area of the circle with center P at (5, 5) is $n\pi$, what is the value of n?

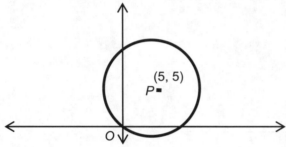

Solution: Since we know that the coordinates of the center of the circle, P, are (5, 5), we can make a 45°-45°-90° triangle by connecting the center of the circle, P, with the origin, O, and with the x-axis at Q.

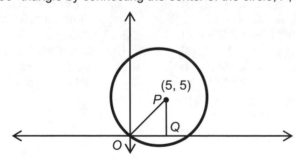

Sides of this 45°-45°-90° $\Delta OPQ \Rightarrow 5, 5, 5\sqrt{2}$

Radius of the Circle = $OP = 5\sqrt{2}$

Area of Circle $\Rightarrow \pi r^2 = n\pi$ [Set the formula of area equal to the given area]
$\Rightarrow \pi \left(5\sqrt{2}\right)^2 = n\pi$ [Substitute the known values]
$\Rightarrow \left(5\sqrt{2}\right)^2 = n$ [Divide both sides by π]
$\Rightarrow n = 50$ [Simplify the expression]

Question #35:   In a xy-coordinate plane, a circle with center (8, 0) is tangent to the line $y = x$. What is the diameter of the circle?
Solution: Let's first draw a diagram to better visualize the problem:

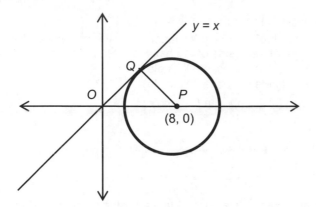

The line $y = x$ makes a 45° angle with each axis in the first and the third quadrant.
Connect the center of the circle to the point of tangency of the circle and the line $y = x$.
The radius of a circle is perpendicular to the tangent of the circle at point of tangency.
In $\Delta OPQ \Rightarrow \angle QOP = 45°$, $\angle OQP = 90°$, and $\angle OPQ = 45°$

Therefore, ΔOPQ is a 45°-45°-90° triangle with sides in the ratio of $x : x : x\sqrt{2}$
Since coordinates of point P are (8,0), length of $OP = 8$
Side opposite 90° angle $= OP = 8 \Rightarrow x\sqrt{2} = 8$

$$\Rightarrow x = \frac{8}{\sqrt{2}} = \frac{8}{\sqrt{2}} \times \frac{\sqrt{2}}{\sqrt{2}} = \frac{8\sqrt{2}}{2} = 4\sqrt{2}$$

Side opposite 45° angle $= PQ =$ radius of the circle $= 4\sqrt{2}$

Diameter of Circle $= 2\left(4\sqrt{2}\right) = 8\sqrt{2}$

Question #36:   In the figure given below, $PQRST$ is a regular hexagon. What is the slope of line QR?

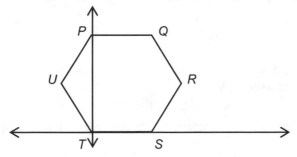

Solution: Sum of Measure of Interior Angles of Hexagon $\Rightarrow (n - 2) \times 180° = (6 - 2) \times 180° = 720°$
Measure of each Interior Angle of Hexagon $\Rightarrow$ Sum ÷ No = 720 ÷ 6 = 120°
Now, make some modifications in the given diagram: draw a vertical line from point U to the x-axis and
name the point at which it touches the x-axis as V, as shown in the figure given below:

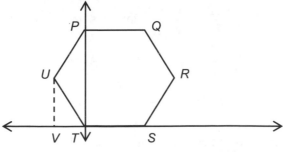

In ΔUVT $\Rightarrow \angle UVT = 90°$
$\Rightarrow \angle UTV = 180° - \angle UTS = 180° - 120° = 60°$
$\Rightarrow \angle VUT = 180° - 90° - 60° = 30°$

ΔUVT is a 30°-60°-90° triangle with sides in the ratio of $x : \sqrt{3}x : 2x$

Since we ultimately want to find the slope, it doesn't matter what the measure of each side of the hexagon is, so let's assume the length of each side of the hexagon, or side $UT = 2$

In ΔUVT $\Rightarrow$ Measure of $UT = 2$ (side opposite 90° angle)

              $\Rightarrow$ Measure of $VT = 1$ (side opposite 30° angle)

              $\Rightarrow$ Measure of $UV = \sqrt{3}$ (side opposite 60° angle)

Coordinate of point U $\Rightarrow \left(-1, \sqrt{3}\right)$

Coordinate of point T $\Rightarrow (0, 0)$

Slope of UT $\Rightarrow \dfrac{y_1 - y_2}{x_1 - x_2} = \dfrac{\sqrt{3} - 0}{-1 - 0} = -\sqrt{3}$

Directly opposite sides in a regular hexagon are parallel to each other, and since parallel sides have same slopes $\Rightarrow$ Slope of QR = Slope of $UT = -\sqrt{3}$

MULTIPLE FIGURES:

Question #37: In the figure given below, the smaller circle is inscribed in the square and the square is inscribed in the larger circle. If the length of each side of the square is n, what is the ratio of the area of the larger circle to the area of the smaller circle?

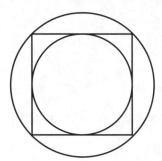

Solution: Side of Square $\Rightarrow n$

Diagonal of Square $\Rightarrow$ side times $\sqrt{2} = n\sqrt{2}$

Note: Side of square = Diameter of smaller circle

Small Circle: Diameter $\Rightarrow n$ [Given]

                Radius $\Rightarrow$ ½ of $n = \dfrac{n}{2}$ [Radius is half of diameter]

                Area $\Rightarrow \pi r^2 = \pi \left(\dfrac{n}{2}\right)^2 = \pi \dfrac{n^2}{4}$ [Apply appropriate formula and simplify]

Note : Diameter of Big Circle = Diagonal of Square

Big Circle: Diameter $\Rightarrow n\sqrt{2}$ [Given]

                Radius $\Rightarrow$ ½ $(n\sqrt{2}) = \dfrac{n\sqrt{2}}{2} = \dfrac{n}{\sqrt{2}}$ [Radius is half of diameter]

                Area $\Rightarrow \pi r^2 = \pi \left(\dfrac{n}{\sqrt{2}}\right)^2 = \pi \dfrac{n^2}{2}$ [Apply appropriate formula and simplify]

Ratio of Area of Larger Circle to Area of Smaller Circle $\Rightarrow \pi \dfrac{n^2}{2} : \pi \dfrac{n^2}{4} = 2{:}1 = 2$

Question #38: If the area of a rectangle A with length $x + 8$ and width $x + 1$ is 100, what is the area of rectangle B with length $x + 7$ and width $x + 2$?

Solution: Area of Rectangle $A \Rightarrow LW = 100$ [Equate the area formula with the given area]

                               $\Rightarrow (x + 8)(x + 1) = 100$ [Substitute the known values]

$$\Rightarrow x^2 + 9x + 8 = 100 \qquad \text{[Apply distributive property]}$$
$$\Rightarrow x^2 + 9x = 92 \qquad \text{[Subtract 8 from both sides]}$$

Area of Rectangle $B \Rightarrow LW$ [Write the appropriate formula]

$$\Rightarrow (x + 7)(x + 2) \qquad \text{[Substitute the known values]}$$
$$\Rightarrow x^2 + 9x + 14 \qquad \text{[Apply distributive property]}$$
$$\Rightarrow 92 + 14 = 106 \qquad \text{[Substitute } x^2 + 9x = 92 \text{ from above]}$$

Question #39: If A is the area and C is the circumference of a circle, what is A in terms of C?

Solution: Circumference of Circle $\Rightarrow C = 2\pi r$ [Write the appropriate formula]

$$\Rightarrow r = \frac{C}{2\pi} \qquad \text{[Divide both sides by } 2\pi\text{]}$$

Area of Circle $= A$ $\Rightarrow \pi r^2$ [Write the appropriate formula]

$$\Rightarrow \pi \left(\frac{C}{2\pi}\right)^2 \qquad \text{[Substitute the known values]}$$

$$\Rightarrow \pi \left(\frac{C^2}{4\pi^2}\right) \qquad \text{[Solve the exponent]}$$

$$\Rightarrow \frac{C^2}{4\pi} \qquad \text{[Simplify the expression]}$$

Question #40: In the figure given below, a semicircle is attached to the narrow sides of the two rectangles. If the length of the rectangle is 100 and width is 50, what is the total area enclosed by the figure?

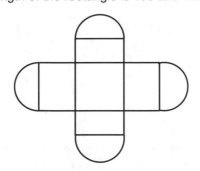

Solution:
Length of Rectangle $\Rightarrow 100$
Width of Rectangle $\Rightarrow 50$
Area of 2 Rectangles $\Rightarrow 2(LW) = 2(100 \times 50) = 10,000$
Area of Middle Square $\Rightarrow s^2 = 50^2 = 2,500$
Note: Diameter of Semicircle is same as width of rectangle
Diameter of Semicircle $\Rightarrow 50$
Radius of Semicircle $\Rightarrow \frac{1}{2}(d) = \frac{1}{2}(50) = 25$
Area of 4 Semicircles $\Rightarrow 2(\text{Area of Circle}) = 2(\pi r^2) = 2(\pi \times 25^2) = 2(625\pi) = 1,250\pi$
Note: 4 semicircles makes 2 semicircles.
Area of Whole Figure $\Rightarrow$ Area of 2 Rectangles + Area of 4 Semicircles – Area of Square (overlap)
                            $\Rightarrow 10,000 + 1,250\pi - 2,500 = 7,500 + 1,250\pi$

Question #41: In the figure given below, all the circles are tangent to one another, and the total area of four equal circles is 100π. What is the diameter of the small circle in the center?

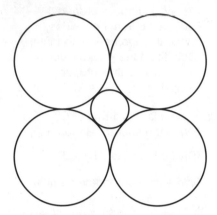

Solution: First thing to do in this problem is to make some addition to the given figure.
Connect the centers of circle *P*, *Q*, and *R* so that it forms a right triangle *PQR*.

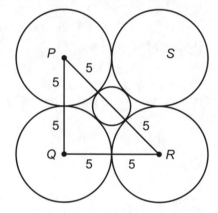

Area of all 4 Equal Circle $\Rightarrow 100\pi$ [Given]
Area of Each Circle $\Rightarrow 100\pi \div 4 = 25\pi$ [Divide by 4 to get area of each circle]
                           $\Rightarrow \pi r^2 = 25\pi$ [Equate the area formula with the actual area]
                           $\Rightarrow r^2 = 25$ [Divide both sides by π]
Radius of Each Circle $\Rightarrow r = 5$ [Square root both sides]
Each leg of triangle *PQR* $\Rightarrow PQ = QR = r + r = 5 + 5 = 10$
Apply Pythagorean Theorem $\Rightarrow PQ^2 + QR^2 = PR^2$ [Write the Pythagorean Theorem]
                           $\Rightarrow 10^2 + 10^2 = PR^2$ [Substitute the known values]
                           $\Rightarrow 100 + 100 = PR^2$ [Solve the exponents]
                           $\Rightarrow 200 = PR^2$ [Combine like terms]
                           $\Rightarrow PR = 10\sqrt{2}$ [Square root both sides]
EZ Problem Set-Up $\Rightarrow$ Hypotenuse PR = 2 radii + Diameter of Small Circle
                   $\Rightarrow 10\sqrt{2} = 2(5)$ + Diameter of Small Circle [Set up the equation]
                   $\Rightarrow$ Diameter of Small Circle = $10\sqrt{2} - 10$ [Subtract 10 from both sides]

Question #42:   A certain recipe makes enough batter for identical 8 large circular cookies that are each 20 inches in diameter. How many circular identical small cookies, each with ¼ the diameter of large cookie and of the same thickness as the large cookie, can be made with the same batter?

Solution: Diameter of Each Large Cookie $\Rightarrow 20$
Radius of Each Large Cookie $\Rightarrow \frac{1}{2}(d) = \frac{1}{2}(20) = 10$
Area of Each Large Cookie $\Rightarrow \pi r^2 = \pi(10)^2 = 100\pi$
Area of 8 Large Cookies $\Rightarrow 100\pi \times 8 = 800\pi$
Diameter of Each Small Cookie $\Rightarrow \frac{1}{4}$(diameter of large cookie) = $\frac{1}{4}(20) = 5$
Radius of Each Small Cookie $\Rightarrow \frac{1}{2}(d) = \frac{1}{2}(5) = 2.5$
Area of Each Small Cookie $\Rightarrow \pi r^2 = \pi(2.5)^2 = 6.25\pi$

No. of Small Cookies that can be made with the same (800π) batter $\Rightarrow \dfrac{Area\,of\,8\,Big\,Cookies}{Area\,of\,Each\,Small\,Cookie}$

$$\Rightarrow \frac{800\pi}{6.25\pi} = 128$$

Question #43: The internal dimensions of a rectangular cargo container are 16 meters by 18 meters by 20 meters. A cylindrical oil tank is to be packed inside the box so that it's placed straight up when the closed box stands on one of its six sides. What should be the radius of the cylindrical tank so that it can contain the maximum amount of oil?

Solution: Since the rectangular container can stand on any of its six sides, or any of its three different sides, let's consider each option and see which one yields the maximum volume:

Stands on 16 by 18 side $\Rightarrow r = 8$ $\Rightarrow h = 20$ $\Rightarrow$ Volume = $\pi r^2 h = \pi(8^2)(20) = 1280\pi$
Stands on 16 by 20 side $\Rightarrow r = 8$ $\Rightarrow h = 18$ $\Rightarrow$ Volume = $\pi r^2 h = \pi(8^2)(18) = 1152\pi$
Stands on 18 by 20 side $\Rightarrow r = 9$ $\Rightarrow h = 16$ $\Rightarrow$ Volume = $\pi r^2 h = \pi(9^2)(16) = 1296\pi$
Therefore, the radius of the cylindrical tank should be 9, which has the maximum volume.

Question #44: Three identical balls fit snuggly into a cylindrical can, meaning, the radius of the spheres equals the radius of the can, and the balls just touch the bottom and the top of the can. What fraction of the volume of the can is taken up by the balls?

Solution: Let's draw the following diagram to help visualize the problem:

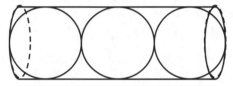

Let the radii of Can and Spheres $\Rightarrow 1$

Volume of each Sphere (ball) $\Rightarrow \dfrac{4}{3}\pi r^3 = \dfrac{4}{3}\pi(1)^3 = \dfrac{4}{3}\pi$

Volume of all Three Spheres $\Rightarrow \dfrac{4}{3}\pi \times 3 = 4\pi$

Height of Cylindrical Can $\Rightarrow 1 + 1 + 1 + 1 + 1 + 1 = 6$
Volume of Cylindrical Can $\Rightarrow \pi r^2 h = \pi(1)^2(6) = 6\pi$

Fraction of the volume of the cylindrical can taken up by the balls $\Rightarrow \dfrac{4\pi}{6\pi} = \dfrac{2}{3} = 0.67$

Question #45: There are five small circles, all of which are of exactly same size, lie inside a large circle as shown below. The diameter of the large circle passes through the centers of the small circles. If each of the smaller circles has a circumference of 10π, what is the area of the shaded region?

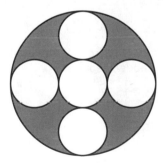

Solution: Circumference of Small Circle $\Rightarrow 2\pi r = 10\pi$ [Equate circumference formula with given value]
                                        $\Rightarrow r = 5$ [Divide both sides by 2π]
Radius of Small Circle $\Rightarrow 5$ [From above]
Diameter of Small Circle $\Rightarrow 2r = 5 \times 2 = 10$ [Diameter is twice of radius]
Diameter of Large Circle $\Rightarrow$ Diameter of Small Circle $\times 3 = 10 \times 3 = 30$ [Substitute the values and]

Radius of Large Circle ⇒ ½d = ½(30) = 15   [Radius is half of diameter]
Area of Large Circle ⇒ $\pi r^2 = \pi(15)^2 = 225\pi$ [Apply appropriate formula and simplify]
Area of 1 Small Circle ⇒ $\pi r^2 = \pi(5)^2 = 25\pi$ [Apply appropriate formula and simplify]
Area of 5 Small Circles ⇒ $25\pi \times 5 = 125\pi$ [Multiply by 5]
Area of Shaded Region ⇒ Area of Large Circle – Area of 5 Small Circles
                              ⇒ $225\pi - 125\pi = 100\pi$ [Substitute the values and simplify]

Question #46: In the figure given below, the rectangular plot, which is x units by y units, is surrounded by a walkway, which is 2.5 units wide. What is the area of the shaded walkway in terms of x and y?

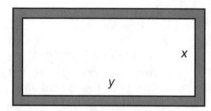

Solution: Dimensions of Inner Rectangle ⇒ x units by y units
Area of Inner Rectangle ⇒ $L \times W = xy$ unit^2
Dimensions of Outer Rectangle ⇒ (x + 2.5 + 2.5) units by (y + 2.5 + 2.5) units
Area of Outer Rectangle ⇒ $L \times W = (x + 5)(y + 5) = xy + 5x + 5y + 25$ unit^2
Area of the Walkway ⇒ Area of Outer Rectangle – Area of Inner Rectangle
                             ⇒ $(xy + 5x + 5y + 25) - xy = 5x + 5y + 25$ unit^2

Question #47: In the figure given below, trapezoid ABCDEF is divided into rectangle ABDE, ΔAEF, and ΔBDC. What is the combined area of the two shaded triangles?

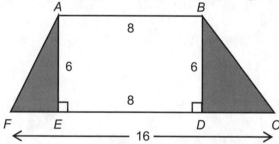

Solution: Following are the different methods to find the area of the shaded region:
Method #1: Area of Trapezoid ABCDEF   = ½(b₁ + b₂) × h   = ½(8 + 16) × 6   ⇒   72
             –Area of Rectangle ABDE   = lw   = 8 × 6   ⇒ <u>–48</u>
             Total Shaded Area   ⇒ <u> 24</u>
Method #2: Merge ΔAEF and ΔBDC to form one big triangle
             Base = 16 – 8 = 8   &   Height = 6
             Shaded Area of Merged Triangle   = ½bh   = ½(8)(6)   ⇒ 24

Question #48: The figure given below consists of four semicircles in a large semicircle. If the small semicircles have radii of 1, 2, 3, and 4, what is the perimeter and area of the shaded region?

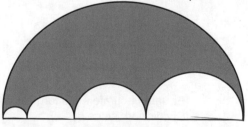

Solution: Radii of Small Semicircles   ⇒ 1, 2, 3, and 4
Diameters of Small Semicircles   ⇒ 2, 4, 6, and 8

Diameter of Big Semicircle $\Rightarrow 2 + 4 + 6 + 8 = 20$
Radius of Big Semicircle $\Rightarrow \frac{1}{2}(d) = \frac{1}{2}(20) = 10$
For Perimeter of Shaded Region:
Perimeter of Semicircle $\Rightarrow \pi r$
Perimeter of Big Semicircle $\Rightarrow \pi r = 10\pi$
Perimeter of Small Semicircle $\Rightarrow 1\pi + 2\pi + 3\pi + 4\pi = 10\pi$
Perimeter of Shaded Region $\Rightarrow$ Perimeter of Big Semicircle + Perimeter of Small Semicircle
         $\Rightarrow 10\pi + 10\pi = 20\pi$

For Area of Shaded Region:
Area of Big Semicircle $\Rightarrow \frac{1}{2}\pi r^2 = \frac{1}{2}\pi (10)^2 = \frac{1}{2}\pi (100) = 50\pi$
Area of Small Semicircles   First $\Rightarrow \frac{1}{2}\pi r^2 = \frac{1}{2}\pi (1)^2 = \frac{1}{2}\pi (1) = 0.5\pi$
                     Second $\Rightarrow \frac{1}{2}\pi r^2 = \frac{1}{2}\pi (2)^2 = \frac{1}{2}\pi (4) = 2\pi$
                     Third $\Rightarrow \frac{1}{2}\pi r^2 = \frac{1}{2}\pi (3)^2 = \frac{1}{2}\pi (9) = 4.5\pi$
                     Fourth $\Rightarrow \frac{1}{2}\pi r^2 = \frac{1}{2}\pi (4)^2 = \frac{1}{2}\pi (16) = 8\pi$
Sum of Area all Small Semicircles $\Rightarrow 0.5\pi + 2\pi + 4.5\pi + 8\pi = 15\pi$
Area of Shaded Region $\Rightarrow$ Area of Big Semicircle – Area of Small Semicircles
         $\Rightarrow 50\pi - 15\pi = 35\pi$

Question #49: The figure given below consists of four shaded semicircles. If $AB = 4$, $BC = 2AB$, $CD = 2BC$, and $DE = 2CD$. what is the area of the shaded region?

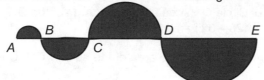

Solution: Radius of circle $AB = \frac{1}{2}(4) = 2$ $\Rightarrow$ Area $= \pi r^2 = \pi(2)^2 = 4\pi$ $\Rightarrow$ Area of Semicircle $= 2\pi$
Radius of circle $BC = 2(2) = 4$ $\Rightarrow$ Area $= \pi r^2 = \pi(4)^2 = 16\pi$ $\Rightarrow$ Area of Semicircle $= 8\pi$
Radius of circle $CD = 2(4) = 8$ $\Rightarrow$ Area $= \pi r^2 = \pi(8)^2 = 64\pi$ $\Rightarrow$ Area of Semicircle $= 32\pi$
Radius of circle $DC = 2(8) = 16$ $\Rightarrow$ Area $= \pi r^2 = \pi(16)^2 = 256\pi$ $\Rightarrow$ Area of Semicircle $= 128\pi$
Total Area of Shaded Regions $\Rightarrow 2\pi + 8\pi + 32\pi + 128\pi = 170\pi$

Question #50: In the figure given below, $\angle POQ = 60°$, and OP is 12. What is the area and perimeter of the shaded region?

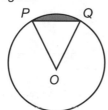

Solution: For Area of Shaded Region:
Area of the Whole Circle $\Rightarrow \pi r^2 = \pi(12)^2 = 144\pi$

Area of Sector POQ $\Rightarrow \dfrac{n}{360} \times$ Area $= \dfrac{60}{360} \times 144\pi = 24\pi$

Area of Equilateral ΔPOQ $\Rightarrow \dfrac{s^2\sqrt{3}}{4} = \dfrac{12^2\sqrt{3}}{4} = 36\sqrt{3}$

Area of Shaded Region $\Rightarrow$ Area of Sector POQ – Area of $\Delta POQ = 24\pi - 36\sqrt{3}$
For Perimeter of Shaded Region:
Circumference of Circle $\Rightarrow 2\pi r = 2\pi(12) = 24\pi$

Length of Arc PQ $\Rightarrow \dfrac{n}{360} \times C = \dfrac{60}{360} \times 24\pi = 4\pi$

Length of Chord PQ $\Rightarrow 12$
Perimeter of Shaded Region $\Rightarrow$ Length of Arc PQ + Length of Chord $PQ = 12 + 4\pi$

Question #51:   In the figure given below, if the radius *OP* is 16 and the area of the right triangle *OPQ* is 128, what is the area of the shaded region?

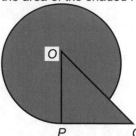

Solution: Area of Circle O $\Rightarrow \pi r^2 = \pi(16)^2 = 256\pi$

Area of $\triangle OPQ$ $\Rightarrow \frac{1}{2}bh = 128$ [Equate the area formula with the given area]

$\Rightarrow \frac{1}{2}(b)(16) = 128$ [Substitute the values]

$\Rightarrow 8b = 128$ [Simplify the left side]

$\Rightarrow b = 16$ [Divide both sides by 8]

Since *OP* = ρQ = 16, $\triangle OPQ$ is a 45°-45°-90° isosceles triangle

Area of Overlapping Sector $\Rightarrow \dfrac{\bullet\bullet}{360} \times$ Area = $\dfrac{45}{360}(256\pi) = 32\pi$

Area of Shaded Region $\Rightarrow$ Area of Circle O + Area of $\triangle OPQ$ – Area of the Overlap

$\Rightarrow 256\pi + 128 - 32\pi = 224\pi + 128$

Question #52:   In the figure given below, if the radius *OP* is 12 and the area of the square *OPXQ* is 144, what is the area of the shaded region?

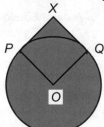

Solution: Area of Circle O $\Rightarrow \pi r^2 = \pi(12)^2 = 144\pi$

Area of Square *OPXQ* $\Rightarrow s^2 = 12^2 = 144$

Note: Since *OPXQ* is a square, $\angle O$ is 90°

Area of Overlapping Sector *POQ* $\Rightarrow \dfrac{n}{360} \times$ Area = $\dfrac{90}{360}(144\pi) = 36\pi$

Area of Shaded Region $\Rightarrow$ Area of Circle O + Area of Square *OPXQ* – Area of the Overlap

$\Rightarrow 144\pi + 144 - 36\pi = 108\pi + 144$

Question #53:   In the figure given below, an equilateral triangle with side 18 is inscribed in a circle. What is the area of the shaded region?

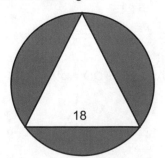

Solution: To find the area of the shaded region, we'll have to find the area of the circle and subtract the area of the triangle from it.

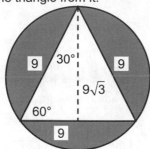 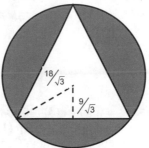

Sides of Half of Equilateral Triangle $\Rightarrow 30° \quad - \quad 60° \quad - \quad 90°$

$\Rightarrow x \quad - \quad x\sqrt{3} \quad - \quad 2x$

$\Rightarrow 9 \quad - \quad 9\sqrt{3} \quad - \quad 18$

Area of Equilateral Triangle $\Rightarrow ½\, b \times h = ½ \times 18 \times 9\sqrt{3} = 81\sqrt{3}$

Sides of Small Equilateral Triangle $\Rightarrow 30° \quad - \quad 60° \quad - \quad 90°$

$\Rightarrow x \quad - \quad x\sqrt{3} \quad - \quad 2x$

$\Rightarrow \dfrac{9}{\sqrt{3}} \quad - \quad 9 \quad - \quad \dfrac{18}{\sqrt{3}}$

Area of Circle $\Rightarrow \pi r^2 = \pi\left(\dfrac{18}{\sqrt{3}}\right)^2 = \dfrac{18 \cdot 18}{\sqrt{3} \cdot \sqrt{3}}\pi = 108\pi$

Area of Shaded Region $\Rightarrow$ Area of Circle – Area of Equilateral Triangle $= 108\pi - 81\sqrt{3}$

Question #54:   In the figure given below, a right circular cylinder is inscribed in a cone with height 25 and radius 15. The radius of the base of the cylinder is 6. What is the volume of the white region?

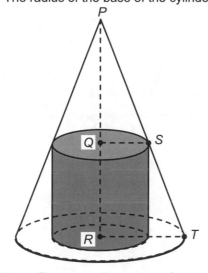

Note: Figure not drawn to scale.

Solution: Let the height of the Cylinder, $QR = h$
Then, $PQ = PR - QR = 25 - h$
In $\triangle PQS$ $\Rightarrow PQ = 25 - h$, $QS = 6$
In $\triangle PRT$ $\Rightarrow PR = 25$, $RT = 15$

$\triangle PQS$ & $\triangle PRT$ are similar triangles $\Rightarrow \dfrac{PQ}{PR} = \dfrac{QS}{RT}$ [Set up the proportion]

$$\Rightarrow \frac{25 - h}{25} = \frac{6}{15}$$ [Substitute the known values]

$$\Rightarrow \frac{25 - h}{25} = \frac{2}{5}$$ [Reduce the fraction]

$\Rightarrow 5(25 - h) = 2(25)$ [Cross multiply]
$\Rightarrow 125 - 5h = 50$ [Apply distributive property]
$\Rightarrow -5h = -75$ [Subtract 125 from both sides]
$\Rightarrow h = 15$ [Divide both sides by −5]

Volume of the Cylinder $\Rightarrow \pi r^2 h = \pi(6)^2(15) = 540\pi$
Volume of the Cone $\Rightarrow 1/3(\pi r^2 h) = 1/3[\pi(15)^2(25)] = 1{,}875\pi$
Volume of White Region: $\Rightarrow$ Volume of the Cone − Volume of the Cylinder = $1{,}875\pi - 540\pi = 1{,}335\pi$

Question #55: If the figure given below, what is the area of the shaded region?

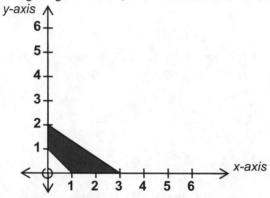

Solution: Area of Bigger Triangle $\Rightarrow \frac{1}{2}(b)(h) = \frac{1}{2}(3)(2) = 3$
Area of Smaller Triangle $\Rightarrow \frac{1}{2}(b)(h) = \frac{1}{2}(1)(1) = \frac{1}{2}$
Area of Shaded Region $\Rightarrow$ Area of Bigger Triangle − Area of Smaller Triangle = $3 - \frac{1}{2} = 2.5$

PART 5.0: WORD PROBLEMS:

TOPICS COVERED:

- Arithmetic Word Problems

- Algebraic Word Problems

- Numeral Problems

- Literal Expressions

- Age & Weight Problems

- Work Problems

- Motion Problems

- Mixture Problems

- Measurements

PRACTICE EXERCISE:

ARITHMETIC PROBLEMS:

Question #1:   At a certain company, two-seventh of the managers attended the company's annual meeting, and one-half of them were females. If one-tenth of the managers who did not attend the annual meeting were females, what fractional part of the total number of managers were males?

Question #2:   If one-fourth of the air in a cylindrical tank is removed after each stroke of a vacuum pump, what fraction of the original amount of air remains in the tank after five strokes?

Question #3:   In a laboratory, there are two test-tube containing certain type of acid. The capacity of the larger test-tube is double the capacity of the smaller test-tube. The larger test-tube is 5/6 full and the smaller test-tube is 1/6 full. If all the content of the smaller test-tube is poured into the larger test-tube, what fraction of the larger test-tube will be filled with acid? (Consider there is no loss of acid while pouring.)

Question #4:   In a laboratory, there are two test-tube containing certain type of acid. The capacity of the larger test-tube is double the capacity of the smaller test-tube. The larger test-tube is ¾ full and the smaller test-tube is ¼ full. If all the content of the smaller test-tube is poured into the larger test-tube, what fraction of the larger test-tube will be filled with acid? (Consider there is no loss of acid while pouring.)

Question #5:   Equal amount of oil were poured into two empty jars of different capacities, which made one jar one-eighth full and the other jar one-fifth full. If the oil in the jar with the lesser capacity is then emptied into the jar with the greater capacity, what percent of the larger jar will be filled with oil?

Question #6:   The height of a hill, which is 170 feet tall, is being eroded at the rate of 1 feet every month. At the same time, the height of another hill, which is 110 feet tall, is being eroded at the rate of ¼ feet per month. If the heights of both hills continue to be reduced at these uniform rates, in how many months will the hills have the same height?

Question #7:   A certain cruise liner charges $200 per person if there are less than 50 people in a group. For more than 50 people in a group, for each additional person over 50 people, they reduce the price per person by $2.50 for every person in the group. How much will be the total cost for a group of 60 people?

Question #8:   A certain manufacturing company produces a line of 20 products with an average sale price of $1,125. If the minimum sale price of any of the products is $580, and the sale price of exactly 10 of the products is less than $750, what is the greatest possible sale price of the most expensive product?

Question #9:   A certain passenger is planning a trip that involves four connecting flights that leave from Airport A, B, C and D, respectively, beginning at 7:00 a.m. The first flight leaves Airport A every hour, and arrives at Airport B 1 ½ hours later. The second flight leaves airport B every 20 minutes, and arrives at Airport C 1 1/6 hours later. The third flight leaves Airport C every half hour, and arrives at airport D 1 ¼ hours later. The fourth flight leaves Airport D every 10 minutes, and arrives at airport E 1 hour later. What is the least amount of time the passenger must spend between flights in transit if all flights are on schedule?

Question #10:   At a distribution center, there are 6/7 as many female workers as there are male workers. If each female worker shipped 5/6 as many orders as each male worker, what fraction of all the orders shipped by all the workers did the female workers ship?

ALGEBRAIC PROBLEMS:

Question #11:   There are three identical boxes and each box is divided into equal number of compartments for packing identical soda cans. A shipment of soda cans is packed into these three boxes and five-sixth of the compartments are filled with soda cans. Each compartment can hold only one soda can. After one-fourth of the soda cans are sold, the remaining cans use only two of the boxes. What fraction of the compartments in the two boxes is now filled?

Question #12: On a certain test, 2 points are given away for every correct answer and ¼ point is taken off for every incorrect answer. If a student answered all 200 questions on the test and received a final score of 121 how many questions did the student answer correctly?

Question #13: A number of people boarded a bus at the main terminal. At the first stop, half of the passengers got off and 1 got on. At the second stop, one-third of the passengers on the bus got off and one got on. If the bus then had 25 passengers, how many were there when the bus left the main terminal?

Question #14: Three sisters, Mary, Maria, and Marian, share the same cash box. In the morning, Mary took half of the money plus $1 more. Then in the afternoon, Maria took half of the remaining money plus $1 more. Finally, in the evening Marian took the remaining $1. How many dollars were originally in the box?

Question #15: A certain auto dealership stocks four types of vehicles, there are one-third as many vans as cars, there are one-half as many trucks as vans, and there are equal number of jeeps and trucks. What percent of the vehicles in the dealership are cars?

Question #16: At what degree does Fahrenheit and Celsius become equal?

Question #17: The speed of a ship pulling out of an anchor is given by the equation $s = t^2 + 2t$, where s is the rate of speed in miles per hour, and t is the time in seconds from the moment when the ship starts moving. The given equation holds true for all situations where $0 \le t \le 8$. In miles per hour, what is the positive difference in the speed of the ship 8 seconds after it starts moving relative to the speed 2 seconds after it starts moving?

Question #18: If $-1 \le x \le 8$ and $-2 \le y \le 9$, what is the range of all possible values of $y - x$?

Question #19: It costs a book publisher $25 each to print 500 copies of a particular book. What must be the selling price per book to ensure that the profit (revenue from sales minus total cost to produce) on the 500 books is at least greater than $16,100?

Question #20: If the average (arithmetic mean) of $5x$ and $8y$ is greater than 90, and x is twice y, what is the least integer value of x?

Question #21: In a certain season of a boxing championship, the last year's champion has won 15 of the 86 games played so far. What is the minimum number of additional games he must play, considering the fact that he is sure to lose at least one-sixth of them, in order to ensure that for the entire season he will have won more games than he lost?

NUMERAL PROBLEMS:

Question #22: If one number exceeds another number by 12 and the larger number is $\dfrac{5}{2}$ times the smaller number, then what is the value of the smaller number?

Question #23: What is the value of the greater of two numbers whose product is 600, if the sum of the two numbers exceeds their difference by 24?

Question #24: What number can be added to the numerator and denominator of $\dfrac{2}{9}$ to get $\dfrac{1}{2}$?

Question #25: If n is a number on the number line between 5 and 25, and n is twice as far from 5 as from 25, then what is the exact position of n on the number line?

Question #26: First, a positive number n is multiplied by 2, then 5 is added to the product, then the sum is squared, and then it is divided by 4. The positive square root of the result of all these operations equals n. What is the value of n?

Question #27:   Let x, y, and z be three consecutive odd integers. If 5 more than the product of 7 and y is 40 more than the sum of x and z, what is the mean of the integers in the set $\{x, y, z, 2x, 2y, 2z\}$?

Question #28:   If the consecutive multiple of 8 from –72 to $8n$, such that $n > 0$, are added together, the total is 168, what is the value of n?

Question #29:   If the product of the integers a, b, c, and d is 770, and if $1 < a < b < c < d$, what is the value of $(a + d) - (b + c)$?

Question #30:   If the product of the integers a, b, c, and d is 210, and if $1 < a < b < c < d$, what is the value of $b + c$?

Question #31:   If x and y are positive integers and $x^2 - y^2 = 17$, what is the value of x?

Question #32:   If x, y, and z are positive integers and $x^2 - y^2 = z^2$, what is the value of $x + y + z$?

Question #33:   If the digits of a two-digit positive integer are reversed, the new integer differs from the original integer by 54. What is the positive difference between the two integers?

Question #34:   If x and y are real numbers, and $\sqrt{25x^2} - 81 = 0$, and $|y - 7| < 2$, what the smallest possible integer value of $x + y$?

Question #35:   The product of the digits of a positive two-digit integer is 16. If the units digit is subtracted from the tens digit, the result is 6. What is the two-digit integer?

Question #36:   A postmaster sold 60 stamps for $8.60. Some were 10-cent stamps and some were 15-cent stamps. How many 15-cent stamps were sold?

LITERAL EXPRESSIONS:

Question #37:   A certain car rental company charges x dollars for the first day and $\dfrac{x}{8}$ dollars for each additional day. How much should be the cost in dollars of renting a car for y days, such that $y > 1$?

Question #38:   Tina goes out for shopping with t dollars. First, she spends one-third of her money on furnishings. Then, she spends one-fourth of what's left on supplies. Finally, she buys an outfit for herself that costs one-fifth of her remaining money. What fraction of the money she took is left?

Question #39:   A certain club has x dollars to be divided equally among y members. If z new members join in, how many fewer dollars will each member receive than each of the original members would have received?

Question #40:   At the beginning of a trading day, the cost of 2 tons of coal was ¼d dollars. At the end of the trading day, the cost of 1 ton of coal was d dollars. What was the percent increase in the price of coal from the beginning to the end of the trading day?

Question #41:   In a certain year, a certain avid reader reads an average of x books per month from January to August and average of y books per month from September to December. What is the average number of books the reader reads each month in that year?

Question #42:   Superman and Spiderman are waiting in line to buy a movie ticket to watch Batman. If superman is seventh in the line, and there are k people ahead of Spiderman, where $k > 7$, how many people are between Superman and Spiderman?

Question #43:   At a certain store, a flower vase costs d dollars and c cents. What is the cost, in dollars, of v vases?

Question #44:   In a certain private farm, g pounds of grass can feed h horses for one day. If f new horses are added to the farm, then, at the same rate, how many more pounds of grass will be needed to feed all the horses for a week?

Question #45: If h hammers can be bought for n nickels, how many hammers can be bought for d dimes and q quarters?

Question #46: At a certain hardware store, each hammer that usually sells for $15 or less is on sale for 75 percent of its usual price, and each hammer that usually sells for more than $15 is on sale for 25 percent of its usual price. If a customer purchases x hammers, each of which usually costs $12, and y hammers, each of which usually costs $24, what is the average (arithmetic mean) amount, in dollars, for each hammer purchased?

Question #47: A certain junk trading company purchases p pounds of scrap material at the rate of c dollars per pound. It then spent e dollars per pound in restoring the material. Eventually, t pounds of the material had to be trashed because it was not sellable. If the trading company sold the remaining at the rate of s dollars per pound, what is the company's direct profit in this whole transaction considering the expenses and wastage?

Question #48: The revenue of a company is R dollars per month. If the company spends F dollars on fixed expenses and then spends 2/7 of the remainder on variable expenses, how much, in dollars, in terms of R and F, is the left over money after paying for fixed and variable expense?

Question #49: In a certain bookstore, the list price of a certain book is p dollars. During a sale, the list price is marked down by q percent. Senior citizens are offered an additional discount of r percent off the sale price. What is the price of the book, in dollars, to a senior citizen customer?

Question #50: If a vehicle travels $d + \dfrac{2}{5}$ miles at the rate of $r + \dfrac{1}{2}$ miles per hour, then in terms of d and r, what would be the travel time of the vehicle, in minutes?

Question #51: In a certain club, which has m member, divided their funds of d dollars evenly among its members. If there were n additional members in the club, how much more funds must the club raise in order for the amount per member to remain the same?

Question #52: In a certain state hit by a tornado, the government allocated a special relief fund of d dollars that would be equally divided among t towns that were known to be hit by the tornado. Later on, it was discovered that there were a additional towns that will also be eligible for the fund, which is now to be divided equally among all eligible towns. How much more money, in dollars, would each initial town have received if the additional towns were not discovered to be eligible for the fund?

Question #53: A self employed landscaper got a contract that pays him x dollars every day He has a direct expense of one-sixth of the money he receives every day for supplies, and he spends one-half of what's left on paying back his business loan. The rest of the remaining money is his income. In terms of x, how many days, will it take the landscaper to earn $100?

AGE & WEIGHT PROBLEMS:

Question #54: If today is John's 15th birthday and his father's 52nd birthday, how many years from today will John's father be twice as old as John at that time?

Question #55: If Monika is 10 years younger than Susan and Susan is 2 years older than Nancy, who is 10 years over one-half of a century old, then how old is Tiffany, who is 5 years shy of one-half Monika's age?

Question #56: If Johnny is 10 years younger than Ricky, and Ricky is 6 years older than Bobby, who is 5 years less than one quarter of a century old, how old is Tommy, who is 2 years shy of one-half Johnny's age?

Question #57: John is now five times as old as Tom was 5 years ago. If the sum of John's and Tom's ages is 35, in how many years will John be twice as old as Tom?

Question #58: 8 years ago, Jack was half as old as Mack. Mack is now 20 years older than Jack is. How old will Jack be 8 year from now?

WORK PROBLEMS:

Question #59: Romeo gets on the elevator at the 51st floor of a building and rides up at a rate of 57 floors per minute. At the same time, Juliet gets on an elevator on the 91st floor of the same building and rides down at a rate of 63 floors per minute. If they continue traveling at these rates, at which floor will their paths cross?

Question #60: Victor reads at an average rate of 60 pages per hour, while Susan reads at an average of 80 pages per hour. If Victor starts reading a book at 5:30, and Susan begins reading an identical copy of the same book at 6:20, at what time will they be reading the same page?

Question #61: While typing a project report, John takes his first break after typing one-fourth of the total number of pages. He takes his second break after he types one-half of the remaining number of pages after taking the first break. He then types the remaining 90 pages to finish typing his project. What is the total number of pages in John's project report?

Question #62: Working independently, Anita can execute a certain job in 8 hours and Usher can execute it in 10 hours. After Anita and Usher work together at the same job for 2 hours, Anita quits the job. If Usher completes the remaining job, working alone, how many hours will it take Usher to complete the job?

Question #63: Machine X and Machine Y, both produces widgets. It takes Machine X 20 hours longer to produce 1,080 widgets, than it takes Machine Y. Machine Y produces 20 percent more widgets per hour than Machine X. How many widgets per hour does Machine X produce?

Question #64: Oil flows into an empty 98-gallon tank at spout X and out of the tank at spout Y. If the rate of flow through spout X is 7 gallons per hour, how many gallons per hour must flow out through spout Y so that the tank is full in exactly 126 hours?

Question #65: For a small home improvement job, Jose and Frank were each paid m dollars from the contractor to complete the job. Jose worked 12 hours on the job and Frank worked five-sixth the number of hours that Jose worked on the job. After completing the job, Frank gave Jose n dollars from his payment for his services so that they both earn equal hourly wages for the job. What is the dollar amount, in terms of n, that Jose and Frank received for their services from the contractor?

MOTION PROBLEMS:

Question #66: A river cruiser leaves point A and travels upstream to point B at an average speed of 8 miles per hour. It returns downstream by the same route at an average speed of 12 miles per hour. What is the average speed for the round trip, in miles per hour?

Question #67: Amber rides a bicycle from her home to her school at rate of 5 miles per hour, and rides back along the same route from her school to her home at the rate of 2 miles per hour. If she spends exactly one hour traveling both ways, what is the distance from her home to her school?

Question #68: A man runs from his home to his work at an average speed of 4 miles per hour, and then walks back home along the same route at an average of 2 miles per hour. If his whole journey took one hour, how many miles is his home from his work?

Question #69: On a 80-mile trip, the driver drives the first one-fifth of the trip at the rate of $2r$ miles per hour and the remaining of the trip at half that rate. What is the average rate for the entire trip?

Question #70: For a certain trip, a car averages 50 miles per hour for the first 6 hours of the trip, and averages 90 miles per hour for each additional hour of the same trip. If the average speed for the entire trip is 75 miles per hour, how many hours long is the entire trip?

Question #71: Car A and Car B are both traveling in the same direction along the same route and Car A is 50 miles behind Car B. Car A is traveling at a constant rate of 60 miles per hour and Car B is traveling at a constant rate of 52 miles per hour. How many hours will it take for Car *A* to overtake Car *B* and drive 16 miles ahead of Car *B*?

MIXTURE PROBLEMS:

Question #72: A certain jar contains one-sixth pound of strawberries. The jar is then filled with a mixture that has equal weights of strawberries, raspberries, blueberries, blackberries, and cranberries. If the total weight is 1 pound, what fraction of the mixture are NOT strawberries?

Question #73: Solution *X* contains 10 percent sodium chloride and Solution *Y* contains 15 percent sodium chloride. Another solution, *Z*, is created by mixing Solution *X* and Solution *Y*. If Solution *Z*, which is 600 gallons, contains exactly 82 gallons of sodium chloride, how many gallons of Solution *X* are in Solution *Z*?

Question #74: Solution *X* is 10 percent alcohol and solution *Y* is 25 percent alcohol. If 50 ounces of solution *X* are mixed with 70 ounces of solution *Y* to form Solution *Z*, what percent of Solution *Z* will be alcohol?

Question #75: A certain artist develops two new shades for his next painting. He names the first shade as "sunrise," and makes it by mixing 7 parts red and 5 parts orange. He names the second shade as "sunset," and makes it by mixing 5 parts red and 7 parts orange. How many ounces of orange paint must be added to 24 ounces of sunrise shade to convert it to sunset shade?

PRACTICE EXERCISE – QUESTIONS & ANSWERS WITH EXPLANATIONS:

ARITHMETIC PROBLEMS:

Question #1: At a certain company, two-seventh of the managers attended the company's annual meeting, and one-half of them were females. If one-tenth of the managers who did not attend the annual meeting were females, what fractional part of the total number of managers were males?

Solution: No. of Managers who DID attend the Annual Meeting $\Rightarrow \dfrac{2}{7}$

$$\Rightarrow \text{Females} = \frac{1}{2} \bullet \frac{2}{7} = \frac{1}{7}$$

$$\Rightarrow \text{Males} \quad = \frac{1}{2} \bullet \frac{2}{7} = \frac{1}{7}$$

No. of Managers who DID NOT attend the Annual Meeting $\Rightarrow 1 - \dfrac{2}{7} = \dfrac{5}{7}$

$$\Rightarrow \text{Females} = \frac{1}{10} \bullet \frac{5}{7} = \frac{1}{14}$$

$$\Rightarrow \text{Males} \quad = \frac{9}{10} \bullet \frac{5}{7} = \frac{9}{14}$$

Total No. of Male Managers $\Rightarrow \dfrac{1}{7} + \dfrac{9}{14} = \dfrac{2}{14} + \dfrac{9}{14} = \dfrac{11}{14}$

Question #2: If one-fourth of the air in a cylindrical tank is removed after each stroke of a vacuum pump, what fraction of the original amount of air remains in the tank after five strokes?

Solution: Since after each stroke of the pump, ¼ the air is removed, so, ¾ the air remains in the tank.
Let the Original Amount of Air in the Tank $\Rightarrow 1$

Fraction of Air that Remains in the Tank after: 1 Stroke $\Rightarrow \dfrac{1}{1} \times \dfrac{3}{4} = \dfrac{3^1}{4^1}$

2 Strokes $\Rightarrow \dfrac{3^1}{4^1} \times \dfrac{3}{4} = \dfrac{3^2}{4^2}$

3 Strokes $\Rightarrow \dfrac{3^2}{4^2} \times \dfrac{3}{4} = \dfrac{3^3}{4^3}$

4 Strokes $\Rightarrow \dfrac{3^3}{4^3} \times \dfrac{3}{4} = \dfrac{3^4}{4^4}$

5 Strokes $\Rightarrow \dfrac{3^4}{4^4} \times \dfrac{3}{4} = \dfrac{3^5}{4^5} = \dfrac{243}{1024}$

Question #3: In a laboratory, there are two test-tube containing certain type of acid. The capacity of the larger test-tube is double the capacity of the smaller test-tube. The larger test-tube is 5/6 full and the smaller test-tube is 1/6 full. If all the content of the smaller test-tube is poured into the larger test-tube, what fraction of the larger test-tube will be filled with acid? (Consider there is no loss of acid while pouring.)

Solution: Let the capacity of larger test-tube $\Rightarrow t$ ounces
Then, the capacity of the smaller test-tube $\Rightarrow \frac{1}{2} t$ ounces

Before pouring $\Rightarrow$ Original content of the larger test-tube $= \dfrac{5}{6} t$ ounces

$\Rightarrow$ Original content of the smaller test-tube $= \dfrac{1}{6}\left(\dfrac{1}{2}t\right) = \dfrac{1}{12}t$ ounces

After pouring $\Rightarrow$ Content of the smaller test-tube $= 0$

$\Rightarrow$ Content of the larger test-tube $= \dfrac{5}{6}t + \dfrac{1}{12}t = \dfrac{10}{12}t + \dfrac{1}{12}t = \dfrac{11}{12}t$

Therefore, after poring all the content of the smaller test-tube into the larger test-tube, the larger test-tube will be 11/12 filled with acid.

Question #4: In a laboratory, there are two test-tube containing certain type of acid. The capacity of the larger test-tube is double the capacity of the smaller test-tube. The larger test-tube is ¾ full and the smaller test-tube is ¼ full. If all the content of the smaller test-tube is poured into the larger test-tube, what fraction of the larger test-tube will be filled with acid? (Consider there is no loss of acid while pouring.)

Solution: Let the capacity of larger test-tube $\Rightarrow t$ ounces
Then, the capacity of the smaller test-tube $\Rightarrow$ ½ t ounces

Before pouring $\Rightarrow$ Original content of the larger test-tube $= \dfrac{3}{4}t$ ounces

$\Rightarrow$ Original content of the smaller test-tube $= \dfrac{1}{4}\left(\dfrac{1}{2}t\right) = \dfrac{1}{8}t$ ounces

After pouring $\Rightarrow$ Content of the smaller test-tube $= 0$

$\Rightarrow$ Content of the larger test-tube $= \dfrac{3}{4}t + \dfrac{1}{8}t = \dfrac{6}{8}t + \dfrac{1}{8}t = \dfrac{7}{8}t$

Therefore, after pouring all the content of the smaller test-tube into the larger test-tube, the larger test-tube will be 7/8 filled with acid.

Question #5: Equal amount of oil were poured into two empty jars of different capacities, which made one jar one-eighth full and the other jar one-fifth full. If the oil in the jar with the lesser capacity is then emptied into the jar with the greater capacity, what percent of the larger jar will be filled with oil?

Solution: It's already given that equal amount of oil was poured into the two jars, which means the amounts of oil in the two jars are equal. After pouring the oil into the two jars, the jar with the greater capacity is one-eighth full, and the jar with the lesser capacity is one-fifth full.
Amount of oil in the larger jar which is 1/8 full = Amount of oil in the smaller jar which is 1/5 full.
The jar which is less full with the same amount of oil has a greater capacity, in this case, it is the jar which is 1/8 (12.5%) full has a greater capacity. Likewise, the jar which is more full with the same amount of oil has a lesser capacity, in this case, it is the jar which is 1/5 (20%) full has a lesser capacity. Therefore, oil from the lesser capacity (which is 1/5 full) jar will be moved to the greater capacity (which is 1/8 full) jar.
Since both jars contain the same amount of oil, when the oil in the smaller jar (which is 1/5 full) is emptied into the larger jar (which is 1/8 full), the larger jar will now have double the amount of oil:

$\Rightarrow 2 \times \dfrac{1}{8} = \dfrac{1}{4} = 25\%$

Question #6: The height of a hill, which is 170 feet tall, is being eroded at the rate of 1 feet every month. At the same time, the height of another hill, which is 110 feet tall, is being eroded at the rate of ¼ feet per month. If the heights of both hills continue to be reduced at these uniform rates, in how many months will the hills have the same height?

Solution: Let's make a table and write what happens to the heights of the hills over the first few months:

	Beginning	1 Month	2 Months	3 Months	4 Months	5 Months	....
1st Hill $\Rightarrow$	170 feet	169	168	167	166	165	
2nd Hill $\Rightarrow$	110 feet	109.75	109.50	109.25	109	108.75	
Difference $\Rightarrow$	60	59.25	58.50	57.75	57	56.25	

Both hills started with a difference of 60 feet, and each month, they are getting closer and closer to the same height, at the rate of 0.75 feet per month.
To reach the same height, it will take 60 (difference) ÷ 0.75 (rate) = 80 months.
Check: The answer can be checked by plugging-in:
After 80 months $\Rightarrow$ 1st Hill's Height = 170 – (80 × 1)   = 90 feet
$\Rightarrow$ 2nd Hill's Height = 110 – (80 × ¼) = 90 feet

Question #7: A certain cruise liner charges $200 per person if there are less than 50 people in a group. For more than 50 people in a group, for each additional person over 50 people, they reduce the price per person by $2.50 for every person in the group. How much will be the total cost for a group of 60 people?

Solution: Price per Person for a Group of less than 50 People $\Rightarrow$ $200

Discount per Person for a Group of 60 People   ⇒ (60 − 50) × $2.50 = 10 × $2.50 = $25
Price per Person for a Group of 60 People   ⇒ $200 − $25 = $175
Total Cost for a Group of 60 People   ⇒ $175 × 60 = $10,500

Question #8: A certain manufacturing company produces a line of 20 products with an average sale price of $1,125. If the minimum sale price of any of the products is $580, and the sale price of exactly 10 of the products is less than $750, what is the greatest possible sale price of the most expensive product?

Solution: Average Price of 20 products ⇒ $1,125
Sum of the prices of all 20 products (one of each) ⇒ $1,125 × 20 = $22,500
Since we are asked to find the maximum possible price of one product, we must try to minimize the price of the rest of the 19 products.
Minimum price of any product ⇒ $580
Since exactly 10 of the products sells for less than $750, let's assume that they all sell for $580 each.
Sum of the prices of 10 products (1 of each) ⇒ $580 × 10 = 5,800
Let's assume that the next 9 of the 20 products sells for $750 each.
Sum of the prices of 9 products (1 of each) ⇒ $750 × 9 = 6,750
Sum of the prices of 19 products (1 of each) ⇒ $5,800 + $6,750 = $12,550
Maximum Price of 24th product ⇒ Sum of Prices of 20 Products − Sum of Prices of 19 Products
⇒ $22,500 − 12,550 = $9950

Question #9: A certain passenger is planning a trip that involves four connecting flights that leave from Airport A, B, C and D, respectively, beginning at 7:00 a.m. The first flight leaves Airport A every hour, and arrives at Airport B 1 ½ hours later. The second flight leaves airport B every 20 minutes, and arrives at Airport C 1 1/6 hours later. The third flight leaves Airport C every half hour, and arrives at airport D 1 ¼ hours later. The fourth flight leaves Airport D every 10 minutes, and arrives at airport E 1 hour later. What is the least amount of time the passenger must spend between flights in transit if all flights are on schedule?

Solution: To solve this problem, the best way is to organize all the information in the following style:
Flights from Airport A to B   ⇒ Every Hour from 7:00 am ⇒ on the hr, every hr
Departure from Airport A   ⇒ 7:00 am
Flight Time   ⇒ 1 ½ hours = 1 hours and 30 minutes
Arrival at Airport B   ⇒ 7:00 am + (1 hr 30 min) = 8:30 am
Flights from Airport B to C   ⇒ Every 20 min ⇒ on the hr, 20 and 40 min passed hr
Transit Time at Airport B   ⇒ **10 minutes**
Departure from Airport B   ⇒ 8:40 am
Flight Time   ⇒ 1 1/6 hours = 1 hour and 10 minutes
Arrival at Airport C   ⇒ 8:40 am + (1 hr 10 min) = 9:50 am
Flights from Airport C to D   ⇒ Every 30 min ⇒ on the hr, 30 min passed hr
Transit Time at Airport C   ⇒ **10 minutes**
Departure from Airport C   ⇒ 10:00 pm
Flight Time   ⇒ 1 ¼ hours = 1 hour and 15 minutes
Arrival at Airport D   ⇒ 10:00 pm + (1 hr 15 min) = 11:15 am
Flights from Airport D to E   ⇒ Every 10 min ⇒ on the hr, 10, 20, 30, 40, and 50 min passed hr
Transit Time at Airport D   ⇒ **5 minutes**
Departure from Airport D   ⇒ 11:20 am
Flight Time   ⇒ 1 hour
Arrival at Airport E   ⇒ 12:20 pm
Total Transit Time   ⇒ 10 + 10 + 5 = 25 minutes

Question #10: At a distribution center, there are 6/7 as many female workers as there are male workers. If each female worker shipped 5/6 as many orders as each male worker, what fraction of all the orders shipped by all the workers did the female workers ship?

Solution: Let, the No. of Male Workers   ⇒ w

Then, the No. of Female Workers   ⇒ $\frac{6}{7}w$

Let, the No. of Orders Shipped by Male Workers   ⇒ s

Then, the No. of Orders Shipped by Female Workers $\Rightarrow \dfrac{5}{6}s$

Total No. of Orders Shipped by Male Workers $\Rightarrow ws$

Total No. of Orders Shipped by Female Workers $\Rightarrow \left(\dfrac{6}{7}w\right)\left(\dfrac{5}{6}s\right) = \dfrac{5}{7}ws$

Total No. of Orders Shipped by all Workers $\Rightarrow ws + \dfrac{5}{7}ws = \dfrac{12}{7}ws$

Fraction of Orders Shipped by Male Workers $\Rightarrow \dfrac{ws}{\dfrac{12}{7}ws} = \dfrac{7}{12}$

Fraction of Orders Shipped by Female Workers $\Rightarrow \dfrac{\dfrac{5}{7}ws}{\dfrac{12}{7}ws} = \left(\dfrac{5}{7}\right)\left(\dfrac{7}{12}\right) = \dfrac{5}{12}$

ALGEBRAIC PROBLEMS:

Question #11: There are three identical boxes and each box is divided into equal number of compartments for packing identical soda cans. A shipment of soda cans is packed into these three boxes and five-sixth of the compartments are filled with soda cans. Each compartment can hold only one soda can. After one-fourth of the soda cans are sold, the remaining cans use only two of the boxes. What fraction of the compartments in the two boxes is now filled?

Solution: Let, the No. of compartments in each box $\Rightarrow x$
Then, the total No. of compartments in three boxes $\Rightarrow 3x$

Originally, the fraction of compartments that are filled in all three boxes $\Rightarrow \left(\dfrac{5}{6}\right)(3x) = \dfrac{5}{2}x$

After selling ¼ of the soda cans, the fraction of compartments that are still filled in three boxes

$\Rightarrow \left(\dfrac{5}{2}x\right)\dfrac{3}{4} = \dfrac{15}{8}x$

The fraction that the remaining soda uses in two boxes $\Rightarrow \dfrac{15}{8}x \div 2x = \left(\dfrac{15}{8}x\right)\left(\dfrac{1}{2x}\right) = \dfrac{15}{16}$

Question #12: On a certain test, 2 points are given away for every correct answer and ¼ point is taken off for every incorrect answer. If a student answered all 200 questions on the test and received a final score of 121 how many questions did the student answer correctly?

Solution: Total No. of Questions in the test $\Rightarrow 200$
Let, the No. of Questions Answered Correctly $\Rightarrow n$
Then, the No. of Questions Answered Incorrectly $\Rightarrow 200 - n$
Points Added for Each Correct Answer $\Rightarrow 2$
Points Subtracted for Each Incorrect Answer $\Rightarrow 0.25$
Final Score $\Rightarrow 121$
EZ Problem Set-Up $\Rightarrow$ Points Added – Points Subtracted = Final Score
$\Rightarrow 2(n) - 0.25(200 - n) = 121$ [Set up the equation]
$\Rightarrow 2n - 50 + 0.25n = 121$ [Apply distributive property]
$\Rightarrow 2.25n = 171$ [Combine like-terms]
$\Rightarrow n = 76$ [Divide both sides by 2.25]
Therefore, the No. of correct answers = 76

Question #13: A number of people boarded a bus at the main terminal. At the first stop, half of the passengers got off and 1 got on. At the second stop, one-third of the passengers on the bus got off and one got on. If the bus then had 25 passengers, how many were there when the bus left the main terminal?

Solution: Let, the No. of passengers originally on the bus = n
Now, let's keep track of the passenger who got on and got off.

At the First Stop   ⇒ Half of the passengers got off ⇒ Subtract ½n
                         ⇒ 1 passenger got on ⇒ Add 1
Remaining Passengers on the Bus after the First Stop ⇒ $n - ½n + 1 = ½n + 1$
At the Second Stop   ⇒ One-third of the passengers got off ⇒ Subtract one-third of (½n + 1)
                      ⇒ 1 passenger got on ⇒ Add 1

Remaining Passengers on the Bus after the Second Stop ⇒ $\dfrac{2}{3}\left(\dfrac{1}{2}n + 1\right) + 1$

EZ Problem Set-Up ⇒ After the second stop, the bus had 25 passengers:

$$\Rightarrow \frac{2}{3}\left(\frac{1}{2}n + 1\right) + 1 = 25 \qquad \text{[Set up the equation]}$$

$$\Rightarrow \frac{1}{3}n + \frac{2}{3} + 1 = 25 \qquad \text{[Apply distributive property]}$$

$$\Rightarrow \frac{1}{3}n + \frac{2}{3} = 24 \qquad \text{[Subtract 1 from both sides]}$$

$$\Rightarrow \frac{1}{3}n = 24 - \frac{2}{3} \qquad \text{[Subtract 2/3 from both sides]}$$

$$\Rightarrow \frac{1}{3}n = \frac{72}{3} - \frac{2}{3} \qquad \text{[Scale-Up the fractions to their LCD, which is 3]}$$

$$\Rightarrow \frac{1}{3}n = \frac{70}{3} \qquad \text{[Combine like-terms]}$$

$$\Rightarrow n = 70 \qquad \text{[Multiply both sides by 3]}$$

Question #14: Three sisters, Mary, Maria, and Marian, share the same cash box. In the morning, Mary took half of the money plus $1 more. Then in the afternoon, Maria took half of the remaining money plus $1 more. Finally, in the evening Marian took the remaining $1. How many dollars were originally in the box?

Solution: Let, original amount in the cash box   ⇒ n

Amount of Money Mary took   ⇒ $\dfrac{1}{2}n + 1$

Amount of Money Remaining   ⇒ $n - \left(\dfrac{1}{2}n + 1\right) = \dfrac{1}{2}n - 1$

Amount of Money Maria took   ⇒ $\dfrac{1}{2}\left(\dfrac{1}{2}n - 1\right) + 1 = \dfrac{1}{4}n - \dfrac{1}{2} + 1 = \dfrac{1}{4}n + \dfrac{1}{2}$

Amount of Money Remaining   ⇒ $1
Amount of Money Marian took   ⇒ $1
EZ Problem Set-Up ⇒ Amt. Mary took + Amt. Maria took + Amt. Marian took = Original Amount

$$\Rightarrow n = \left(\frac{1}{2}n + 1\right) + \left(\frac{1}{4}n + \frac{1}{2}\right) + 1 \qquad \text{[Set up the equation]}$$

$$\Rightarrow n = \left(\frac{1}{2}n + \frac{1}{4}n\right) + \left(\frac{1}{2} + 2\right) \qquad \text{[Re-write the equation with like-terms combined]}$$

$$\Rightarrow n = \frac{3}{4}n + \frac{5}{2} \qquad \text{[Combine like-terms]}$$

$$\Rightarrow n - \frac{3}{4}n = \frac{5}{2} \qquad \text{[Subtract ¾n from both sides]}$$

$$\Rightarrow \frac{1}{4}n = \frac{5}{2} \qquad \text{[Combine like-terms]}$$

$$\Rightarrow 2n = 20 \qquad \text{[Cross multiply]}$$

$$\Rightarrow n = 10 \qquad \text{[Divide both sides by 2]}$$

Therefore, there was originally $10 in the cash box.

Question #15: A certain auto dealership stocks four types of vehicles, there are one-third as many vans as cars, there are one-half as many trucks as vans, and there are equal number of jeeps and trucks. What percent of the vehicles in the dealership are cars?

Solution:

There are 1/3 as many vans as cars	$\Rightarrow V = \dfrac{1}{3}C$	$\Rightarrow$ Equation #1
There are 1/2 as many trucks as vans	$\Rightarrow T = \dfrac{1}{2}V$	$\Rightarrow$ Equation #2
	$\Rightarrow V = 2T$	$\Rightarrow$ Equation #3
Substitute the value of V from Eq #1 into #2	$\Rightarrow T = \dfrac{1}{2}\left(\dfrac{1}{3}C\right) = \dfrac{1}{6}C$	$\Rightarrow$ Equation #4
	$\Rightarrow C = 6T$	$\Rightarrow$ Equation #5
There are equal number of jeeps and trucks	$\Rightarrow J = T$	$\Rightarrow$ Equation #6

Let the total No. of vehicles = 100

EZ Problem Set-Up $\Rightarrow$ No. of Vans + No. of Cars + No. of Trucks + No. of Jeeps = No. of Vehicles
$\Rightarrow C + V + J + T = 100$ [Set up the equation]
$\Rightarrow 6T + 2T + T + T = 100$ [Substitute the value of C, V, and J in terms of T]
$\Rightarrow 10T = 100$ [Combine like-terms]
$\Rightarrow T = 10$ [Divide both sides by 10]

No. of Trucks $\Rightarrow T = 10$ $\Rightarrow 10\%$
No. of Jeeps $\Rightarrow J = T$ $\Rightarrow 10\%$
No. of Vans $\Rightarrow V = 2T$ $\Rightarrow 2(10) = 20\%$
No. of Cars $\Rightarrow C = 6T$ $\Rightarrow 6(10) = 60\%$

Question #16: At what degree does Fahrenheit and Celsius become equal?

Solution: EZ Problem Set-Up $\Rightarrow$ Equate C & F by substituting them with X in the conversion formula
$\Rightarrow 9C = 5F - 160$ [Write the conversion formula]
$\Rightarrow 9X = 5X - 160$ [Substitute X for C and F]
$\Rightarrow 4X = -160$ [Subtract $5X$ from both sides]
$\Rightarrow X = -40$ [Divide both sides by 4]
Therefore, $-40°F = -40°C$

Question #17: The speed of a ship pulling out of an anchor is given by the equation $s = t^2 + 2t$, where s is the rate of speed in miles per hour, and t is the time in seconds from the moment when the ship starts moving. The given equation holds true for all situations where $0 \le t \le 8$. In miles per hour, what is the positive difference in the speed of the ship 8 seconds after it starts moving relative to the speed 2 seconds after it starts moving?

Solution: Speed of ship $\Rightarrow s = t^2 + 2t$ [Given]
When $t = 0$ $\Rightarrow s = 0^2 + 2(0) = 0 + 0 = 0$ mph   [Substitute $t = 0$ in the given equation]
When $t = 1$ $\Rightarrow s = 1^2 + 2(1) = 1 + 2 = 3$ mph   [Substitute $t = 1$ in the given equation]
When $t = 2$ $\Rightarrow s = 2^2 + 2(2) = 4 + 4 = 8$ mph   [Substitute $t = 2$ in the given equation]
When $t = 8$ $\Rightarrow s = 8^2 + 2(8) = 64 + 16 = 80$ mph   [Substitute $t = 8$ in the given equation]
Therefore, the positive difference in the speed of the ship 8 seconds after it starts moving compared to the speed 2 seconds after it starts moving = $80 - 8 = 72$

Question #18: If $-1 \le x \le 8$ and $-2 \le y \le 9$, what is the range of all possible values of $y - x$?

Solution: The range of all possible values of anything is given by the difference between the greatest possible value and the least possible value.
Greatest possible value of $y - x$ $\Rightarrow y - x = 9 - (-1) = 9 + 1 = 10$
[When y is the largest possible and x is the smallest possible]
Smallest possible value of $y - x$ $\Rightarrow y - x = -2 - (8) = -2 - 8 = -10$
[When y is the smallest possible and x is the largest possible]
Range of all possible values of $y - x$ $\Rightarrow -10 \le y - x \le 10$

Question #19: It costs a book publisher $25 each to print 500 copies of a particular book. What must be the selling price per book to ensure that the profit (revenue from sales minus total cost to produce) on the 500 books is at least greater than $16,100?

Solution:

Cost to print each book	$\Rightarrow$ $25
No. of books printed	$\Rightarrow$ 500
Let the selling price of the book	$\Rightarrow$ n
Profit Margin per book sold	$\Rightarrow$ Selling Price – Cost Price = n – $25
Total profit from selling books	$\Rightarrow$ (No. of books sold) times (Profit per book) = $500($n$ – 25)
EZ Problem Set-Up	$\Rightarrow$ The profit from book sales must be greater than or equal to 16,100

$\Rightarrow$ $500($n$ – 25) $\geq$ $16,100   [Set up the inequality]

$\Rightarrow$ 500n$ – 12,500 $\geq$ $16,100 [Apply distributive property]

$\Rightarrow$ 500n$ $\geq$ $28,600   [Add 12,500 to both sides]

$\Rightarrow$ n $\geq$ $57.20   [Divide both sides by 500]

Therefore, the selling price of the book must be equal to or greater than $57.20 per book to make the total profit equal to or greater than $16,100.

Question #20: If the average (arithmetic mean) of $5x$ and $8y$ is greater than 90, and x is twice y, what is the least integer value of x?

Solution: EZ Problem Set-Up $\Rightarrow$ Average of $5x$ and $8y$ is greater than 90

$\Rightarrow \dfrac{5x + 8y}{2} > 90$ [Set up the inequality]

$\Rightarrow \dfrac{5x + 8(0.5x)}{2} > 90$ [Since x is twice of y, or y is half of x, replace $y = 0.5x$]

$\Rightarrow \dfrac{5x + 4x}{2} > 90$ [Apply distributive property]

$\Rightarrow \dfrac{9x}{2} > 90$ [Combine like-terms]

$\Rightarrow 9x > 180$ [Multiply both sides by 2]

$\Rightarrow x > 20$ [Divide both sides by 9]

Therefore, the least integer value of x is 21.

Question #21: In a certain season of a boxing championship, the last year's champion has won 15 of the 86 games played so far. What is the minimum number of additional games he must play, considering the fact that he is sure to lose at least one-sixth of them, in order to ensure that for the entire season he will have won more games than he lost?

Solution:
So far, No. of games played $\Rightarrow$ 86
So far, No. of games won $\Rightarrow$ 15
So far, No. of games lost $\Rightarrow$ 86 – 15 = 71
Since we want to find the minimum number of games that he must play to win more than half of them, let's assume that he loses the minimum number of the remaining games, that is, he loses x games and wins $5x$ games.
Now, in all, total No. of games won $\Rightarrow$ 15 + $5x$
And, in all, total No. of games lost $\Rightarrow$ 71 + x
EZ problem Set-Up $\Rightarrow$ Total No. of games won must be greater than total No. of games lost

        $\Rightarrow$ 15 + $5x$ > 71 + x [Set up the inequality]
        $\Rightarrow$ 15 + $4x$ > 71   [Subtract x from both sides]
        $\Rightarrow$ $4x$ > 56   [Subtract 15 from both sides]
        $\Rightarrow$ x > 14   [Divide both sides by 4]

So the least x can be is 15.
This means the champion will have at least 15 losses and 15 × 5 = 75 wins, for a total of 15 + 75 = 90 additional games.

NUMERAL PROBLEMS:

Question #22: If one number exceeds another number by 12 and the larger number is $\dfrac{5}{2}$ times the smaller number, then what is the value of the smaller number?

Solution: Let the value of larger number = x, and the smaller number = y

One number exceeds another number by 12 $\Rightarrow x = y + 12$ $\qquad \Rightarrow$ Equation #1

The larger number is 5/2 times the smaller number $\Rightarrow x = \dfrac{5}{2}y$ $\qquad \Rightarrow$ Equation #2

EZ Problem Set-Up $\Rightarrow$ Equate Equation #1 and Equation #2

$\Rightarrow \dfrac{5}{2}y = y + 12$ $\qquad$ [Set up the equation]

$\Rightarrow \dfrac{5}{2}y - y = 12$ $\qquad$ [Subtract y from both sides]

$\Rightarrow \dfrac{3}{2}y = 12$ $\qquad$ [Combine like-terms]

$\Rightarrow y = 12 \times \dfrac{2}{3} = 8$ $\qquad$ [Multiply both sides by 2/3]

Question #23: What is the value of the greater of two numbers whose product is 600, if the sum of the two numbers exceeds their difference by 24?

Solution: Let, the value of the greater number $\Rightarrow a$
And, the value of the smaller number $\Rightarrow b$

Sum of two numbers exceeds their difference by 24 $\qquad \Rightarrow (a + b) = (a - b) + 24$
$\qquad\qquad\qquad\qquad\qquad\qquad\qquad\qquad\qquad \Rightarrow 2b = 24$ $\quad$ [Simplify the equation]
$\qquad\qquad\qquad\qquad\qquad\qquad\qquad\qquad\qquad \Rightarrow b = 12$ $\quad$ [Divide both sides by 2]

Product of the two numbers is 600 $\qquad\qquad\qquad \Rightarrow ab = 600$
$\qquad\qquad\qquad\qquad\qquad\qquad\qquad\qquad\qquad \Rightarrow 12a = 600$ $\quad$ [Substitute $b = 12$]
$\qquad\qquad\qquad\qquad\qquad\qquad\qquad\qquad\qquad \Rightarrow a = 50$ $\quad$ [Divide both sides by 12]

Value of the smaller number $\Rightarrow a = 50$
Value of the greater number $\Rightarrow b = 12$

Question #24: What number can be added to the numerator and denominator of $\dfrac{2}{9}$ to get $\dfrac{1}{2}$?

Solution: Le, the number that is added to the numerator and denominator = x

EZ Problem Set-Up $\Rightarrow$ What number can be added to the numerator and denominator of $\dfrac{2}{9}$ to get $\dfrac{1}{2}$

$\Rightarrow \dfrac{2 + x}{9 + x} = \dfrac{1}{2}$ $\qquad$ [Set up the equation]

$\Rightarrow 2(2 + x) = 1(9 + x)$ $\qquad$ [Cross-multiply]
$\Rightarrow 4 + 2x = 9 + x$ $\qquad$ [Apply distributive property]
$\Rightarrow 4 + x = 9$ $\qquad$ [Subtract x from both sides]
$\Rightarrow x = 5$ $\qquad$ [Subtract 4 from both sides]

Check: $\dfrac{2 + 5}{9 + 5} = \dfrac{7}{14} = \dfrac{1}{2}$

Therefore, 5 can be added to the numerator and denominator of $\dfrac{2}{9}$ to get $\dfrac{1}{2}$

Question #25: If n is a number on the number line between 5 and 25, and n is twice as far from 5 as from 25, then what is the exact position of n on the number line?

Solution: Difference between 5 and 25 on the number line = $25 - 5 = 20$

EZ Problem Set-Up $\Rightarrow$ Since n is twice as far from 5 as from 25, this means, if n is "x units" away from 25, then it would be "2x units" away from 5.

$\Rightarrow 2x + x = 25 - 5$ $\qquad$ [Set up the equation]
$\Rightarrow 3x = 20$ $\qquad$ [Combine like-terms]

$$\Rightarrow x = \frac{20}{3} \qquad\qquad \text{[Divide both sides by 3]}$$

To find the exact position of n on the number line, add twice of x to 5, or subtract x from 25:

$$\Rightarrow 5 + (2)\frac{20}{3} = 5 + \frac{40}{3} = \frac{15}{3} + \frac{40}{3} = \frac{55}{3} = 18\frac{1}{3}$$

Question #26: First, a positive number n is multiplied by 2, then 5 is added to the product, then the sum is squared, and then it is divided by 4. The positive square root of the result of all these operations equals n. What is the value of n?

Solution: EZ Problem Set-Up $\Rightarrow$ Follow the directions given in the problem

$$\Rightarrow \sqrt{\frac{(2n+5)^2}{4}} = n \qquad\qquad \text{[Set up the equation]}$$

$$\Rightarrow \frac{(2n+5)^2}{4} = n^2 \qquad\qquad \text{[Square both sides]}$$

$\Rightarrow (2n+5)^2 = 4n^2 \qquad\qquad$ [Multiply both sides by 4]
$\Rightarrow 4n^2 + 20n + 25 = 4n^2 \qquad$ [Apply distributive property]
$\Rightarrow 20n + 25 = 0 \qquad\qquad$ [Subtract $4n^2$ from both sides]
$\Rightarrow 20n = -25 \qquad\qquad$ [Subtract 25 from both sides]
$\Rightarrow n = -1\frac{1}{4} \qquad\qquad$ [Divide both sides by 20]

Question #27: Let x, y, and z be three consecutive odd integers. If 5 more than the product of 7 and y is 40 more than the sum of x and z, what is the mean of the integers in the set $\{x, y, z, 2x, 2y, 2z\}$?

Solution: Let the value of the three consecutive odd integers be n, $n + 2$, and $n + 4$
Then, the value of $x = n$, $y = n + 2$, and $z = n + 4$
EZ Problem Set-Up $\Rightarrow$ 5 more than the product of 7 and y is 40 more than the sum of x and z
$\Rightarrow 7y + 5 = (x + z) + 40 \qquad\qquad$ [Set up the equation]
$\Rightarrow 7(n + 2) + 5 = (n + n + 4) + 40 \qquad$ [Substitute the value of x, y, and z]
$\Rightarrow 7n +14 + 5 = 2n + 44 \qquad\qquad$ [Apply distributive property]
$\Rightarrow 7n +19 = 2n + 44 \qquad\qquad$ [Combine like-terms]
$\Rightarrow 5n +19 = 44 \qquad\qquad$ [Subtract $2n$ from both sides]
$\Rightarrow 5n = 25 \qquad\qquad$ [Subtract 19 from both sides]
$\Rightarrow n = 5 \qquad\qquad$ [Divide both sides by 5]
Value of the integers in the set $\quad \Rightarrow \{5, 7, 9, 10, 14, 18\}$
Mean of the integers in the set $\quad \Rightarrow (5 + 7 + 9 + 10 + 14 + 18) \div 6 = 63 \div 6 = 10.5$

Question #28: If the consecutive multiple of 8 from -72 to $8n$, such that $n > 0$, are added together, the total is 168, what is the value of n?

Solution: Sum of consecutive multiple of 8 from -72 to $8n \quad \Rightarrow 168$
Sum of consecutive multiple of 8 from -72 to $72 \quad \Rightarrow (-72) + (-64) + \ldots 0 \ldots + 64 + 72 = 0$
Next two multiples of 8 are 80 & 88 $\quad \Rightarrow [(-72) + (-64) + 0 + 64 + 72] + 80 + 88 = 168$
$\Rightarrow 8n = 88$
$\Rightarrow n = 11$
Value of $n \quad \Rightarrow 11$

Question #29: If the product of the integers a, b, c, and d is 770, and if $1 < a < b < c < d$, what is the value of $(a + d) - (b + c)$?

Solution: Since the product of a, b, c, and d is 770, let's start by factoring it:
Factors of $a \times b \times c \times d \quad \Rightarrow 770 = (2)(385) = (2)(5)(77) = (2)(5)(7)(11) \Rightarrow$ prime factors of 770
Since $1 < a < b < c < d \quad \Rightarrow a = 2; b = 5; c = 7; d = 11$
Value of $(a + d) - (b + c) \Rightarrow (2 + 11) - (5 + 7) = 13 - 12 = 1$

Question #30: If the product of the integers a, b, c, and d is 210, and if $1 < a < b < c < d$, what is the value of $b + c$?
Solution: Since the product of a, b, c, and d is 210, let's start by factoring it:
Factors of $a \times b \times c \times d \quad \Rightarrow 210 = (2)(105) = (2)(3)(35) = (2)(3)(5)(7) \Rightarrow$ prime factors of 210
Since $1 < a < b < c < d$, this means that b and c must the middle two factors $\Rightarrow b = 3$ and $c = 5$

Value of $(b + c) \Rightarrow 3 + 5 = 8$

Question #31: If x and y are positive integers and $x^2 - y^2 = 17$, what is the value of x?
Solution: There is only one way to solve this problem and that is to pick numbers and see which one works.
Find two consecutive integers whose sum is 17 and difference is 1
$\Rightarrow x^2 - y^2 = 17$ [Given]
$\Rightarrow (x + y)(x - y) = 17$ [Factor the left side]
$\Rightarrow (9 + 8)(9 - 8) = 17$ [Pick numbers that satisfy the equation]
$\Rightarrow (17)(1) = 17$ [Check if the equation holds true]
Since $9^2 - 8^2 = 81 - 64 = 17$, the value of x is 9 and $y = 8$

Question #32: If x, y, and z are positive integers and $x^2 - y^2 = z^2$, what is the value of $x + y + z$?
Solution: There is only one way to solve this problem and that is to pick numbers and see which one works.
There is only one set of integers that will satisfy the given condition.
$\Rightarrow x^2 - y^2 = z^2$ [Given]
$\Rightarrow (x + y)(x - y) = z^2$ [Factor the left side]
$\Rightarrow (5 + 4)(5 - 4) = 3^2$ [Pick numbers that satisfy the equation]
$\Rightarrow (9)(1) = 9$ [Check if the equation holds true]
Since $5^2 - 4^2 = 3^2$, the value of $x = 5$, $y = 4$, $z = 3$, and the value of $x + y + z = 5 + 4 + 3 = 12$

Question #33: If the digits of a two-digit positive integer are reversed, the new integer differs from the original integer by 54. What is the positive difference between the two integers?
Solution: Let, the original two-digit number be $10t + u$
Then, the new two-digit number with the digits reversed will be $10u + t$
EZ problem Set-Up $\Rightarrow$ Difference between the new and the original integer is 18
$\Rightarrow (10t + u) - (10u + t) = 54$ [Set up the equation]
$\Rightarrow 10t + u - 10u - t = 54$ [Eliminate the parentheses]
$\Rightarrow 9t - 9u = 54$ [Combine like-terms]
$\Rightarrow 9(t - u) = 54$ [Factor out 9 on the left side]
$\Rightarrow t - u = 6$ [Divide both sides by 9]
Positive difference between the two integers is 6.

Question #34: If x and y are real numbers, and $\sqrt{25x^2} - 81 = 0$, and $|y - 7| < 2$, what the smallest possible integer value of $x + y$?

Solution: Solve for x: $\Rightarrow \sqrt{25x^2} - 81 = 0$ [Given]

$\Rightarrow \sqrt{25x^2} = 81$ [Add 81 to both sides]

$\Rightarrow 5x = 9$ [Square root both sides]

$\Rightarrow x = \dfrac{9}{5} = 1\dfrac{4}{5}$ [Divide both sides by 5]

Solve for y: $\Rightarrow |y - 7| < 2$ [Given]
$\Rightarrow -2 < y - 7 < 2$ [Apply law of absolute value]
$\Rightarrow 5 < y < 9$ [Add 7 to all parts of the inequality]
We have a fixed value for x and range of value for y, and since we want to find the smallest possible integer value for the sum of x and y, we need to pick the smallest possible value of y which will result in the smallest possible integer value of $x + y$.

Smallest possible integer value of $x + y$ $\Rightarrow 1\dfrac{4}{5} + 5\dfrac{1}{5} = 7$

Question #35: The product of the digits of a positive two-digit integer is 16. If the units digit is subtracted from the tens digit, the result is 6. What is the two-digit integer?
Solution: Let, the tens digit of the two-digit integer $\Rightarrow a$
And, the units digit of the two-digit integer $\Rightarrow b$
The product of the digits of a positive two-digit integer is 16 $\Rightarrow ab = 16$ $\Rightarrow$ Equation #1
If the units digit is subtracted from the tens digit, the result is 6 $\Rightarrow a - b = 6$
                                                       $\Rightarrow a = b + 6$ $\Rightarrow$ Equation #2

Substitute the value of a from Equation #2 into #1 $\Rightarrow ab = 16$ [Rewrite Equation #1]

$\Rightarrow b(b + 6) = 16$ [Substitute $a = b + 6$]

$\Rightarrow b^2 + 6b - 16 = 0$ [Apply distributive property]

$\Rightarrow (b + 8)(b - 2) = 0$ [Factor out the trinomial]

$\Rightarrow b = +2$ [Solve for the +ve value of b]

Substitute the value of b into Equation #1 $\Rightarrow ab = 16$ [Rewrite Equation #1]

$\Rightarrow a(2) = 16$ [Substitute $b = 2$]

$\Rightarrow a = 8$ [Divide both sides by 2]

Therefore, the two digit number ab is 82.

Question #36: A postmaster sold 60 stamps for $8.60. Some were 10-cent stamps and some were 15-cent stamps. How many 15-cent stamps were sold?

Solution: Let, the No. of 10-cent stamps $\Rightarrow x$

Then, the No. of 15-cent stamps $\Rightarrow 60 - x$

Value of 10-cent stamps $\Rightarrow 10x$

Value of 15-cent stamps $\Rightarrow 15(60 - x) = 900 - 15x$

Total value of stamps sold $\Rightarrow$ $8.60 or 860 cents

EZ Problem Set-Up $\Rightarrow$ Value of 10-cent stamps + Value of 15-cent stamps = 860 cents

$\Rightarrow 10x + 900 - 15x = 860$ [Substitute the value of stamps in cents]

$\Rightarrow 5x = 40$ [Combine like-terms]

$\Rightarrow x = 8$ [Divide both sides by 5]

Therefore, the postman sold 8 ten-cent stamps and $60 - 8 = 52$ fifteen-cent stamps

LITERAL EXPRESSIONS:

Question #37: A certain car rental company charges x dollars for the first day and $\dfrac{x}{8}$ dollars for each additional day. How much should be the cost in dollars of renting a car for y days, such that $y > 1$?

Solution: Rental Cost for the First Day $\Rightarrow \$x$

Rental Cost for each additional Day $\Rightarrow \$\dfrac{x}{8}$

Rental Cost for y days $\Rightarrow \$x$ (for the first day) $+ \$\dfrac{x}{8}$ (for $y - 1$ days)

$$\Rightarrow x + \frac{x}{8}(y - 1) = \frac{8x}{8} + \frac{xy}{8} - \frac{x}{8} = \frac{8x + xy - x}{8} = \frac{7x + xy}{8}$$

Question #38: Tina goes out for shopping with t dollars. First, she spends one-third of her money on furnishings. Then, she spends one-fourth of what's left on supplies. Finally, she buys an outfit for herself that costs one-fifth of her remaining money. What fraction of the money she took is left?

Solution: Starting Money $\Rightarrow \$t$

Cost of Furnishings $\Rightarrow \dfrac{1}{3}t$

Remaining Money $\Rightarrow t - \dfrac{1}{3}t = \dfrac{3}{3}t - \dfrac{1}{3}t = \dfrac{2}{3}t$

Cost of Supplies $\Rightarrow \dfrac{1}{4} \times \dfrac{2}{3}t = \dfrac{2}{12}t = \dfrac{1}{6}t$

Remaining Money $\Rightarrow \dfrac{2}{3}t - \dfrac{1}{6}t = \dfrac{4}{6}t - \dfrac{1}{6}t = \dfrac{3}{6}t = \dfrac{1}{2}t$

Cost of Outfit $\Rightarrow \dfrac{1}{5} \times \dfrac{1}{2}t = \dfrac{1}{10}t$

Remaining Money $\Rightarrow \dfrac{1}{2}t - \dfrac{1}{10}t = \dfrac{5}{10t} - \dfrac{1}{10}t = \dfrac{4}{10}t = \dfrac{2}{5}t$

Question #39: A certain club has x dollars to be divided equally among y members. If z new members join in, how many fewer dollars will each member receive than each of the original members would have received?

Solution: Amount of funds to be divided $\Rightarrow \$x$

With the original y members, share of each member $\Rightarrow \dfrac{x}{y}$

With the original y members plus z new member, share of each member $\Rightarrow \dfrac{x}{y+z}$

Difference in share per member $\Rightarrow \dfrac{x}{y} - \dfrac{x}{y+z} = \dfrac{x(y+z)-xy}{y(y+z)} = \dfrac{xy+xz-xy}{y^2+yz} = \dfrac{xz}{y^2+yz}$

Question #40: At the beginning of a trading day, the cost of 2 tons of coal was ¼d dollars. At the end of the trading day, the cost of 1 ton of coal was d dollars. What was the percent increase in the price of coal from the beginning to the end of the trading day?

Solution: Price in the beginning of the trading day for 2 tons of coal $\Rightarrow$ ¼d dollars

Price in the beginning of the trading day for 1 ton of coal $\Rightarrow \dfrac{1}{2}\left(\dfrac{1}{4}d\right) = \dfrac{1}{8}d$ dollars

Price at the end of the trading day for 1 ton of coal $\Rightarrow d$ dollars

Change in price of 1 ton of coal from the beginning to the end of the trading day $\Rightarrow d - \dfrac{1}{8}d = \dfrac{7}{8}d$

Percent Increase in price of 1 ton of coal from the beginning to the end of the trading day:

$$\Rightarrow \dfrac{\frac{7}{8}d}{\frac{1}{8}d} \times 100 = 700\%$$

Question #41: In a certain year, a certain avid reader reads an average of x books per month from January to August and average of y books per month from September to December. What is the average number of books the reader reads each month in that year?

Solution:
Average No. of books read from January through August (8 months) $\Rightarrow x$
Total No. of books read from January through August (8 months) $\Rightarrow 8x$
Average No. of books read from September through December (4 months) $\Rightarrow y$
Total No. of books read from September through December (4 months) $\Rightarrow 4y$
Total No. of Books read from January through December (12 months) $\Rightarrow 8x+4y$

Average No. of books read from January through December (12 months)
$$\Rightarrow \dfrac{8x+4y}{12}$$
$$\Rightarrow \dfrac{4(2x+y)}{12}$$
$$\Rightarrow \dfrac{2x+y}{3}$$

Question #42: Superman and Spiderman are waiting in line to buy a movie ticket to watch Batman. If superman is seventh in the line, and there are k people ahead of Spiderman, where $k > 7$, how many people are between Superman and Spiderman?

Solution: There are 6 people ahead of Superman, and Superman is the 7th one.
There are k people ahead of Spiderman, one of whom is Superman.
In all, there are 7 people who are not behind Superman.
This means, all the remaining people, or $k - 7$ people are behind Superman and in front of Spiderman.
Therefore, there are $k - 7$ people between Superman and Spiderman.

Question #43: At a certain store, a flower vase costs d dollars and c cents. What is the cost, in dollars, of v vases?

Solution: Cost of 1 vase $\Rightarrow d$ dollars $+ c$ cents $= d$ dollars $+ \dfrac{c}{100}$ dollars $= d + \dfrac{c}{100} = \dfrac{100d+c}{100}$ dollars

$$\text{Cost of } v \text{ vases } \Rightarrow v\left(\frac{100d + c}{100}\right) = \frac{100vd + vc}{100} \text{ dollars}$$

Question #44: In a certain private farm, g pounds of grass can feed h horses for one day. If f new horses are added to the farm, then, at the same rate, how many more pounds of grass will be needed to feed all the horses for a week?

Solution:

No. of pounds of grass needed to feed h horses for 1 day $\Rightarrow g$

No. of pounds of grass needed to feed 1 horse for 1 day $\Rightarrow \dfrac{g}{h}$

No. of pounds of grass needed to feed $(h + f)$ horses for 1 day $\Rightarrow \dfrac{g}{h}(h + f) = g + \dfrac{gf}{h}$

Additional No. of pounds of grass needed to feed all horses for 1 day $\Rightarrow g + \dfrac{gf}{h} - g = \dfrac{gf}{h}$

Additional No. of pounds of grass needed to feed all horses for 1 week $\Rightarrow \dfrac{7gf}{h}$

Question #45: If h hammers can be bought for n nickels, how many hammers can be bought for d dimes and q quarters?

Solution:

No. of hammers that can be bought for n nickels $\Rightarrow h$

No. of hammers that can be bought for 1 nickel $\Rightarrow \dfrac{h}{n}$

Since 1 dime = 2 nickels   &   Since 1 quarter = 5 nickels

$\Rightarrow d$ dimes = $2d$ nickels $\Rightarrow q$ quarters = $5q$ nickels

$\Rightarrow d$ dimes and q quarters = $(2d + 5q)$ nickels

No. of hammers that can be bought for $(2d + 5q)$ nickels $\Rightarrow \dfrac{h}{n}(2d + 5q)$

Question #46: At a certain hardware store, each hammer that usually sells for $15 or less is on sale for 75 percent of its usual price, and each hammer that usually sells for more than $15 is on sale for 25 percent of its usual price. If a customer purchases x hammers, each of which usually costs $12, and y hammers, each of which usually costs $24, what is the average (arithmetic mean) amount, in dollars, for each hammer purchased?

Solution:

Cost of one $12 hammer $\Rightarrow$ 75% of $12   Cost of x $12 hammers $\Rightarrow x(75\%$ of $12)

Cost of one $24 hammer $\Rightarrow$ 25% of $24   Cost of y $24 hammers $\Rightarrow y(25\%$ of $24)

Cost per hammer $\Rightarrow \dfrac{12x(75\%) + 24y(25\%)}{x + y} = \dfrac{12x(0.75) + 24y(0.25)}{x + y} = \dfrac{9x + 6y}{x + y}$

Question #47: A certain junk trading company purchases p pounds of scrap material at the rate of c dollars per pound. It then spent e dollars per pound in restoring the material. Eventually, t pounds of the material had to be trashed because it was not sellable. If the trading company sold the remaining at the rate of s dollars per pound, what is the company's direct profit in this whole transaction considering the expenses and wastage?

Solution:

Purchase Details	$\Rightarrow$ Quantity Purchased	= p pounds
	$\Rightarrow$ Cost Price per pound	= c dollars
	$\Rightarrow$ Total Cost of Purchase	= pc dollars
Expenses	$\Rightarrow$ Expenses per pound	= e dollars
	$\Rightarrow$ Total Expenses	= pe dollars
Wastage	$\Rightarrow$ Total Quantity Wasted	= t pounds
Sale Details	$\Rightarrow$ Quantity Sold	= $p - t$ pounds
	$\Rightarrow$ Selling price per pound	= s dollars
	$\Rightarrow$ Total Sale Proceeds	= $s(p - t)$ dollars
Direct Profit	$\Rightarrow$ Total Sale Proceeds – Total Cost of Purchase – Total Expenses	

$\Rightarrow s(p - t) - pc - pe = s(p - t) - p(c + e)$

Question #48: The revenue of a company is R dollars per month. If the company spends F dollars on fixed expenses and then spends 2/7 of the remainder on variable expenses, how much, in dollars, in terms of R and F, is the left over money after paying for fixed and variable expense?

Solution:

Total revenues of the company	$\Rightarrow R$ dollars
Fixed Expenses of the company	$\Rightarrow F$ dollars
Remaining money after paying Fixed Expenses	$\Rightarrow R - F$ dollar

Variable Expenses of the company $\Rightarrow \dfrac{2}{7}(R-F) = \dfrac{2}{7}R - \dfrac{2}{7}F$ dollars

Total Fixed Expenses and Variable Expenses $\Rightarrow F + \dfrac{2}{7}R - \dfrac{2}{7}F = \dfrac{7}{7}F + \dfrac{2}{7}R - \dfrac{2}{7}F = \dfrac{2}{7}R + \dfrac{5}{7}F$

Remaining money after paying Fixed & Variable Expenses $\Rightarrow R - \dfrac{2}{7}R - \dfrac{5}{7}F$

$$\Rightarrow \dfrac{7}{7}R - \dfrac{2}{7}R - \dfrac{5}{7}F = \dfrac{5}{7}R - \dfrac{5}{7}F = \dfrac{5}{7}(R-F)$$

Question #49: In a certain bookstore, the list price of a certain book is p dollars. During a sale, the list price is marked down by q percent. Senior citizens are offered an additional discount of r percent off the sale price. What is the price of the book, in dollars, to a senior citizen customer?

Solution:

List Price of the book	$\Rightarrow \$p$
Sale Discount	$\Rightarrow q\%$

Price after First Discount $\Rightarrow p\left(\dfrac{100-q}{100}\right)$

Senior Citizen Discount $\Rightarrow r\%$

Price after Second Discount $\Rightarrow p\left(\dfrac{100-q}{100}\right)\left(\dfrac{100-r}{100}\right) = p\left(1-\dfrac{q}{100}\right)\left(1-\dfrac{r}{100}\right)$

Question #50: If a vehicle travels $d + \dfrac{2}{5}$ miles at the rate of $r + \dfrac{1}{2}$ miles per hour, then in terms of d and r, what would be the travel time of the vehicle, in minutes?

Solution: Set up the problem, just like any motion problem and solve for the time:

Distance $\Rightarrow d + \dfrac{2}{5}$ miles

Rate $\Rightarrow r + \dfrac{1}{2}$ miles per hour

Time $\Rightarrow \dfrac{D}{R} = \dfrac{d + \dfrac{2}{5}}{r + \dfrac{1}{2}} = \dfrac{\dfrac{5d}{5} + \dfrac{2}{5}}{\dfrac{2r}{2} + \dfrac{1}{2}} = \dfrac{\dfrac{5d+2}{5}}{\dfrac{2r+1}{2}} = \dfrac{5d+2}{5} \div \dfrac{2r+1}{2} = \dfrac{5d+2}{5} \times \dfrac{2}{2r+1} = \dfrac{2(5d+2)}{5(2r+1)}$ hours

$$\Rightarrow \dfrac{2(5d+2)}{5(2r+1)} \times 60 = \dfrac{120(5d+2)}{5(2r+1)} = \dfrac{24(5d+2)}{(2r+1)}$ \text{ minutes}$$

Question #51: In a certain club, which has m member, divided their funds of d dollars evenly among its members. If there were n additional members in the club, how much more funds must the club raise in order for the amount per member to remain the same?

Solution:

With original number of members:

	Amount of funds available	$\Rightarrow \$d$
	No. of members	$\Rightarrow m$
	Share of each member	$\Rightarrow \dfrac{d}{m}$

With n additional number of members: No. of towns eligible for share of funds $\Rightarrow m + n$

	Let, the amount of funds available	$\Rightarrow \$x$
	Share of each member	$\Rightarrow \dfrac{x}{m+n}$

Since the share of each member is to remain the same, equate the share of each member with original number of members and with additional number of members:

$$\Rightarrow \frac{d}{m} = \frac{x}{m+n}$$

$$\Rightarrow mx = d(m + n)$$

$$\Rightarrow x = \frac{d(m+n)}{m} = \frac{dm+dn}{m}$$

Amount of additional funds required in order for the amount per member to remain the same is the difference between the amount of funds available with n additional member and the amount of funds available with original number of members:

$$\Rightarrow x - d \Rightarrow \frac{dm+dn}{m} - d = \frac{dm+dn}{m} - \frac{dm}{m} = \frac{dm+dn-dm}{m} = \frac{dn}{m}$$

Question #52: In a certain state hit by a tornado, the government allocated a special relief fund of d dollars that would be equally divided among t towns that were known to be hit by the tornado. Later on, it was discovered that there were a additional towns that will also be eligible for the fund, which is now to be divided equally among all eligible towns. How much more money, in dollars, would each initial town have received if the additional towns were not discovered to be eligible for the fund?

Solution: Total relief fund available $\Rightarrow d$ dollars

Before additional towns were discovered: No. of towns eligible for fund $\Rightarrow t$

Share of each town in the fund $\Rightarrow \frac{d}{t}$

After additional towns were discovered: No. of towns eligible for fund $\Rightarrow t + a$

Share of each town in the fund $\Rightarrow \frac{d}{t+a}$

Difference in share of a town if additional towns were not discovered:

$$\Rightarrow \frac{d}{t} - \frac{d}{t+a}$$

$$\Rightarrow \frac{(t+a)d - d(t)}{t(t+a)}$$

$$\Rightarrow \frac{ad+td-td}{t(t+a)}$$

$$\Rightarrow \frac{ad}{t(t+a)}$$

Question #53: A self employed landscaper got a contract that pays him x dollars every day He has a direct expense of one-sixth of the money he receives every day for supplies, and he spends one-half of what's left on paying back his business loan. The rest of the remaining money is his income. In terms of x, how many days, will it take the landscaper to earn $100?

Solution: Daily Pay for the contract $\Rightarrow \$x$

Payment for Supplies $\Rightarrow \frac{x}{6}$

Remaining Money $\Rightarrow x - \frac{x}{6} = \frac{5x}{6}$

Payment for Loan $\Rightarrow \frac{1}{2} \bullet \frac{5x}{6} = \frac{5x}{12}$

Remaining Money $\Rightarrow \frac{5x}{6} - \frac{5x}{12} = \frac{5x}{12}$

No. of Days required to earn $\$\frac{5x}{12}$ $\Rightarrow 1$

No. of Days required to earn $1 $\Rightarrow \frac{12}{5x}$

No. of Days required to earn $100 $\Rightarrow \dfrac{12}{5x} \bullet 100 = \dfrac{240}{x}$

AGE & WEIGHT PROBLEMS:

Question #54: If today is John's 15th birthday and his father's 52nd birthday, how many years from today will John's father be twice as old as John at that time?

Solution: Organize all the given information in the following grid:

Year	John's Age	Father's Age
Today	15	52
x year later	15 + x	52 + x

EZ Problem Set-Up $\Rightarrow$ Father's age after x years = 2(John's Age after x years)

$\Rightarrow 52 + x = 2(15 + x)$ [Set up the equation]

$\Rightarrow 52 + x = 30 + 2x$ [Apply distributive property]

$\Rightarrow 52 = 30 + x$ [Subtract x from both sides]

$\Rightarrow x = 22$ [Subtract 30 from both sides]

Therefore, 22 years after today, John's father will be twice as old as John at that time.

Question #55: If Monika is 10 years younger than Susan and Susan is 2 years older than Nancy, who is 10 years over one-half of a century old, then how old is Tiffany, who is 5 years shy of one-half Monika's age?

Solution:
Let, Susan's Age $\Rightarrow S$

And, Monika's Age $\Rightarrow M$

And, Nancy's Age $\Rightarrow N$

And, Tiffany's Age $\Rightarrow T$

Monika is 10 years younger than Susan	$\Rightarrow M = S - 10$	$\Rightarrow$ Equation #1
Susan is 2 years older than Nancy	$\Rightarrow S = N + 2$	$\Rightarrow$ Equation #2
Nancy is 10 years over one-half of a century	$\Rightarrow N = 10 + 50 = 60$	$\Rightarrow$ Equation #3
Tiffany is 5 years shy of one-half Monika's age	$\Rightarrow T = \frac{1}{2}M - 5$	$\Rightarrow$ Equation #4

Substitute the value of N into #2 $\Rightarrow S = N + 2$ [Rewrite Equation #2]

$\Rightarrow S = 60 + 2$ [Substitute N = 60]

$\Rightarrow S = 62$ [Do the addition]

Substitute the value of S into #1 $\Rightarrow M = S - 10$ [Rewrite Equation #1]

$\Rightarrow M = 62 - 10$ [Substitute S = 62]

$\Rightarrow M = 52$ [Do the subtraction]

Substitute the value of M into #4 $\Rightarrow T = \frac{1}{2}M - 5$ [Rewrite Equation #4]

$\Rightarrow T = \frac{1}{2}(52) - 5$ [Substitute M = 52]

$\Rightarrow T = 26 - 5$ [Apply distributive property]

$\Rightarrow T = 21$ [Do the subtraction]

Therefore: Susan's Age $\Rightarrow S = 62$ years

Monika's Age $\Rightarrow M = 52$ years

Nancy's Age $\Rightarrow N = 60$ years

Tiffany's Age $\Rightarrow T = 21$ years

Question #56: If Johnny is 10 years younger than Ricky, and Ricky is 6 years older than Bobby, who is 5 years less than one quarter of a century old, how old is Tommy, who is 2 years shy of one-half Johnny's age?

Solution:
Let, Johnny's Age $\Rightarrow J$

And, Ricky's Age $\Rightarrow R$

And, Bobby's Age $\Rightarrow B$

And, Tommy's Age $\Rightarrow T$

Johnny is 10 years younger than Ricky $\Rightarrow J = R - 10$ $\Rightarrow$ Equation #1

Ricky is 6 years older than Bobby $\Rightarrow R = B + 6$ $\Rightarrow$ Equation #2

Bobby is 5 years less than ¼ of a century $\Rightarrow B = \frac{1}{4}(100) - 5$

$\Rightarrow B = 25 - 5$ [Apply distributive property]

$\Rightarrow B = 20$ [Do the subtraction]

Tommy is 2 years shy of ½ Johnny's age $\Rightarrow T = 1/2J - 2$ $\Rightarrow$ Equation #3

Substitute the value of B into Equation #2 $\Rightarrow R = B + 6$ [Rewrite Equation #2]

	$\Rightarrow R = 20 + 6$	[Substitute $B = 20$]
	$\Rightarrow R = 26$	[Do the addition]
Substitute the value of R into Equation #1	$\Rightarrow J = R - 10$	[Rewrite Equation #1]
	$\Rightarrow J = 26 - 10$	[Substitute $R = 26$]
	$\Rightarrow J = 16$	[Do the subtraction]
Substitute the value of J into Equation #3	$\Rightarrow T = \frac{1}{2}J - 2$	[Rewrite Equation #3]
	$\Rightarrow T = \frac{1}{2}(16) - 2$	[Substitute $J = 16$]
	$\Rightarrow T = 8 - 2$	[Do the multiplication]
	$\Rightarrow T = 6$	[Do the subtraction]

Therefore: Johnny's Age $\Rightarrow J = 16$ years
     Ricky's Age $\Rightarrow R = 26$ years
     Bobby's Age $\Rightarrow B = 20$ years
     Tommy's Age $\Rightarrow T = 6$ years

Question #57: John is now five times as old as Tom was 5 years ago. If the sum of John's and Tom's ages is 35, in how many years will John be twice as old as Tom?

Solution: Let, John's current age $\Rightarrow J$
And, Tom's current age $\Rightarrow T$

John's current age is 5 times Tom's age 5 years ago	$\Rightarrow J = 5(T - 5)$	$\Rightarrow$ Equation #1
Sum of John's & Tom's age is 35	$\Rightarrow J + T = 35$	$\Rightarrow$ Equation #2
Substitute the value of J from Equation #1 into #2	$\Rightarrow 5(T - 5) + T = 35$	[Substitute $J = 5(T - 5)$]
	$\Rightarrow 5T - 25 + T = 35$	[Apply distributive property]
	$\Rightarrow 6T - 25 = 35$	[Combine like-terms]
	$\Rightarrow 6T = 60$	[Add 25 to both sides]
	$\Rightarrow T = 60 \div 6 = 10$	[Divide both sides by 6]
Substitute the value of T in Equation #2	$\Rightarrow J + T = 35$	[Rewrite Equation #2]
	$\Rightarrow J + 10 = 35$	[Substitute $T = 10$]
	$\Rightarrow J = 25$	[Subtract 10 from both sides]

John is currently 25 and Tom is currently 10
Let n be the number of years from now when John will be twice as old as Tom.

EZ Problem Set-Up	$\Rightarrow$ After n years, John will be twice as old as Tom	
	$\Rightarrow 25 + n = 2(10 + n)$	[Set up the equation]
	$\Rightarrow 25 + n = 20 + 2n$	[Apply distributive property]
	$\Rightarrow 25 = 20 + n$	[Subtract n from both sides]
	$\Rightarrow n = 5$	[Subtract 20 from both sides]

Therefore, John will be twice as old as Tom in 5 years.

Question #58: 8 years ago, Jack was half as old as Mack. Mack is now 20 years older than Jack is. How old will Jack be 8 year from now?

Solution: Organize all the given information in the following grid:
Let, Jack's Age $\Rightarrow J$
And, Mack's Age $\Rightarrow M$

Year	Jack's Age	Mack's Age
8 years ago	$J - 8$	$M - 8$
Now	J	M
8 year later	$J + 8$	$M + 8$

8 years ago, Jack was half as old as Mack	$\Rightarrow J - 8 = \frac{1}{2}(M - 8)$	
	$\Rightarrow 2(J - 8) = M - 8$	[Multiply both sides by 2]
	$\Rightarrow 2J - 16 = M - 8$	[Apply distribute property]
		$\Rightarrow$ Equation #1
Mack is now 20 years older than Jack	$\Rightarrow M = J + 20$	$\Rightarrow$ Equation #2
Substitute the value of M from Equation #2 into #1	$\Rightarrow 2J - 16 = (J + 20) - 8$	
	$\Rightarrow 2J - 16 = J + 12$	[Apply distributive property]
	$\Rightarrow J - 16 = 12$	[Subtract J from both sides]
	$\Rightarrow J = 28$	[Add 16 to both sides]

Therefore, Jack is now 28 years old and will be 36 in 8 years.

WORK PROBLEMS:

Question #59: Romeo gets on the elevator at the 51st floor of a building and rides up at a rate of 57 floors per minute. At the same time, Juliet gets on an elevator on the 91st floor of the same building and rides down at a rate of 63 floors per minute. If they continue traveling at these rates, at which floor will their paths cross?

Solution: Both people are traveling at about one floor per second and there are 91 − 51 or exactly 40 floors between them. So it would take one person about 40 seconds to cover this distance, and it would take two people about ½ of 40, which is 20 seconds when they are traveling towards each other. So each person will travel for about 20 seconds.

20 seconds is one-third of a minute   ⇒ Romeo travels 57 floors a minute
                                         ⇒ In 20 seconds Romeo travels 57 × 1/3 = 57/3 = 19 floors.
                                         ⇒ Juliet travels 63 floors a minute
                                         ⇒ In 20 seconds Juliet travels 63 × 1/3 = 63/3 = 21 floors

This makes 19 + 21, or exactly 40 floors that the two would travel
Romeo moves up 19 stories and Juliet descends 21 stories.
Therefore, they cross each other at 51 + 19 = 91 − 21 = 70th floor

Alternative Method: You could also have solved this question by adding the two rates. Romeo travels at 57 floors per minute and Juliet at 63 floors per minute. So, they are reducing the number of floors between them at a rate of 57 + 63 or 120 floors per minute, which is 2 floors per second. Since they start out 40 floors apart, it'll take them 40/2 or 20 seconds to cross each other. After 20 seconds, which is 1/3 of a minute, Romeo will have moved 57 × 1/3 or 19 floors and he will be on the 70th floor, and Juliet will have moved 63 × 1/3 or 21 floors and she will also be on the 70th floor.

Question #60: Victor reads at an average rate of 60 pages per hour, while Susan reads at an average of 80 pages per hour. If Victor starts reading a book at 5:30, and Susan begins reading an identical copy of the same book at 6:20, at what time will they be reading the same page?

Solution: Susan reads at the rate of 80 pages per hour and Victor reads at the rate of 60 pages per hour.
Victor starts reading 50 minutes ahead of Susan. Since 50 minutes is 5/6 of an hour, by the time Susan starts reading at 6:20, Victor has already read 5/6 × 60 = 50 pages.
The number of pages Susan has read at any given time after 5:30 is $80t$, where t is the time in hours from 6:20.
The number of pages that Victor has read at any time after 6:20 is $50 + 60t$.

EZ Problem Set-Up ⇒ Time when both, Victor and Susan will be reading the same page
                   ⇒ $80t = 50 + 60t$ [Set up the equation]
                   ⇒ $80t − 60t = 50$ [Subtract 60t from both sides]
                   ⇒ $20t = 50$ [Combine like-terms]
                   ⇒ $t = 2½$ [Divide both sides by 20]

So it takes 2½ hours for Susan to catch Victor
Since Susan started at 6:20, this means she will catch Victor at precisely 8:50

Alternative Method: You could have saved yourself some time by observing that Susan gains 20 pages an hour on Victor, as Susan reads 20 pages an hour faster. Since Victor has a head start of 50

pages at 6:20, it should take Susan ⇒ $\dfrac{50\,pages}{20\,(pages/hour)}$ = 2.5 hours for her to catch Victor.

Question #61: While typing a project report, John takes his first break after typing one-fourth of the total number of pages. He takes his second break after he types one-half of the remaining number of pages after taking the first break. He then types the remaining 90 pages to finish typing his project. What is the total number of pages in John's project report?

Solution: Let, the total No. of pages in the project report   ⇒ x

No. of pages typed before taking the first break   ⇒ $\dfrac{1}{4}x$

No. of remaining pages after taking the first break   ⇒ $x - \dfrac{1}{4}x = \dfrac{3}{4}x$

No. of pages typed between the first and second break $\Rightarrow \dfrac{1}{2}\left(\dfrac{3}{4}x\right)=\dfrac{3}{8}x$

No. of pages typed after the second break to the completion of job $\Rightarrow$ 90 pages

EZ Problem Set-Up $\Rightarrow$ No. of pages typed before taking the first break + No. of pages typed between the first and second break + No. of pages typed after the second break to the completion of the job = Total No. of pages in the project report.

$$\Rightarrow \frac{1}{4}x + \frac{3}{8}x + 90 = x \qquad\qquad \text{[Set up the equation]}$$

$$\Rightarrow \frac{1}{4}x + \frac{3}{8}x = x - 90 \qquad\qquad \text{[Subtract 90 from both sides]}$$

$$\Rightarrow \frac{1}{4}x + \frac{3}{8}x - x = -90 \qquad\qquad \text{[Subtract } x \text{ from both sides]}$$

$$\Rightarrow \frac{2}{8}x + \frac{3}{8}x - \frac{8}{8}x = -90 \qquad\qquad \text{[Scale-Up all the fractions to their LCD]}$$

$$\Rightarrow -\frac{3}{8}x = -90 \qquad\qquad \text{[Combine like-terms]}$$

$$\Rightarrow \frac{3}{8}x = 90 \qquad\qquad \text{[Multiply both sides by } -1\text{]}$$

$$\Rightarrow x = 90 \times \frac{8}{3} = 240 \qquad\qquad \text{[Multiply both sides by 8/3]}$$

Question #62: Working independently, Anita can execute a certain job in 8 hours and Usher can execute it in 10 hours. After Anita and Usher work together at the same job for 2 hours, Anita quits the job. If Usher completes the remaining job, working alone, how many hours will it take Usher to complete the job?

Solution: Since Anita can execute the whole job in 8 hours, amount of job that Anita can do in 1 hour $\Rightarrow \dfrac{1}{8}$

Since Usher can execute the whole job in 10 hours, amount of job that Usher can do in 1 hour $\Rightarrow \dfrac{1}{10}$

Amount of job that Anita and Usher can do in 1 hour $\Rightarrow \dfrac{1}{8} + \dfrac{1}{10} = \dfrac{10}{80} + \dfrac{8}{80} = \dfrac{18}{80} = \dfrac{9}{40}$

Amount of job that Anita and Usher can do in 2 hours $\Rightarrow 2 \times \dfrac{9}{40} = \dfrac{9}{20}$

Amount of job remaining after Anita quits the job $\Rightarrow 1 - \dfrac{9}{20} = \dfrac{20}{20} - \dfrac{9}{20} = \dfrac{11}{20}$

Amount of time in which Usher can complete the whole job $\Rightarrow$ 10 hours

Amount of time in which Usher can complete 11/20 of the job $\Rightarrow 10 \times \dfrac{11}{20} = \dfrac{110}{20} = \dfrac{11}{2} = 5\dfrac{1}{2}$ hours

Question #63: Machine X and Machine Y, both produces widgets. It takes Machine X 20 hours longer to produce 1,080 widgets, than it takes Machine Y. Machine Y produces 20 percent more widgets per hour than Machine X. How many widgets per hour does Machine X produce?

Solution: Let the amount of time taken by Machine Y to produce 1080 widgets be $\Rightarrow x$ hours

Then, the number of widgets produced by Machine Y in 1 hour $\Rightarrow \dfrac{1080}{x}$

Now, the amount of time taken by Machine X to produce 1080 widgets $\Rightarrow x + 20$ hours

Then, the number of widgets produced by Machine X in 1 hour $\Rightarrow \dfrac{1080}{x + 20}$

EZ Problem Set-Up $\Rightarrow$ Machine Y produces 20 percent more widgets per hour than Machine X:

$$\Rightarrow \frac{1080}{x} = 120\%\left(\frac{1080}{x + 20}\right) \qquad\qquad \text{[Set up the equation]}$$

$$\Rightarrow \frac{1080}{x} = \frac{120}{100}\left(\frac{1080}{x+20}\right) \qquad \text{[Convert the percent into a fraction]}$$

$$\Rightarrow \frac{1080}{x} = \frac{6}{5}\left(\frac{1080}{x+20}\right) \qquad \text{[Reduce the fraction to its lowest terms]}$$

$$\Rightarrow \left(\frac{5}{6}\right)\frac{1080}{x} = \frac{6}{5}\left(\frac{1080}{x+20}\right)\left(\frac{5}{6}\right) \qquad \text{[Multiply both sides by 5/6]}$$

$$\Rightarrow \frac{5400}{6x} = \frac{1080}{x+20} \qquad \text{[Apply distributive property]}$$

$$\Rightarrow 5400(x+20) = 1080(6x) \qquad \text{[Cross-multiply]}$$

$$\Rightarrow 5400x + 108000 = 6480x \qquad \text{[Apply distributive property]}$$

$$\Rightarrow 1080x = 108000 \qquad \text{[Subtract 5400x from both sides]}$$

$$\Rightarrow x = 108000 \div 1080 = 100 \qquad \text{[Divide both sides by 1080]}$$

Therefore, the amount of time it takes Machine X to produce 1,080 widgets $\Rightarrow 100 + 20 = 120$ hours

And, the number of widgets produced by Machine X in 1 hour $= \dfrac{1080}{x+20} = \dfrac{1080}{100+20} = \dfrac{1080}{120} = 9$ widgets

Question #64: Oil flows into an empty 98-gallon tank at spout X and out of the tank at spout Y. If the rate of flow through spout X is 7 gallons per hour, how many gallons per hour must flow out through spout Y so that the tank is full in exactly 126 hours?

Solution: Rate of Retention: Rate of Inflow through X $\Rightarrow$ 7 gallons per hour
Let the Rate of Outflow through $Y \Rightarrow g$ gallons per hour
Rate of Retention $\Rightarrow$ Inflow (X) – Outflow (Y)
$\Rightarrow (7 - g)$ gallons per hour

Rate of Filling the Tank: Capacity or Volume of Tank $\Rightarrow$ 98 gallons
Time to Completely Fill the Tank $\Rightarrow$ 126 hours
Rate of Filling the Tank $\Rightarrow \dfrac{98\,gallons}{126\,hours} = \dfrac{7}{9}$ gallons per hour

EZ Problem Set-Up $\Rightarrow$ Rate of Retention = Rate of Filling the Tank

$$\Rightarrow 7 - g = \frac{7}{9} \qquad \text{[Set up the equation]}$$

$$\Rightarrow -g = \frac{7}{9} - 7 \qquad \text{[Subtract 7 from both sides]}$$

$$\Rightarrow g = 7 - \frac{7}{9} \qquad \text{[Multiply both sides –1]}$$

$$\Rightarrow g = \frac{63}{9} - \frac{7}{9} = \frac{56}{9} = 6\frac{2}{9} \qquad \text{[Do the subtraction]}$$

Therefore, $6\dfrac{2}{9}$ gallons per hr must flow out through spout Y so that the tank is full in exactly 126 hrs.

Question #65: For a small home improvement job, Jose and Frank were each paid m dollars from the contractor to complete the job. Jose worked 12 hours on the job and Frank worked five-sixth the number of hours that Jose worked on the job. After completing the job, Frank gave Jose n dollars from his payment for his services so that they both earn equal hourly wages for the job. What is the dollar amount, in terms of n, that Jose and Frank received for their services from the contractor?

Solution:

	Jose	Frank
Gross Wages	$\Rightarrow \$m$	$\Rightarrow \$m$
Hours Worked	$\Rightarrow$ 12 hours	$\Rightarrow 12 \times \dfrac{5}{6} = 10$ hours
Net Wages after Frank gave $\$n$ to Jose	$\Rightarrow m + n$	$\Rightarrow m - n$
Net Hourly Wages	$\Rightarrow \dfrac{m+n}{12}$	$\Rightarrow \dfrac{m-n}{10}$

After everything is said and done, the net hourly wages are equal for Jose and Frank:

EZ Problem Set-Up $\Rightarrow$ Jose's Net Hourly Wages = Franks' Hourly Wages

$\Rightarrow \dfrac{m+n}{12} = \dfrac{m-n}{10}$ [Set up the equation]

$\Rightarrow 10(m+n) = 12(m-n)$ [Cross multiply]

$\Rightarrow 10m + 10n = 12m - 12n$ [Apply distributive property]

$\Rightarrow 10m + 22n = 12m$ [Add $12n$ to both sides]

$\Rightarrow 22n = 2m$ [Subtract $10m$ from both sides]

$\Rightarrow m = 11n$ [Divide both sides by 2]

Jose's Wages for his services $\Rightarrow \$m = \$11n$

Frank's Wages for his services $\Rightarrow \$m = \$11n$

Combined Wages of Jose and Frank $\Rightarrow \$11n + \$11n = \$22n$

MOTION PROBLEMS:

Question #66: A river cruiser leaves point A and travels upstream to point B at an average speed of 8 miles per hour. It returns downstream by the same route at an average speed of 12 miles per hour. What is the average speed for the round trip, in miles per hour?

Solution: Organize all the given information in the following grid:

Upstream Trip   **Downstream Trip**

$R_1 \Rightarrow 8$ mph $R_2 \Rightarrow 12$ mph

$D_1 \Rightarrow d$ (assumption) $D_2 \Rightarrow d$ (same as upstream trip)

$T_1 \Rightarrow \dfrac{d}{8}$ $T_2 \Rightarrow \dfrac{d}{12}$

Total Trip

Total Distance $\Rightarrow d + d = 2d$ m   [Add the total distance]

Total Time $\Rightarrow \dfrac{d}{8} + \dfrac{d}{12} = \dfrac{3d}{24} + \dfrac{2d}{24} = \dfrac{5d}{24}$ hours   [Add the total time]

Average Rate $\Rightarrow \dfrac{2d}{\frac{5}{24}d} = 2 \div \dfrac{5}{24} = 2 \times \dfrac{24}{5} = 9.6$ mph   [Find the total average rate]

Question #67: Amber rides a bicycle from her home to her school at rate of 5 miles per hour, and rides back along the same route from her school to her home at the rate of 2 miles per hour. If she spends exactly one hour traveling both ways, what is the distance from her home to her school?

Solution: Organize all the given information in the following grid:

Home to School   **School to Home**

$D_1 \Rightarrow d$ (assumption) $D_2 \Rightarrow d$ (same as home to school)

$R_1 \Rightarrow 5$ mph $R_2 \Rightarrow 2$ mph

$T_1 \Rightarrow \dfrac{d}{5}$ $T_2 \Rightarrow \dfrac{d}{2}$

EZ Problem Set-Up $\Rightarrow$ Total Time = $T_1 + T_2$ = 1 hour

$\Rightarrow \dfrac{d}{5} + \dfrac{d}{2} = 1$ [Set up the equation]

$\Rightarrow \dfrac{2d}{10} + \dfrac{5d}{10} = 1$ [Scale up the fractions to their LCD, which is 10]

$\Rightarrow \dfrac{7d}{10} = 1$ [Add the fractions with common denominator]

$\Rightarrow d = \dfrac{10}{7} = 1\dfrac{3}{7}$ miles   [Multiply both sides by 10/7]

Question #68: A man runs from his home to his work at an average speed of 4 miles per hour, and then walks back home along the same route at an average of 2 miles per hour. If his whole journey took one hour, how many miles is his home from his work?

Solution: Organize all the given information in the following grid:

Going Trip (Home to Work)
$R_1 \Rightarrow 4$ mph
$D_1 \Rightarrow n$
$T_1 \Rightarrow n \div 4$ hrs

Return Trip (Work to Home)
$R_2 \Rightarrow 2$ mph
$D_2 \Rightarrow n$
$T_2 \Rightarrow n \div 2$ hrs

EZ Problem Set-Up $\Rightarrow$ Time of Outbound Trip (T_1) + Time of Inbound Trip (T_2) = 1 hr

$$\Rightarrow \frac{n}{4} + \frac{n}{2} = 1 \qquad \text{[Set up the equation]}$$

$$\Rightarrow \frac{n}{4} + \frac{2n}{4} = 1 \qquad \text{[Scale up the fractions to their LCD, which is 4]}$$

$$\Rightarrow \frac{3n}{4} = 1 \qquad \text{[Add the fractions with common denominator]}$$

$$\Rightarrow n = \frac{4}{3} = 1\frac{1}{3} \text{ miles} \qquad \text{[Multiply both sides by 4/3]}$$

Question #69: On a 80-mile trip, the driver drives the first one-fifth of the trip at the rate of $2r$ miles per hour and the remaining of the trip at half that rate. What is the average rate for the entire trip?

Solution: Organize all the given information in the following grid:

First Part of Trip
$R_1 \Rightarrow 2r$ mph

$D_1 \Rightarrow \dfrac{1}{5} \times 80 = 16$ m

$T_1 \Rightarrow \dfrac{16}{2r} = \dfrac{8}{r}$

Second Part of Trip
$R_2 \Rightarrow r$ mph

$D_2 \Rightarrow 80 - 16 = 64$ m

$T_2 \Rightarrow \dfrac{64}{r}$

Total Trip

Total Distance $\Rightarrow 80$ miles   [Add the total distance]

Total Time $\Rightarrow \dfrac{8}{r} + \dfrac{64}{r} = \dfrac{72}{r}$ [Add the total time]

Average Rate $\Rightarrow 80 \div \dfrac{72}{r} = 80 \times \dfrac{r}{72} = \dfrac{10}{9}r$ [Find the total average rate]

Question #70: For a certain trip, a car averages 50 miles per hour for the first 6 hours of the trip, and averages 90 miles per hour for each additional hour of the same trip. If the average speed for the entire trip is 75 miles per hour, how many hours long is the entire trip?

Solution: Organize all the given information in the following grid:

First Part pf Trip
$R_1 \Rightarrow 50$ mph
$T_1 \Rightarrow 6$ hours
$D_1 \Rightarrow 50 \times 6 = 300$ miles

Second Part of Trip
$R_2 \Rightarrow 90$ mph
$T_2 \Rightarrow t$ hours
$D_2 \Rightarrow 90t$ hours

Total Trip

Average Rate $\Rightarrow 75$ mph   [Given]

Total Distance $\rightarrow 300 + 90t$ [Add the total distance]

Total Time $\Rightarrow \dfrac{300 + 90t}{75}$ [Find the total time]

EZ Problem Set-Up $\Rightarrow$ Time of First Part + Time of Second Part = Total Time of the Entire trip

$$\Rightarrow t + 6 = \frac{300 + 90t}{75} \qquad \text{[Set up the equation]}$$

$$\Rightarrow 75(t + 6) = 300 + 90t \qquad \text{[Multiply both sides by 75]}$$
$$\Rightarrow 75t + 450 = 300 + 90t \qquad \text{[Apply distributive property]}$$
$$\Rightarrow 15t + 300 = 450 \qquad \text{[Subtract 75t from both sides]}$$
$$\Rightarrow 15t = 150 \qquad \text{[Subtract 300 from both sides]}$$
$$\Rightarrow t = 10 \text{ hours} \qquad \text{[Divide both sides by 15]}$$

Total time of the entire trip = 6 + 10 = 16 hours

Question #71: Car A and Car B are both traveling in the same direction along the same route and Car A is 50 miles behind Car B. Car A is traveling at a constant rate of 60 miles per hour and Car B is traveling at a constant rate of 52 miles per hour. How many hours will it take for Car A to overtake Car B and drive 16 miles ahead of Car B?

Solution: Let's try to solve this problem by mathematical reasoning:

Facts   ⇒ Since Car A is 50 miles behind Car B, Car A has to travel an additional 50 miles to catch up with Car B

          ⇒ Since Car A has to drive 16 miles ahead of Car B, Car A is required to travel an additional 16 miles ahead of Car B

Hence   ⇒ Car A has to travel an extra 50 + 16 = 66 miles in comparison to Car B

Facts   ⇒ Rate of Speed of Car A = 60 mph
          ⇒ Rate of Speed of Car B = 52 mph

Hence   ⇒ Rate of Speed of Car A is 60 − 52 = 8 mph faster than the Rate of Speed of Car B

Car A has to travel 66 miles at 8 mph ⇒ Time = $\dfrac{distance}{rate} = \dfrac{66}{8}$ = 8.25 hrs

Therefore, it will take Car A 8.25 hours to overtake and drive 16 miles ahead of Car B.

MIXTURE PROBLEMS:

Question #72: A certain jar contains one-sixth pound of strawberries. The jar is then filled with a mixture that has equal weights of strawberries, raspberries, blueberries, blackberries, and cranberries. If the total weight is 1 pound, what fraction of the mixture are NOT strawberries?

Solution: Total Weight of Mixture   ⇒ 1 pound

Original Amount of Strawberries   ⇒ $\dfrac{1}{6}$ pound

Remaining Mixture   ⇒ $1 - \dfrac{1}{6} = \dfrac{5}{6}$

Equal weight of strawberries, raspberries, blueberries, blackberries, and cranberries are added, this means, each one weighs $\dfrac{5}{6} \div 5 = \dfrac{5}{6} \times \dfrac{1}{5} = \dfrac{1}{6}$

Fraction of mixture, which are strawberries   ⇒ $\dfrac{1}{6} + \dfrac{1}{6} = \dfrac{2}{6} = \dfrac{1}{3}$

Fraction of mixture, which are NOT strawberries   ⇒ $1 - \dfrac{1}{3} = \dfrac{2}{3}$

Question #73: Solution X contains 10 percent sodium chloride and Solution Y contains 15 percent sodium chloride. Another solution, Z, is created by mixing Solution X and Solution Y. If Solution Z, which is 600 gallons, contains exactly 82 gallons of sodium chloride, how many gallons of Solution X are in Solution Z?

Solution: Total volume of solution Z = 600 gallons

Let, the No. of gallons of Solution X in the mixture Solution Z   ⇒ n

Then, the No. of gallons of Solution Y in the mixture Solution Z   ⇒ 600 − n

EZ Problem set-Up   ⇒ Amount of sodium chloride from solution X + Amount of sodium chloride from solution Y = Amount of sodium chloride in mixture Z = 82

                  ⇒ 10% of n + 15% of (600 − n) = 82

                  ⇒ 0.10n + 0.15(600 − n) = 82   [Convert the percents into decimals]

                  ⇒ 0.10n + 90 − 0.15n = 82   [Apply distributive property]

                  ⇒ −0.05n + 90 = 82   [Combine like-terms]

                  ⇒ −0.05n = −8   [Subtract 90 from both sides]

                  ⇒ 0.05n = 8   [Multiply both sides by −1]

                  ⇒ n = 8 ÷ 0.05 = 160   [Divide both sides by 0.05]

Therefore, there are 160 gallons of Solution X in the mixture Solution Z.

Question #74: Solution X is 10 percent alcohol and solution Y is 25 percent alcohol. If 50 ounces of solution X are mixed with 70 ounces of solution Y to form Solution Z, what percent of Solution Z will be alcohol?

Solution:

Solution X	$\Rightarrow$ Volume of Solution	$\Rightarrow$ 50 oz	[Given]
	$\Rightarrow$ Percent of Alcohol	$\Rightarrow$ 10%	[Given]
	$\Rightarrow$ Alcohol content	$\Rightarrow$ 10% of 50	[Given]
		$\Rightarrow$ 0.10 × 50	[Convert the percent to decimal]
		$\Rightarrow$ 5 oz	[Simplify the expression]
Solution Y	$\Rightarrow$ Volume of Solution	$\Rightarrow$ 70 oz	[Given]
	$\Rightarrow$ Percent of Alcohol	$\Rightarrow$ 25%	[Given]
	$\Rightarrow$ Alcohol Content	$\Rightarrow$ 25% of 70	[Given]
		$\Rightarrow$ 0.25 × 70	[Convert the percent to decimal]
		$\Rightarrow$ 17.5 oz	[Simplify the expression]
Solution Z	$\Rightarrow$ Volume of Solution	$\Rightarrow X + Y$	[Add the volume of solution X and Y]
		$\Rightarrow$ 50 + 70	[Substitute the values]
		$\Rightarrow$ 120 oz	[Simplify the expression]
	$\Rightarrow$ Alcohol Content	$\Rightarrow X + Y$	[Add the alcohol content of solution X and Y]
		$\Rightarrow$ 5 + 17.5	[Substitute the values]
		$\Rightarrow$ 22.50 oz	[Simplify the expression]

Percent Alcohol in Solution Z $\Rightarrow \dfrac{22.50}{120} \times 100$ [Calculate the percent]

$\Rightarrow$ 18.75%   [Simplify the expression]

Question #75:   A certain artist develops two new shades for his next painting. He names the first shade as "sunrise," and makes it by mixing 7 parts red and 5 parts orange. He names the second shade as "sunset," and makes it by mixing 5 parts red and 7 parts orange. How many ounces of orange paint must be added to 24 ounces of sunrise shade to convert it to sunset shade?

Solution:

Sunrise Shade	$\Rightarrow$ Composition	$\Rightarrow$ 7 parts red + 5 parts orange
	$\Rightarrow$ Total Parts	$\Rightarrow$ 7 + 5 = 12 parts
	$\Rightarrow$ Fraction of Orange	$\Rightarrow \dfrac{5}{12}$
Sunset Shade	$\Rightarrow$ Composition	$\Rightarrow$ 5 parts red + 7 parts orange
	$\Rightarrow$ Total Parts	$\Rightarrow$ 5 + 7 = 12 parts
	$\Rightarrow$ Fraction of Orange	$\Rightarrow \dfrac{7}{12}$

Total Amount of Sunrise Shade $\Rightarrow$ 24 ounces

$\Rightarrow$ Amount of Red in the mixture $\Rightarrow \dfrac{7}{12} \times 24 = 14$ ounces

$\Rightarrow$ Amount of Orange in the mixture $\Rightarrow \dfrac{5}{12} \times 24 = 10$ ounces

Set up a proportion to find amount of orange that the mixture must contain in order to convert it from Sunrise shade to Sunset shade.

Set up the proportion $\Rightarrow \dfrac{5\,red}{7\,orange} = \dfrac{14\,red}{x\,orange}$

$\Rightarrow 5x = 98$ [Cross multiply]

$\Rightarrow x = 19.6$ ounces   [Divide both sides by 5]

Therefore, the mixture must contain 19.6 ounces of orange in order to convert it from Sunrise shade to Sunset shade. The given Sunrise shade already contains 10 ounces of orange, so 19.6 − 10 = 9.6 ounces of orange must be added to convert it from Sunrise shade to Sunset shade.

THIS PAGE HAS BEEN INTENTIONALLY LEFT BLANK

PART 6.0: LOGIC & STATS:

TOPICS COVERED:

- Pure Logic

- Permutation Combination

- Probability

- Sets

- Sequence & Patterns

- Miscellaneous Problems

- Stats – Averages

PRACTICE EXERCISE:

PURE LOGIC:

Question #1:   A certain security code has 5 digits. All the digits in the code must appear in descending numerical order and no digit can be used more than once. One example of such a code is 97510. What is the difference between the largest and smallest possible codes?

Question #2:   A certain rectangular tomb can only hold 8-ounce blocks of gold and 5-ounce blocks of silver. If there are a total of 90 ounces of gold and silver, what is the greatest amount of gold that the tomb can contain?

Question #3:   In a certain private university, there are three schools and each school has 10 advisors. Exactly 5 advisors are in all three schools and each pair of school has 6 advisors in common. How many distinct advisors are there in the entire university?

Question #4:   John weighs twice as much as Mack. Mack's weight is 75% of Tom's weight. Nick weighs 50% of George's weight. George weighs 190% of John's weight. Which of these 5 persons weigh the least?

Question #5:   A certain box contains 20 slips of paper, each with an integer from 1 to 20, inclusive written on it. If one slip at a time is randomly drawn from the box without replacing the slips already drawn, how many slips must be drawn in order to ensure that sum of the numbers on the all slips drawn is even? (Assume that more than one slip needs to be drawn.)

Question #6:   A 100-inch rope needs to be cut into five pieces. Each piece must have an integer length in inches, and no two pieces can have the same length. If the largest piece of rope is 50 inches and the smallest piece is 10 inches, what is the maximum length of the third largest piece of rope?

PERMUTATION & COMBINATION:

Question #7:   A five-digit pin must satisfy the following condition: the first digit is an even number, the second digit is an odd number, the third digit is an even prime number, the fourth digit is an odd prime number, and the fifth digit is a random number that is not used anywhere in the number. How many such pins can be generated?

Question #8:   How many five-digit numbers are there, if the first two digits are even, the rest of the digits are odd, and the digit 8 cannot appear more than once in any number?

Question #9:   A nine-digit (from 1 to 9) employee id must satisfy the following condition: the first two digits are fixed as 79 in that order, the third digit is bigger than 7, the fourth digit is smaller than 5, the fifth digit is divisible by 3, the sixth digit is a multiple of 2, the seventh digit is twice the eighth digit, and the ninth digit is a prime number. How many different employee ids' can be generated?

Question #10:   A certain company used a 9-digit id to identify each customer, and now wants to add a two-digit prefix to every id. The two digits are composed of 115 different special symbols. If the company used 110 of the symbols completely and five remains unused, how many additional prefixes can be generated if the company uses all 115 symbols?

Question #11:   In a certain exam, each examinee was assigned a three-letter code from the set {a, b, c, d, e, f, g}. If 25 of the possible codes were not assigned to anyone, how many people took the exam?

Question #12:   In how many ways can 11 red balls and 8 blue balls be arranged in a row so that no two blue balls are next to each other?

Question #13:   To obtain a certain certification, each student must choose 5 out of 7 tests and 6 out of 8 projects. How many different combinations of tests and projects are available to each student?

Question #14: To obtain a certain certification, each student must choose 2 out of 5 tests and 2 out of 6 projects. How many different combinations of tests and projects are available to each student?

Question #15: There is a group of 8 people, 7 boys and 1 girl who needs to be seated in a row of 8 seats in a theater. In how many ways can the 8 people be seated if the girl won't sit on the either end or in the middle?

PROBABILITY:

Question #16: A certain shade card for wall paint contains 900 different shades, and a certain shade card for vinyl flooring contains 600 different shades. Among all these shades, only 50 shades are common to both shade cards. If one shade is to be selected at random from each shade card, what is the probability that the two shades selected will be of the same shade?

Question #17: A big bowl contains 100 slips of paper, each with a distinct integer 1 to 100, inclusive, written on it. If a slip of paper is drawn at random, what is the probability that the slip of paper will have a number written on it that is a multiple of 5 or a multiple of 7?

Question #18: Tracy, Stacy, and Macy, each independently tried to solve the same crossword puzzle. If their individual probabilities to solve the puzzle are 1/2 1/5, and 2/9, respectively, what is the probability that Tracy and Stacy, but not Macy, will be able to solve the puzzle?

Question #19: In a certain college, 110 students participate in football and 120 students participate in hockey. Of these, 50 students participate in both football and hockey. The remaining 20 students participate in neither football nor hockey. If one student is randomly chosen from this college, what is the probability that the chosen student participates in hockey but not in football?

Question #20: In a certain game, the number 1 is written on 1 slip of paper, the number 2 is written on 2 slips of paper, the number 3 is written on 3 slips of paper, the number 4 is written on 4 slips of paper, and so on, until the number 10 is written on 10 slips pf paper. All these slips are folded and placed in a big jar. All the slips with a prime number written on them are the winning slips. If one slip of paper is randomly drawn from the jar, what is the probability that it will have a winning number written on it?

Question #21: Each integer from 1 to 100 whose units digit is a 7 is written on a separate piece of paper. If all the pieces of paper are kept in a big jar, and one piece is picked at random, what is the probability that the picked piece of paper would have a prime number written on it?

Question #22: The three finalists of a wrestling championship, Stacy, Tracy, and Lucy are playing with no ties, meaning one of the two players playing the game must win and the other must lose the game. There are only two games left. The first game is between Stacy and Tracy, and the winner will play with Lucy. The probability that Stacy will beat Tracy is $\frac{5}{6}$, that Lucy will beat Stacy is $\frac{7}{8}$, and that Lucy will beat Tracy is $\frac{8}{9}$. What is the probability that Tracy will win the championship?

Question #23: A certain windmill gets its energy from a simple turbine, which is made up of two rotors. Each rotor either functions or fails. The functioning or failure of one rotor is exclusive of the functioning or failure of the other rotor. The turbine works only if both rotors function. If the probability that a rotor functions is $\frac{7}{9}$, what is the probability that the turbine works?

Question #24: In jar A there are 2 red balls and 5 blue balls, and in jar B there are 5 red and 2 blue balls. If one of the two jars is randomly picked and then one ball from that jar is randomly picked, what is the probability of picking a red ball from jar A?

Question #25: In a family with three children, what is the probability that all the three children are of the same gender? (Assume that the probability of having a boy or a girl is equal.)

Question #26:   In a family with three children, what is the probability of having 2 boys and 1 girl? (Assume that the probability of having a boy or a girl is equal.)

Question #27:   The probability of John passing the test is 1/6. The probability of John passing the test and George getting a job is 1/8. What is the probability of George getting a job?

Question #28:   The probability of drawing a red ball out of a blue jar is $1/x$. The probability of drawing a red ball from the blue jar and breaking the jar is $1/y$. What is the probability of breaking the jar?

Question #29:   In a certain jar, there are 3 red balls and 2 blue balls. What is the probability of drawing at least one red ball when drawing two consecutive balls randomly?

Question #30:   In a certain jar, there are four colors of balls: red, blue, green, and yellow. The probability of randomly drawing a red ball is 1/5, blue ball is 1/9, and green ball is 1/10. If the jar cannot contain more than 90 balls, what is the maximum number of yellow balls that could be in the jar?

Question #31:   In a certain organization, there are 4 projects and only 3 project managers. If the projects are randomly assigned to the project managers, what is the probability that all three project-managers are assigned at least one project?

Question #32:   What is the probability of getting a sum of 8 or 14 when rolling 3 dice at the same time?

Question #33:   A certain bookstore sells only 10 different titles of books. A customer buys 3 different titles out of the 10 tiles offered by the bookstore. Another customer walks into the bookstore and randomly picks 2 of the 10 titles offered by the bookstore. What is the probability that the second customer picks the title that the first customer didn't?

Question #34:   A jar contains 7 red balls and 3 blue balls. If two balls are drawn randomly, what is the probability that at least one of the drawn balls is red?

Question #35:   In a box there are 12 pencils, only 2 of which are sharpened. If 3 pencils are drawn at random, what is the probability that at least 1 of the chosen pencils is sharpened?

Question #36:   There are three boxers, X, Y, and Z, and each one will play against the other exactly once. Boxer X has a 80 percent chance of winning whenever it plays. Boxer Y and Z, each has equal chances of winning whenever they play against each other. What is the probability that boxer X will lose both of its games, and boxer Y will win both of its games?

Question #37:   In a certain jar, there are 6 red marbles, 4 blue marbles, and 2 green marbles. If two marbles are randomly drawn, what is the probability that the two marbles will be of different colors?

Question #38:   In a certain jar, there are 5 red marbles, 5 blue marbles, and 5 green marbles. If two marbles are randomly drawn, what is the probability that the two marbles will be of different colors?

SETS:

Question #39:   If A is the solution set of $x^2 - 25 = 0$ and B is the solution set of $x^2 - 7x + 10 = 0$, what is the intersection of Set A and Set B?

Question #40:   In the figure below, circular region A represents the set of all numbers of the form $2m$, circular region B represents the set of all numbers of the form n^2, and circular region C represents the set of all numbers of the form 10^k, where m, n, and k are positive integers. What is a number that belongs in the common set represented by all the sets?

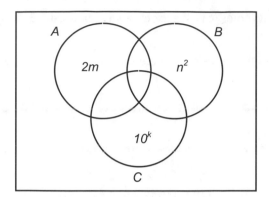

Question #41: In a certain club that has 100 members, more number of members speaks Spanish than the number of members who speaks French. If 70 members speak French and 25 speak neither Spanish nor French, what is the minimum number of members who speak both Spanish and French?

Question #42: At a certain high school of 191 students, every student has to take a foreign language in at least one of the three semesters; 78 students take it in fall, 82 take it in winter, 96 take it in spring. If 29 students take a foreign language in exactly two semesters, how many students take it in all three semesters?

Question #43: In a certain ethical group of 150 people, every person speaks at least one of the three foreign languages; 50 speak French, 75 speak Spanish, and 100 speak Italian. If 35 people speak exactly two foreign languages, how many people speak all three languages?

SEQUENCE & PATTERNS:

Question #44: There were 125 days between two major hurricanes. If the first hurricane was on a Saturday, how many Sundays were there between the two hurricanes?

Question #45: Consider the following infinite sequence: 1, 5, 2, 8, 7, 9, 6, 1, 5, 2, 8, 7, 9, 6, ..., where the seven digits 1, 5, 2, 8, 7, 9, and 6, keep on repeating in that order indefinitely. What is the sum of the 900th through 907th terms of the sequence?

Question #46: In a sequence of numbers, each term after the first one is twice the preceding term. If the difference between the 5th and the 1st term is 18, what is the value of the middle term?

Question #47: The first term is the sequence given below is 2, and each term after the first term is determined by multiplying the preceding term by m and then adding n. What is the value of $m + n$?
2, 9, 23, 51, 107, ...

Question #48: There is a sequence of 5 numbers. A number is chosen for the first term, and each successive term is found by adding 8 to the preceding term and then doubling it. If the fifth term is 1,200, what is the value of the first term?

Question #49: What is the sum of the units digit of 2^{79} and the units digit of 5^{68}?

Question #50: What is the sum of the units digit of 9^{60} and the units digit of 6^{90}?

Question #51: In a certain restaurant, a jukebox plays songs in a regularly repeated cycle of 20 different songs. If a dime buys 1 song, then, in dollars, what is the minimum amount of money that must be spent before the same song is played five times?

MISCELLANEOUS PROBLEMS:

Question #52: A certain clock chimes one note at 10 minutes past every hour, two notes at 20 minutes past every hour, three note at 30 minutes past every hour, four notes at 40 minutes past every hour, and five notes at 50 minutes past every hour. On the onset of every hour, it chimes six notes plus the number of notes equal to that hour. How many notes will the clock chime between 6 P.M. and 11 P.M., inclusive?

Question #53: If all the letters represent single digits in the correctly worked computation shown below, what is the value of $X + Y + Z$?

```
    X   2   6   9
    8   Y   2   1
    2   1   Z   2
+   1   7   1   5
─────────────────
1   7   7   7   7
```

STATS – AVERAGES:

Question #54: The average (arithmetic mean) rating of the students in the south campus is 150 points and the average rating of the students in the north campus is 120 points. There are no common students between the south and north campus. If the average rating of all the students is 132 points, and if there are 50 students in the south campus, how many students are in the north campus?

Question #55: In a certain technology company, a senior programmer can execute 5 web applications in 2 hours and a junior programmer can execute 2 web applications in 5 hours. If a senior programmer and a junior programmer, each execute the same number of applications, what is the average amount of time, in minutes, to process one web application?

Question #56: If the average of 17 consecutive odd integers is 685, what is the least of these integers?

Question #57: If the average of 18 consecutive odd integers is 876, what is the least of these integers?

Question #58: What is the median of the following set: $\{n, 2, 5, 11, 11, 15, 19\}$, where n is a positive number.

Question #59: If A is the average (arithmetic mean) of the first 25 positive multiple of 2 and if B is the median of the first 25 positive multiples of 2, what is the value of $A - B$?

Question #60: If the average (arithmetic mean) of 8, m, and n is 6, and the average of 9, m, and $-n$ is 7, what is the value of m?

Question #61: If the average (arithmetic mean) of x and y is 85 and the average (arithmetic mean) of y and z is 80, what is the value of $(x - z)^2$?

Question #62: If the average (arithmetic mean) of m, n, and 7 is 25, what is the average of $m + 2$, $n - 9$, and 8?

Question #63: The average (arithmetic mean) of $2a + 12$ and another number is $5a$. What is the average of the other number and $6a$?

Question #64: A students' average score for a series of test was 95. However, after taking one last test, in which the student scored a score of 50, it lowered the overall average score to 90. How many tests were there in the series before taking the last test?

Question #65: During a group vocation, the average (arithmetic mean) daily expense of 10 members was $90. If 2 of the members had no expenses at all, and each of the others had a daily expense of at least $75, including one member, who had a daily expense of exactly $170 dollars, what is the maximum possible daily expenses, in dollars, that any one of the members in the group could have?

Question #66: The average (arithmetic mean) weight of a group of five people is 175.2 pounds. If no two people weigh less than 155 pounds and if no two peoples' weights are within 5 pounds of each other, then, in pounds, what is the maximum possible weight that any of the five people can have?

Question #67: A certain student's average (arithmetic mean) score on six tests is 70. Assuming that the students can't earn more than 100 on any one test, what is the least the student can score on the seventh test and still have a chance of getting an average score of 75 after taking nine tests?

Question #68   A student has taken seven math tests so far this semester. If he gets a 60 on his next test, that score will lower his average (arithmetic mean) by 2 points. What is his average now?

Question #69:   In a certain store, the average (arithmetic mean) daily sales for the last n days was 70 units. If today's sale of 160 units increases the average to 75 units per day, what is the value of n?

Question #70:   There are 7 books placed on a certain bookshelf. Each book is at least 90 pages long, and the total number of pages of all 7 books is 777 pages. If the average number of pages of the first 5 books is 105 pages, what is the greatest possible number of pages of any of the 7 books?

PRACTICE EXERCISE – QUESTIONS & ANSWERS WITH EXPLANATIONS:

PURE LOGIC:

Question #1: A certain security code has 5 digits. All the digits in the code must appear in descending numerical order and no digit can be used more than once. One example of such a code is 97510. What is the difference between the largest and smallest possible codes?

Solution: We need to find the difference between the largest and smallest possible 5 digit codes. A digit cannot be repeated. All digits must appear in descending numerical order.

    Largest Possible Code   ⇒ The largest code must have the largest digit in the ten-thousands place, which is 9, followed by next largest digits, which are 8, 7, 6, and 5, in the next four places. So the largest possible code is 98765

    Smallest Possible Code   ⇒The smallest code must have the smallest digit in the units place, which is 0, followed by next smallest digits, which are 1, 2, 3, and 4, in the next four places. So the smallest possible code is 43210

The difference between the largest and smallest possible codes ⇒ 98765 – 43210 = 55555

Question #2: A certain rectangular tomb can only hold 8-ounce blocks of gold and 5-ounce blocks of silver. If there are a total of 90 ounces of gold and silver, what is the greatest amount of gold that the tomb can contain?

Solution: The tomb has a total capacity of 90 ounces of gold and silver. Each block of gold weighs 8 ounces and each block of silver weighs 5 ounces. We have to find the greatest amount of gold that the tomb can contain.

It's not possible to have all 90 ounces as blocks of gold, since 90 is not a multiple of 8. So now we know that there has to be some blocks of silver as well.

The largest multiple of 8 that is less than 90 is 88, but again this can't be the amount of gold either, since this leaves only 90 – 88 = 2 ounces leftover for silver, and each block of silver is of 5 ounces.

Now let's take a look at the multiple of 8 that is less than 88, until we find the one that leaves a leftover which is a multiple of 5.

The next largest multiple of 8 that is less than 88, is 80, which leaves us a leftover of 10, which is also a multiple of 5. So, this amount works. We can have 10 blocks of gold for a total of 10 × 8 = 80 ounces, and 2 blocks of silver for a total of 2 × 5 = 10 ounces.

Therefore, the greatest amount of gold that the tomb can contain is 80 ounces.

Question #3: In a certain private university, there are three schools and each school has 10 advisors. Exactly 5 advisors are in all three schools and each pair of school has 6 advisors in common. How many distinct advisors are there in the entire university?

Solution: This problem is extremely confusing but it can be extremely easy if you tackle it intelligently.

The best way to tackle this problem is by systematically putting everything in a grid.

List advisors for each school and use numbers for each advisor.

School A ⇒	1	2	3	4	5	6	7	9	12	15
School B ⇒	1	2	3	4	5	6	8	10	13	16
School C ⇒	1	2	3	4	5	7	8	11	14	17

Note   ⇒ The first 5 advisors are common for all three schools.

            ⇒ Now we need one more member to be common for each pair of school.

            ⇒ Make the 6th advisor to be common for School A and School B

            ⇒ Make the 7th advisor to be common for School C and School A

            ⇒ Make the 8th advisor to be common for School B and School C

            ⇒ Now we have exactly 5 advisors who are in all three schools and each pair of school has 6 advisors in common

            ⇒ The remaining advisors are only in one School each.

Therefore, there are 17 distinct advisors in the entire university.

Question #4: John weighs twice as much as Mack. Mack's weight is 75% of Tom's weight. Nick weighs 50% of George's weight. George weighs 190% of John's weight. Which of these 5 persons weigh the least?

Solution: The best way to solve this problem is to get all the weights of the five people in a common variable.
Let's try to represent all weights in term of J, which is John's weight.

Let, Johns weight = J

John weighs twice as much as Mack:	$\Rightarrow J = 2M$	$\Rightarrow$ Equation #1
	$\Rightarrow M = 0.5J$	[Divide both sides by 2]
Mack's weight is 75% of Tom's weight:	$\Rightarrow M = 0.75T$	$\Rightarrow$ Equation #2
	$\Rightarrow 0.5J = 0.75T$	[Substitute $M = 0.5J$]
	$\Rightarrow T = 0.66J$	[Divide both sides by 0.75]
George weighs 190% of John's weight:	$\Rightarrow G = 1.90J$	$\Rightarrow$ Equation #3
Nick weighs 50% of George's weight:	$\Rightarrow N = 0.50G$	$\Rightarrow$ Equation #4
	$\Rightarrow N = 0.50 (1.90J)$	[Substitute $G = 1.90J$]
	$\Rightarrow N = 0.95J$	[Do the multiplication]

Now we have the following weights:

John's Weight $\Rightarrow J$
Mack's Weight $\Rightarrow 0.5J$
Tom's Weight $\Rightarrow 0.66J$
George's Weight $\Rightarrow 1.90J$
Nick's Weight $\Rightarrow 0.95J$

Now that we have all the weights in a common variable it's easy to compare – Mack's weight is the least and George's weight is the most.

Note: To answer this problem, you don't have to find the actual weight of anyone; you are simply asked to compare the weights and find the person who weighs the least.

Question #5: A certain box contains 20 slips of paper, each with an integer from 1 to 20, inclusive written on it. If one slip at a time is randomly drawn from the box without replacing the slips already drawn, how many slips must be drawn in order to ensure that sum of the numbers on the all slips drawn is even? (Assume that more than one slip needs to be drawn.)

Solution: To be assured of something, we have to consider the worst-case scenario. We have to find the least number of slips that must be drawn from the box to be assured that the sum of the numbers on the all slips drawn is even.

Best-case scenario $\Rightarrow$ The best-case scenario would be that the first 2 slips drawn has an even number written on them – this is possible, but may not always happen. However, to be assured that the sum of the numbers on the all the slips drawn is even, let's consider the worst-case scenario.

Worst-case scenario $\Rightarrow$ Since the box contains 20 slips of paper, each with an integer from 1 to 20, inclusive written on it, half of the slips have an even number written on them and half have an odd number.

Case #1: Assume that the first slip drawn has an odd number written on it. Then the next slip drawn has an even number written on it. This adds up to: odd + even = odd. Furthermore, assume that the next 9 slips has an even number written on them. This still adds up to an odd number. Now, all the even numbered slips have been exhausted. The next slip drawn has to have an odd number written on it. Now, the sum of the numbers written on the slips is odd + odd = even.

Total Number of Slips Drawn $\Rightarrow$ odd (first slip) + even (10 slips) + odd (twelfth slip) = even (12 slips)

Case #2: Assume that the first slip drawn has an even number written on it. Then the next slip drawn has an odd number written on it. This adds up to even + odd = odd. Furthermore, assume that the next 9 slips drawn has an even number written on them. This still adds up to an odd number. Now, all the even numbered slips have been exhausted. The next slip drawn has to have an odd number written on it. Now, the sum of the numbers written on the slips is odd + odd = even.

Total Number of Slips Drawn $\Rightarrow$ even (first slip) + odd (second slips) + even (9 slips) +odd (twelfth slip) = even (12 slips)

Therefore, in either case, 12 slips must be drawn in order to ensure that sum of the numbers on the all slips drawn is even.

Question #6: A 100-inch rope needs to be cut into five pieces. Each piece must have an integer length in inches, and no two pieces can have the same length. If the largest piece of rope is 50 inches and the smallest piece is 10 inches, what is the maximum length of the third largest piece of rope?

Solution:
Total length of rope $\Rightarrow$ 100 inches
Length of the first largest piece of rope $\Rightarrow$ 50 inches
Length of the fifth largest piece of rope $\Rightarrow$ 10 inches

Keep in mind that for the third place to be as large as possible, the fourth place must be as small as possible, but it must be more than the fifth place.

Length of the first largest piece of rope $\Rightarrow$ 50 inches
Length of the fourth largest piece of rope $\Rightarrow$ 11 inches
Length of the fifth largest piece of rope $\Rightarrow$ 10 inches

Now we have already used a total of 50 + 10 + 11 = 71 inches of rope. The remaining length of rope is 100 – 71 = 29 inches, which must be used for the second and third place.

Since we want to maximize the length of the third place, but the second place must still be greater than the third place, divide 29 into two integer lengths, which are 14 and 15.

Length of the first largest piece of rope $\Rightarrow$ 50 inches
Length of the second largest piece of rope $\Rightarrow$ 15 inches
Length of the third largest piece of rope $\Rightarrow$ 14 inches
Length of the fourth largest piece of rope $\Rightarrow$ 11 inches
Length of the fifth largest piece of rope $\Rightarrow$ 10 inches

Therefore, the maximum length of the third largest piece of rope is 14 inches.

PERMUTATION & COMBINATION:

Question #7: A five-digit pin must satisfy the following condition: the first digit is an even number, the second digit is an odd number, the third digit is an even prime number, the fourth digit is an odd prime number, and the fifth digit is a random number that is not used anywhere in the number. How many such pins can be generated?

Solution: List all the options for each digit:
No. of options for the first digit $\Rightarrow$ 4 (even number: 2, 4, 6, 8; 0 can't be included here)
No. of options for the second digit $\Rightarrow$ 5 (odd number: 1, 3, 5, 7, 9)
No. of options for the third digit $\Rightarrow$ 1 (even prime number: 2)
No. of options for the fourth digit $\Rightarrow$ 3 (odd prime number: 3, 5, or 7)
No. of options for the fifth digit $\Rightarrow$ 6 (10 – 4 used as the first four digits)
Total No. of options for the five-digit pin $\Rightarrow$ 4 × 5 × 1 × 3 × 6 = 360

Question #8: How many five-digit numbers are there, if the first two digits are even, the rest of the digits are odd, and the digit 8 cannot appear more than once in any number?

Solution: If there was no restriction of the number 8 not being able to appear more than once in a number, then the total options for the five-digit numbers:
No. of options for the first digit $\Rightarrow$ 4 (even number: 2, 4, 6, 8; 0 can't be included here)
No. of options for the second digit $\Rightarrow$ 5 (even number: 0, 2, 4, 6, 8)
No. of options for the third digit $\Rightarrow$ 5 (odd number: 1, 3, 5, 7, 9)
No. of options for the fourth digit $\Rightarrow$ 5 (odd number: 1, 3, 5, 7, 9)
No. of options for the fifth digit $\Rightarrow$ 5 (odd number: 1, 3, 5, 7, 9)
No. of options for the five-digit numbers $\Rightarrow$ 4 × 5 × 5 × 5 × 5 = 2,500

Now, let's subtract the options where the number 8 does appear more than once in the number. Since 8 is an even number, and in our five-digit numbers, only the first two digits can be even numbers, the only place where the number 8 can appear twice is only in the first two places. In this case, the total number of options for this would be $\Rightarrow$ 1 × 1 × 5 × 5 × 5 = 125

Total No. of Options for the five-digit numbers $\Rightarrow$ 2,500 – 125 = 2,375

Question #9: A nine-digit (from 1 to 9) employee id must satisfy the following condition: the first two digits are fixed as 79 in that order, the third digit is bigger than 7, the fourth digit is smaller than 5, the fifth digit is divisible by 3, the sixth digit is a multiple of 2, the seventh digit is twice the eighth digit, and the ninth digit is a prime number. How many different employee ids' can be generated?

Solution: List all the options for each digit:
No. of options for the first digit $\Rightarrow$ 1 (it is fixed as 7)
No. of options for the second digit $\Rightarrow$ 1 (it is fixed as 9)
No. of options for the third digit $\Rightarrow$ 2 (bigger than 7: 8 or 9)
No. of options for the fourth digit $\Rightarrow$ 4 (smaller than 5: 1, 2, 3, or 4; 0 is not allowed)
No. of options for the fifth digit $\Rightarrow$ 3 (divisible by 3: 3,6, or 9)
No. of options for the sixth digit $\Rightarrow$ 4 (multiple of 2: 2, 4, 6, or 8)

No. of options for the seventh/eighth digit $\Rightarrow$ 4 (seventh is twice of eighth: 2 &1, 4 & 2, 6 & 3, 8 & 4)
No. of options for the ninth digit $\Rightarrow$ 4 (prime number: 2, 3, 5, or 7)
Total No. of different nine-digit ids possible $\Rightarrow$ 1 × 1 × 2 × 4 × 3 × 4 × 4 × 4 = 1,536

Question #10: A certain company used a 9-digit id to identify each customer, and now wants to add a two-digit prefix to every id. The two digits are composed of 115 different special symbols. If the company used 110 of the symbols completely and five remains unused, how many additional prefixes can be generated if the company uses all 115 symbols?

Solution: In this problem, since we are asked to determine the prefixes, the 9-digit customer id is irrelevant.

Total No. of Prefixes that can be generated $\rightarrow$ 115 × 115 = 115^2
No. of Prefixes that are already generated $\Rightarrow$ 110 × 110 = 110^2
No. of additional Prefixes that can be generated $\Rightarrow$ $115^2 - 110^2$
$\Rightarrow$ (115 + 110) (115 − 110)
$\Rightarrow$ 225 × 5 = 1,125

Question #11: In a certain exam, each examinee was assigned a three-letter code from the set {a, b, c, d, e, f, g}. If 25 of the possible codes were not assigned to anyone, how many people took the exam?

Solution: No. of possible 3-letter codes:

Permutation $\Rightarrow {}_mP_n \Rightarrow \dfrac{m!}{(m-n)!}$

$\Rightarrow {}_7P_3 \Rightarrow \dfrac{7!}{(7-3)!} = \dfrac{7!}{4!} = \dfrac{7 \times 6 \times 5 \times 4!}{4!} = 7 \times 6 \times 5 = 210$

No. of unassigned codes $\Rightarrow$ 25
No of examinees $\Rightarrow$ No. of possible codes – No. of unassigned codes
$\Rightarrow$ 210 − 25 = 185

Question #12: In how many ways can 11 red balls and 8 blue balls be arranged in a row so that no two blue balls are next to each other?

Solution: First, place all the 11 red balls in a row so that there is enough space between them for another ball.
Now, there will be 10 spots in between the 11 red balls and 2 more on each side, for a total of 12 available spots for the blue balls.
Next, place the 8 blue balls on any of these 12 available spots and there will be no two blue balls next to each other.
Total No. of arrangements:

Combination $\Rightarrow {}_mC_n \Rightarrow \dfrac{m!}{n!(m-n)!}$

$\Rightarrow {}_{12}C_8 \Rightarrow \dfrac{12!}{8!(12-8)!} = \dfrac{12 \times 11 \times 10 \times 9 \times 8!}{8!(4!)} = \dfrac{12 \times 11 \times 10 \times 9}{4 \times 3 \times 2 \times 1} = \dfrac{11880}{24} = 495$

Question #13: To obtain a certain certification, each student must choose 5 out of 7 tests and 6 out of 8 projects. How many different combinations of tests and projects are available to each student?

Solution: No. of different combos for tests:

Combination $\Rightarrow {}_mC_n \Rightarrow \dfrac{m!}{n!(m-n)!}$

$\Rightarrow \dfrac{7!}{5!(7-5)!} = \dfrac{7!}{5!2!} = \dfrac{7 \times 6 \times \cancel{5!}}{\cancel{5!}2!} = \dfrac{7 \times 6}{2 \times 1} = \dfrac{42}{2} = 21$

No. of different combos for projects:

Combination $\Rightarrow {}_mC_n \Rightarrow \dfrac{m!}{n!(m-n)!}$

$\Rightarrow \dfrac{8!}{6!(8-6)!} = \dfrac{8!}{6!2!} = \dfrac{8 \times 7 \times \cancel{6!}}{\cancel{6!}2!} = \dfrac{8 \times 7}{2 \times 1} = \dfrac{56}{2} = 28$

Total No. of Different Combinations of Tests and Projects $\Rightarrow$ 21 × 28 = 588

Question #14: To obtain a certain certification, each student must choose 2 out of 5 tests and 2 out of 6 projects. How many different combinations of tests and projects are available to each student?

Solution: No. of different combos for tests:

$$\text{Combination} \Rightarrow {}_mC_n \Rightarrow \frac{m!}{n!(m-n)!}$$

$$\Rightarrow \frac{5!}{2!(5-2)!} = \frac{5!}{2!3!} = \frac{5 \times 4 \times \cancel{3!}}{\cancel{3!}\, 2!} = \frac{5 \times 4}{2 \times 1} = \frac{20}{2} = 10$$

No. of different combos for projects:

$$\text{Combination} \Rightarrow {}_mC_n \Rightarrow \frac{m!}{n!(m-n)!}$$

$$\Rightarrow \frac{6!}{2!(6-2)!} = \frac{6!}{2!4!} = \frac{6 \times 5 \times \cancel{4!}}{\cancel{4!}\, 2!} = \frac{6 \times 5}{2 \times 1} = \frac{30}{2} = 15$$

Total No. of Different Combinations of Tests and Projects $\Rightarrow 10 \times 15 = 150$

Question #15: There is a group of 8 people, 7 boys and 1 girl who needs to be seated in a row of 8 seats in a theater. In how many ways can the 8 people be seated if the girl won't sit on the either end or in the middle?

Solution: Total No. of People $\Rightarrow 8$; 7 boys and 1 girl who cant be seated on either end or in the middle.
Total No. of Seating Options for the Girl $\Rightarrow 8 - (2 \text{ for the two ends}) - 1 \text{ (for the middle)} = 5$
Total No. of Seating Options for the Boys $\Rightarrow 8 - 1 \text{ (for the girl)} = 7! = 5,040$
Total No. of Seating Options for all 8 people $\Rightarrow 5 \times (7!) = 5 \times 5,040 = 25,200$

PROBABILITY:

Question #16: A certain shade card for wall paint contains 900 different shades, and a certain shade card for vinyl flooring contains 600 different shades. Among all these shades, only 50 shades are common to both shade cards. If one shade is to be selected at random from each shade card, what is the probability that the two shades selected will be of the same shade?

Solution: Probability of selecting a shade from the wall shade card that is of the common shade $\Rightarrow \dfrac{50}{900}$

Probability of selecting that one shade from the vinyl shade card that is of the same shade $\Rightarrow \dfrac{1}{600}$

Probability of selecting the two shades of the same shade $\Rightarrow \left(\dfrac{50}{900}\right)\left(\dfrac{1}{600}\right) = \dfrac{1}{10,800}$

Question #17: A big bowl contains 100 slips of paper, each with a distinct integer 1 to 100, inclusive, written on it. If a slip of paper is drawn at random, what is the probability that the slip of paper will have a number written on it that is a multiple of 5 or a multiple of 7?

Solution: The two events are mutually non-exclusive, since there are common elements in both sets.

Integers that are multiples of 5: $\Rightarrow A = \{5, 10, 15, 20, 25, ..., 100\} \Rightarrow 20 \text{ items} \Rightarrow P(A) = \dfrac{20}{100}$

Integers that are multiples of 7: $\Rightarrow B = \{7, 14, 21, 28, 35, ..., 98\} \Rightarrow 14 \text{ items} \Rightarrow P(B) = \dfrac{14}{100}$

Integers that are multiples of 5 & 7 $\Rightarrow A \cap B = \{35, 70\}$ $\Rightarrow P(A \cap B) = \dfrac{2}{100}$

Probability (multiple of 5 or multiple of 7) $\Rightarrow P(A \text{ or } B) \Rightarrow P(A) + P(B) - P(A \cap B)$

$$\Rightarrow \frac{20}{100} + \frac{14}{100} - \frac{2}{100} = \frac{32}{100} = \frac{8}{25}$$

Question #18: Tracy, Stacy, and Macy, each independently tried to solve the same crossword puzzle. If their individual probabilities to solve the puzzle are 1/2 1/5, and 2/9, respectively, what is the probability that Tracy and Stacy, but not Macy, will be able to solve the puzzle?

Solution: Probability that Tracy will solve the puzzle $\Rightarrow \dfrac{1}{2}$

Probability that Stacy will solve the puzzle $\Rightarrow \dfrac{1}{5}$

Probability that Macy will solve the puzzle $\Rightarrow \dfrac{2}{9}$

Probability that Macy will NOT solve the puzzle $\Rightarrow 1 - \dfrac{2}{9} = \dfrac{7}{9}$

Probability that Tracy and Stacy, but not Macy, will be able to solve the puzzle $\Rightarrow \left(\dfrac{1}{2}\right)\left(\dfrac{1}{5}\right)\left(\dfrac{7}{9}\right) = \left(\dfrac{7}{90}\right)$

Question #19: In a certain college, 110 students participate in football and 120 students participate in hockey. Of these, 50 students participate in both football and hockey. The remaining 20 students participate in neither football nor hockey. If one student is randomly chosen from this college, what is the probability that the chosen student participates in hockey but not in football?

Solution:
No. of students who participates in Football $\Rightarrow 110$
No. of students who participates in Hockey $\Rightarrow 120$
No. of students who participates in Football & Hockey $\Rightarrow 50$
No. of students who participates only in Football $\Rightarrow 110 - 50 = 60$
No. of students who participates only in Hockey $\Rightarrow 120 - 50 = 70$
No. of students who participates in neither Football nor Hockey $\Rightarrow 20$
Total No. of Students:
$\Rightarrow$ Only Football + Only Hockey + Both Football & Hockey + Neither Football nor Hockey
$\Rightarrow 60 + 70 + 50 + 20 = 200$

Probability of randomly picking a student who participates in hockey but not in football $\Rightarrow \dfrac{70}{200} = \dfrac{7}{20}$

Question #20: In a certain game, the number 1 is written on 1 slip of paper, the number 2 is written on 2 slips of paper, the number 3 is written on 3 slips of paper, the number 4 is written on 4 slips of paper, and so on, until the number 10 is written on 10 slips pf paper. All these slips are folded and placed in a big jar. All the slips with a prime number written on them are the winning slips. If one slip of paper is randomly drawn from the jar, what is the probability that it will have a winning number written on it?

Solution:
Total No. of slips placed in the jar $\Rightarrow 1 + 2 + 3 + 4 + 5 + 6 + 7 + 8 + 9 + 10 = 55$
Total No. of prime numbered slips $\Rightarrow 2 + 3 + 5 + 7 = 17$

Probability of drawing a prime numbered slip $\Rightarrow \dfrac{17}{55}$

Question #21: Each integer from 1 to 100 whose units digit is a 7 is written on a separate piece of paper. If all the pieces of paper are kept in a big jar, and one piece is picked at random, what is the probability that the picked piece of paper would have a prime number written on it?

Solution:
List of integer from 1 - 100 whose units digit is 7 $\Rightarrow$ 7, 17, 27, 37, 47, 57, 67, 77, 87, 97
Total No. of integer from 1 – 100 whose units digit is 7 $\Rightarrow 10$
List of integer from 1 - 100 whose units digit is 7 and are prime $\Rightarrow$ 7, 17, 37, 47, 67, 97
Total No. of integer from 1 – 100 whose units digit is 7 and are prime $\Rightarrow 6$

Probability of picking a prime $\Rightarrow \dfrac{6}{10} = \dfrac{3}{5}$

Question #22: The three finalists of a wrestling championship, Stacy, Tracy, and Lucy are playing with no ties, meaning one of the two players playing the game must win and the other must lose the game. There are only two games left. The first game is between Stacy and Tracy, and the winner will play with Lucy.

The probability that Stacy will beat Tracy is $\dfrac{5}{6}$, that Lucy will beat Stacy is $\dfrac{7}{8}$, and that Lucy will beat

Tracy is $\dfrac{8}{9}$. What is the probability that Tracy will win the championship?

Solution: For Tracy to win the championship, she has to first beat Stacy and then beat Lucy.

Probability that Stacy will beat Tracy $\Rightarrow \dfrac{5}{6}$

Probability that Tracy will beat Stacy $\Rightarrow 1 - \dfrac{5}{6} = \dfrac{1}{6}$

Probability that Lucy will beat Tracy $\Rightarrow \dfrac{8}{9}$

Probability that Tracy will beat Lucy $\Rightarrow 1 - \dfrac{8}{9} = \dfrac{1}{9}$

Probability that Tracy will beat Stacy and Lucy and win the championship $\Rightarrow \dfrac{1}{6} \times \dfrac{1}{9} = \dfrac{1}{54}$

Question #23: A certain windmill gets its energy from a simple turbine, which is made up of two rotors. Each rotor either functions or fails. The functioning or failure of one rotor is exclusive of the functioning or failure of the other rotor. The turbine works only if both rotors function. If the probability that a rotor functions is $\dfrac{7}{9}$, what is the probability that the turbine works?

Solution: Probability that a rotor does function $\Rightarrow \dfrac{7}{9}$

Probability that a rotor doesn't function $\Rightarrow 1 - \dfrac{7}{9} = \dfrac{2}{9}$

Probability that neither rotor functions $\Rightarrow \dfrac{2}{9} \times \dfrac{2}{9} = \dfrac{4}{81}$

Probability that both rotor functions $\Rightarrow 1 - \dfrac{4}{81} = \dfrac{77}{81}$

Question #24: In jar *A* there are 2 red balls and 5 blue balls, and in jar *B* there are 5 red and 2 blue balls. If one of the two jars is randomly picked and then one ball from that jar is randomly picked, what is the probability of picking a red ball from jar *A*?

Solution: Probability of picking jar *A* (1 out of 2) $\Rightarrow \dfrac{1}{2}$

Probability of picking a red ball from jar *A* (2 out of 7) $\Rightarrow \dfrac{2}{7}$

Probability of picking jar *A* and then picking a red ball from it $\Rightarrow \dfrac{1}{2} \times \dfrac{2}{7} = \dfrac{1}{7}$

Question #25: In a family with three children, what is the probability that all the three children are of the same gender? (Assume that the probability of having a boy or a girl is equal.)

Solution: No. of options for the 1st Child $\Rightarrow 2$
No. of options for the 2nd Child $\Rightarrow 2$
No. of options for the 3rd Child $\Rightarrow 2$
No. of options for all Children $\Rightarrow 2 \times 2 \times 2 = 8$
No of Favorable Options $\Rightarrow$ All Boys (BBB) or All Girls (GGG) = 2

Probability of all the children to be of the same gender $\Rightarrow \dfrac{2}{8} = \dfrac{1}{4}$

Alternate Method: This problem can also be solved by using logic:
Since we want all children to have the same gender, if they are all boys or girls, the gender of the first child is irrelevant; it could be all boys or all girls.
Probability of the second child to have the same gender as the first child $\Rightarrow$ ½
Probability of the third child to have the same gender as the first child $\Rightarrow$ ½
Probability of all the children to be of the same gender $\Rightarrow 1 \times$ ½ $\times$ ½ = ¼

Question #26: In a family with three children, what is the probability of having 2 boys and 1 girl? (Assume that the probability of having a boy or a girl is equal.)

Solution: List of number of arrangements of 2 boys and 1 girl:

$\Rightarrow$ BBG $\Rightarrow$ P(B) = ½; P(B) = ½; P(G) = ½ $\Rightarrow$ Total Probability = ½ × ½ × ½ = 1/8

$\Rightarrow$ GBB $\Rightarrow$ P(G) = ½; P(B) = ½; P(B) = ½ $\Rightarrow$ Total Probability = ½ × ½ × ½ = 1/8

$\Rightarrow$ BGB $\Rightarrow$ P(B) = ½; P(G) = ½; P(B) = ½ $\Rightarrow$ Total Probability = ½ × ½ × ½ = 1/8

Combined probability of having 2 boys and 1 girl $\Rightarrow \dfrac{1}{8} + \dfrac{1}{8} + \dfrac{1}{8} = \dfrac{3}{8}$

Question #27:   The probability of John passing the test is 1/6. The probability of John passing the test and George getting a job is 1/8. What is the probability of George getting a job?

Solution: Let, the probability of George getting the job $\Rightarrow x$

Probability of John passing the test $\Rightarrow \dfrac{1}{6}$

Probability of John passing the test and George getting a job $\Rightarrow \dfrac{1}{8}$

Probability of John passing the test and George getting a job = (Probability of John passing the test) × (Probability of George getting the job)

$\Rightarrow \dfrac{1}{8} = \dfrac{1}{6}(x)$

$\Rightarrow x = \dfrac{6}{8} = \dfrac{3}{4}$

Question #28:   The probability of drawing a red ball out of a blue jar is $1/x$. The probability of drawing a red ball from the blue jar and breaking the jar is $1/y$. What is the probability of breaking the jar?

Solution: Let, the probability of breaking the blue jar $\Rightarrow z$

Probability of drawing a red ball out of the blue jar $\Rightarrow \dfrac{1}{x}$

Probability of drawing a red ball out of the blue jar and breaking the jar $\Rightarrow \dfrac{1}{y}$

(Probability of drawing a red ball out of the blue jar and breaking the jar) = (Probability of drawing a red ball out of a blue jar) × (Probability of breaking the blue jar)

$\Rightarrow \dfrac{1}{y} = \dfrac{1}{x} \bullet z$

$\Rightarrow \dfrac{1}{y} = \dfrac{z}{x}$

$\Rightarrow zy = x$

$\Rightarrow z = \dfrac{x}{y}$

Question #29:   In a certain jar, there are 3 red balls and 2 blue balls. What is the probability of drawing at least one red ball when drawing two consecutive balls randomly?

Solution: We are asked to draw two balls randomly such that at least one of the balls drawn is a red ball

Option #1:   First Ball is Red, Second Ball is Red $\Rightarrow$ Probability = $\dfrac{3}{5} \times \dfrac{2}{4} = \dfrac{6}{20} = \dfrac{3}{10}$

Option #2:   First Ball is Red, Second Ball is Blue $\Rightarrow$ Probability = $\dfrac{3}{5} \times \dfrac{2}{4} = \dfrac{6}{20} = \dfrac{3}{10}$

Option #3:   First Ball is Blue, Second Ball is Red $\Rightarrow$ Probability = $\dfrac{2}{5} \times \dfrac{3}{4} = \dfrac{6}{20} = \dfrac{3}{10}$

Total: Probability of drawing at least one red ball $\Rightarrow \dfrac{3}{10} + \dfrac{3}{10} + \dfrac{3}{10} = \dfrac{9}{10}$

Alternately: Probability of drawing no red ball when drawing two consecutive balls:

First Ball is Blue, Second Ball is Blue $\Rightarrow$ Probability = $\dfrac{2}{5} \times \dfrac{1}{4} = \dfrac{2}{20} = \dfrac{1}{10}$

Probability of drawing at least one red ball $\Rightarrow$ 1 – Probability of drawing no red ball

$$\Rightarrow 1 - \frac{1}{10} = \frac{9}{10}$$

Question #30: In a certain jar, there are four colors of balls: red, blue, green, and yellow. The probability of randomly drawing a red ball is 1/5, blue ball is 1/9, and green ball is 1/10. If the jar cannot contain more than 90 balls, what is the maximum number of yellow balls that could be in the jar?

Solution: Since we are asked to find the maximum possible number of yellow balls, let's assume that there are 90 balls in the jar.

Probability of randomly drawing a red ball $\Rightarrow \dfrac{1}{5}$

No. of red balls in the jar $\Rightarrow \dfrac{1}{5} \times 90 = 18$

Probability of randomly drawing a blue ball $\Rightarrow \dfrac{1}{9}$

No. of blue balls in the jar $\Rightarrow \dfrac{1}{9} \times 90 = 10$

Probability of randomly drawing a green ball $\Rightarrow \dfrac{1}{10}$

No. of green balls in the jar $\Rightarrow \dfrac{1}{10} \times 90 = 9$

Maximum No. of Yellow Balls in the jar $\Rightarrow 90 - 18 - 10 - 9 = 53$

Question #31: In a certain organization, there are 4 projects and only 3 project managers. If the projects are randomly assigned to the project managers, what is the probability that all three project-managers are assigned at least one project?

Solution: Total No. of ways of assigning the 4 projects to the 3 project managers $\Rightarrow 3^4 = 81$
No. of Ways in which the first project manager can be assigned a project $\Rightarrow 4$
No. of Ways in which the second project manager can be assigned a project $\Rightarrow 3$
No. of Ways in which the third project manager can be assigned a project $\Rightarrow 2$
At this point, 3 of the 4 projects has been assigned, one to each project manager, and 1 project still remains unassigned
No. of Ways in which the fourth project can be assigned to one of the 3 project managers $\Rightarrow 3$

Probability that all three project-managers are assigned at least one project $\Rightarrow \dfrac{4 \times 3 \times 2 \times 3}{3 \times 3 \times 3 \times 3} = \dfrac{8}{9}$

Question #32: What is the probability of getting a sum of 8 or 14 when rolling 3 dice at the same time?

Solution: Option for the sum of 8 $\Rightarrow$ (1, 1, 6) $\Rightarrow$ Has 3 options: (116), (161), (611)
$\Rightarrow$ (1, 2, 5) $\Rightarrow$ Has 6 options: (125), (152), (215), (251), (521), (512)
$\Rightarrow$ (1, 3, 4) $\Rightarrow$ Has 6 options: (134), (143), (314), (341), (431), (413)
$\Rightarrow$ (2, 2, 4) $\Rightarrow$ Has 3 options: (224), (242), (422)
$\Rightarrow$ (2, 3, 3) $\Rightarrow$ Has 3 options: (233), (232), (322)
$\Rightarrow$ Total No. of Options = 3 + 6 + 6 + 3 + 3 = 21
Option for the sum of 14 $\Rightarrow$ (2, 6, 6) $\Rightarrow$ Has 3 options: (266), (626), (662)
$\Rightarrow$ (3, 5, 6) $\Rightarrow$ Has 6 options: (356), (365), (536), (563), (653), (635)
$\Rightarrow$ (4, 4, 6) $\Rightarrow$ Has 3 options: (446), (464), (644)
$\Rightarrow$ (4, 5, 5) $\Rightarrow$ Has 3 options: (455), (545), (554)
$\Rightarrow$ Total No. of Options = 3 + 6 + 3 + 3 = 15
Total No. of Options of getting a sum of 8 or 14 when rolling 3 dice simultaneously $\Rightarrow$ 21 + 15 = 36
Total No. of Options when rolling 3 dice simultaneously $\Rightarrow 6 \times 6 \times 6 = 216$

Probability of getting a sum of 8 or 12 when rolling 3 dice simultaneously = $\dfrac{36}{216} = \dfrac{1}{6}$

Question #33: A certain bookstore sells only 10 different titles of books. A customer buys 3 different titles out of the 10 tiles offered by the bookstore. Another customer walks into the bookstore and randomly picks 2 of the 10 titles offered by the bookstore. What is the probability that the second customer picks the title that the first customer didn't?

Solution: No. of ways to pick 2 of the 10 titles $\Rightarrow {}_mC_n \Rightarrow \dfrac{m!}{n!(m-n)!}$

$$\Rightarrow {}_{10}C_2 \Rightarrow \dfrac{10!}{2!(10-2)!} = \dfrac{10!}{2!8!} = \dfrac{10 \times 9 \times 8!}{2!8!} = \dfrac{10 \times 9}{2 \times 1} = 45$$

No. of ways to pick 2 of the 7 titles $\Rightarrow {}_mC_n \Rightarrow \dfrac{m!}{n!(m-n)!}$

(Without picking the 3 that the first picked) $\Rightarrow {}_7C_2 \Rightarrow \dfrac{7!}{2!(7-2)!} = \dfrac{7!}{2!5!} = \dfrac{7 \times 6 \times 5!}{2!5!} = \dfrac{7 \times 6}{2 \times 1} = 21$

Probability that the second customer picks the title that the first customer didn't $\Rightarrow \dfrac{{}_7C_2}{{}_{10}C_2}$

$$\Rightarrow \dfrac{21}{45} = \dfrac{7}{15}$$

Question #34: A jar contains 7 red balls and 3 blue balls. If two balls are drawn randomly, what is the probability that at least one of the drawn balls is red?

Solution: No. of ways to draw two balls from the jar so that at least one of them is red:

$\Rightarrow$ Red Blue $\Rightarrow$ P(Red) = 7/10; P(Blue) = 3/9 $\Rightarrow$ Combined Probability $= \dfrac{7}{10} \times \dfrac{3}{9} = \dfrac{21}{90}$

$\Rightarrow$ Blue Red $\Rightarrow$ P(Blue) = 3/10; P(Red) = 7/9 $\Rightarrow$ Combined Probability $= \dfrac{3}{10} \times \dfrac{7}{9} = \dfrac{21}{90}$

$\Rightarrow$ Red Red $\Rightarrow$ P(Red) = 7/10; P(Red) = 6/9 $\Rightarrow$ Combined Probability $= \dfrac{7}{10} \times \dfrac{6}{9} = \dfrac{42}{90}$

Combined probability that at least one of the drawn balls is red $\Rightarrow \dfrac{21}{90} + \dfrac{21}{90} + \dfrac{42}{90} = \dfrac{84}{90} = \dfrac{14}{15}$

Alternate Method: This problem can also be solved in the following way:

Probability that at least one of the drawn balls is red $\Rightarrow$ 1 – Probability that no red ball is drawn

$$\Rightarrow 1 - \dfrac{{}_3C_2}{{}_{10}C_2} = \dfrac{\dfrac{3!}{2!(3-2)!}}{\dfrac{10!}{2!(10-2)!}} = \dfrac{\dfrac{3!}{2!1!}}{\dfrac{10!}{2!8!}} = \dfrac{\dfrac{3 \times 2!}{2! \times 1!}}{\dfrac{10 \times 9 \times 8!}{2!8!}} = \dfrac{3}{45} = \dfrac{1}{15}$$

Question #35: In a box there are 12 pencils, only 2 of which are sharpened. If 3 pencils are drawn at random, what is the probability that at least 1 of the chosen pencils is sharpened?

Solution: Total No. of Pencils in the Box $\Rightarrow$ 12
No. of Sharpened Pencils in the Box $\Rightarrow$ 2
No. of Unsharpened Pencils in the Box $\Rightarrow$ 12 – 2 = 10
Total No. of Ways of picking 3 of the 12 pencils:

Combination $\Rightarrow {}_mC_n \Rightarrow \dfrac{m!}{n!(m-n)!}$

$$\Rightarrow {}_{12}C_3 \Rightarrow \dfrac{12!}{3!(12-3)!} = \dfrac{12!}{3! \times 9!} = \dfrac{12 \times 11 \times 10 \times \cancel{9!}}{3! \times \cancel{9!}} = \dfrac{12 \times 11 \times 10}{3 \times 2 \times 1} = \dfrac{1320}{6} = 220$$

Total No. of Ways of picking 3 of the 10 Unsharpened Pencils:

Combination $\Rightarrow {}_mC_n \Rightarrow \dfrac{m!}{n!(m-n)!}$

$$\Rightarrow {}_{10}C_3 \Rightarrow \dfrac{10!}{3!(10-3)!} = \dfrac{10!}{3! \times 7!} = \dfrac{10 \times 9 \times 8 \times \cancel{7!}}{3! \times \cancel{7!}} = \dfrac{10 \times 9 \times 8}{3 \times 2 \times 1} = \dfrac{720}{6} = 120$$

Probability (none of the chosen pencils is sharpened) $\Rightarrow \dfrac{120}{220} = \dfrac{6}{11}$

Probability (at least 1 of the chosen pencils is sharpened) $\Rightarrow 1 -$ Probability (none sharpened)

$\Rightarrow 1 - \dfrac{6}{11} = \dfrac{5}{11}$

Question #36:   There are three boxers, X, Y, and Z, and each one will play against the other exactly once. Boxer X has a 80 percent chance of winning whenever it plays. Boxer Y and Z, each has equal chances of winning whenever they play against each other. What is the probability that boxer X will lose both of its games, and boxer Y will win both of its games?

Solution: First thing is to figure out the permutation:

Note: $3! = 3 \times 2 \times 1 = 6 \Rightarrow$ but since half the games are between the same player, i.e., XY and YX are duplicates, actual number of games = $6 \div 2 = 3$

Since each player plays against the other player exactly once, there will be only the following three games: XY, YZ, and XZ

Now let's figure out the probabilities:

List all the individual probabilities and circle the desired outcomes.

First Game between X and Y $\Rightarrow$ Probability of X winning (or Y losing) $= \dfrac{4}{5}$

$\Rightarrow$ Probability of Y winning (or X losing) $= \boxed{\dfrac{1}{5}}$

Second Game between Y and Z $\Rightarrow$ Probability of Y winning (or Z losing) $= \dfrac{1}{2}$

$\Rightarrow$ Probability of Z winning (or Y losing) $= \boxed{\dfrac{1}{2}}$

Third Game between X and Z $\Rightarrow$ Probability of X winning (or Z losing) $= \dfrac{4}{5}$

$\Rightarrow$ Probability of Z winning (or X losing) $= \boxed{\dfrac{1}{5}}$

Probability of $\Rightarrow X$ loosing both games $\Rightarrow X$ losing to Y $\Rightarrow \dfrac{1}{5}$

AND

$\Rightarrow X$ losing to Z $\Rightarrow \dfrac{1}{5}$ (duplicate)

AND

$\Rightarrow Z$ winning both games $\Rightarrow Z$ winning with X $\Rightarrow \dfrac{1}{5}$ (duplicate)

AND

$\Rightarrow Z$ winning with Y $\Rightarrow \dfrac{1}{2}$

Now, note that X losing to Z or Z winning with X is the same thing, and since there are dependent events, we must not count them twice.

Probability that boxer X will lose both of its games, and boxer Y will win both of its games:

$\Rightarrow \left(\dfrac{1}{5}\right)\left(\dfrac{1}{5}\right)\left(\dfrac{1}{2}\right) = \dfrac{1}{20}$

Question #37:   In a certain jar, there are 6 red marbles, 4 blue marbles, and 2 green marbles. If two marbles are randomly drawn, what is the probability that the two marbles will be of different colors?

Solution: Probability that the two marbles will be of different colors = $1 -$ Probability that the two marbles will be of the same color (note: order of color matters)

$\Rightarrow 1 - \dfrac{_6C_2}{_{12}C_2} + \dfrac{_4C_2}{_{12}C_2} + \dfrac{_2C_2}{_{12}C_2}$

$$\Rightarrow 1 - \frac{\dfrac{6!}{2!(6-2)!}}{\dfrac{12!}{2!(12-2)!}} + \frac{\dfrac{4!}{2!(4-2)!}}{\dfrac{12!}{2!(12-2)!}} + \frac{\dfrac{2!}{2!(2-2)!}}{\dfrac{12!}{2!(12-2)!}}$$

$$\Rightarrow 1 - \frac{\dfrac{6!}{2!4!}}{\dfrac{12!}{2!10!}} + \frac{\dfrac{4!}{2!2!}}{\dfrac{12!}{2!10!}} + \frac{\dfrac{2!}{2!0!}}{\dfrac{12!}{2!10!}}$$

$$\Rightarrow 1 - \frac{\dfrac{6\times5\times4!}{2!4!}}{\dfrac{12\times11\times10!}{2!10!}} + \frac{\dfrac{4\times3\times2!}{2!2!}}{\dfrac{12\times11\times10!}{2!10!}} + \frac{\dfrac{2!}{2!0!}}{\dfrac{12\times11\times10!}{2!10!}}$$

$$\Rightarrow 1 - \frac{\dfrac{6\times5}{2}}{\dfrac{12\times11}{2}} + \frac{\dfrac{4\times3}{2}}{\dfrac{12\times11}{2}} + \frac{\dfrac{2}{2}}{\dfrac{12\times11}{2}}$$

$$\Rightarrow 1 - \frac{\dfrac{30}{2}}{\dfrac{132}{2}} + \frac{\dfrac{12}{2}}{\dfrac{132}{2}} + \frac{\dfrac{2}{2}}{\dfrac{132}{2}}$$

$$\Rightarrow 1 - \frac{15}{66} + \frac{6}{66} + \frac{1}{66}$$

$$\Rightarrow 1 - \frac{22}{66}$$

$$\Rightarrow 1 - \frac{1}{3}$$

$$\Rightarrow \frac{2}{3}$$

Question #38: In a certain jar, there are 5 red marbles, 5 blue marbles, and 5 green marbles. If two marbles are randomly drawn, what is the probability that the two marbles will be of different colors?

Solution: Probability that the two marbles will be of different colors = 1 – Probability that the two marbles will be of the same color (note: order of color matters)

$$\Rightarrow 1 - \frac{{}_5C_2}{{}_{15}C_2} + \frac{{}_5C_2}{{}_{15}C_2} + \frac{{}_5C_2}{{}_{15}C_2}$$

$$\Rightarrow 1 - (3)\frac{\dfrac{5!}{2!(5-2)!}}{\dfrac{15!}{2!(15-2)!}}$$

$$\Rightarrow 1 - (3)\frac{\dfrac{5!}{2!3!}}{\dfrac{15!}{2!13!}}$$

$$\Rightarrow 1 - (3)\frac{\dfrac{5\times4\times3!}{2!3!}}{\dfrac{15\times14\times13!}{2!13!}}$$

$$\Rightarrow 1 - (3)\frac{\dfrac{5\times4}{2}}{\dfrac{15\times14}{2}}$$

$$\Rightarrow 1 - (3)\dfrac{\dfrac{20}{2}}{\dfrac{210}{2}}$$

$$\Rightarrow 1 - (3)\dfrac{10}{105}$$

$$\Rightarrow 1 - \dfrac{30}{105}$$

$$\Rightarrow 1 - \dfrac{2}{7}$$

$$\Rightarrow \dfrac{5}{7}$$

SETS:

Question #39: If A is the solution set of $x^2 - 25 = 0$ and B is the solution set of $x^2 - 7x + 10 = 0$, what is the intersection of Set A and Set B?

Solution: Solve the first equation $\Rightarrow x^2 - 25 = 0$
                                           $\Rightarrow (x + 5)(x - 5) = 0$
                                           $\Rightarrow$ Solution Set A: $\{-5, 5\}$
           Solve the second equation $\Rightarrow x^2 - 7x + 10 = 0$
                                           $\Rightarrow (x - 2)(x - 5) = 0$
                                           $\Rightarrow$ Solution Set B: $\{2, 5\}$
           Union of Set A and Set B $\Rightarrow A \cup B = \{-5, 2, 5\}$
           Intersection of Set A and Set B $\Rightarrow A \cap B = \{5\}$

Question #40: In the figure below, circular region A represents the set of all numbers of the form $2m$, circular region B represents the set of all numbers of the form n^2, and circular region C represents the set of all numbers of the form 10^k, where m, n, and k are positive integers. What is a number that belongs in the common set represented by all the sets?

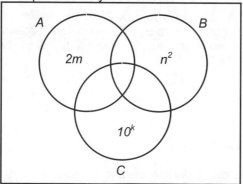

Solution: We are asked to find a number that belongs to all 3 sets. So we are looking for a number such that it obeys the rules of all 3 regions:
In other words we are looking for the intersection of all 3 sets: $A \cap B \cap C$
Set A: $2m$ $\Rightarrow$ this rule means that it can be any positive even number
Set B: n^2 $\Rightarrow$ this rule means that it can be any perfect square
Set C: 10^k $\Rightarrow$ this rule means that it can be any positive integer power of 10
We are looking for a number that obeys all 3 rules given above: it must be a positive even number and a perfect square and a positive integer power of 10.
Since now we know what we are looking for, all we have to do is plug and see which number satisfies all the given rules.
Since there are a lot of positive even numbers, and a lot of perfect squares, we should look for a number that is a power of 10 and also happens to be an even number and a perfect square. Since all

powers of 10 are even, we are essentially looking for a number that is a power of 10 and a perfect square.

Now let's start plugging numbers:

Let's start with $10 \Rightarrow 10$ is a power of 10^1, 10 is an even number, but 10 is not a perfect square

Next let's try $100 \Rightarrow 100$ is a power of 10^2, 100 is an even number, and 100 is a perfect square of 10

$\Rightarrow$ BINGO! We have found a number that satisfies all 3 rules and that is our answer.

Therefore, 100 is the correct answer.

Question #41: In a certain club that has 100 members, more number of members speaks Spanish than the number of members who speaks French. If 70 members speak French and 25 speak neither Spanish nor French, what is the minimum number of members who speak both Spanish and French?

Solution: Total No. of Members in the Club $\Rightarrow 100$

Total No. of Members who speak neither Spanish nor French $\Rightarrow 25$

Total No. of Members who speak either Spanish or French ore both $\Rightarrow 100 - 25 = 75$

Total No. of Members who speak French $\Rightarrow 70$

Total No. of Members who speak Spanish $\Rightarrow 75 - 70 = 5$

Let, the Total No. of Members who speak both French and Spanish $\Rightarrow x$

Since more members speak Spanish than French $\Rightarrow 5 + x > 70$

$\Rightarrow x > 65$

The minimum No. of members who speak both Spanish & French, or the minimum value of $x = 66$

Question #42: At a certain high school of 191 students, every student has to take a foreign language in at least one of the three semesters; 78 students take it in fall, 82 take it in winter, 96 take it in spring. If 29 students take a foreign language in exactly two semesters, how many students take it in all three semesters?

Solution: Let: No. of students who take FL in all three semesters $\Rightarrow x$

No. of students who take FL in fall and winter $\Rightarrow a$

No. of students who take FL in fall and spring $\Rightarrow b$

No. of students who take FL in winter and spring $\Rightarrow c$

No. of students who take FL in exactly two semesters $\Rightarrow a + b + c = 29$

Total No. of students $\Rightarrow 191$

Then, No. of students who take FL only in fall $\Rightarrow 78 - x - a - b$

And, No. of students who take FL only in winter $\Rightarrow 82 - x - a - c$

And, No. of students who take FL only in spring $\Rightarrow 96 - x - b - c$

EZ Problem Set-Up $\Rightarrow$ Only Fall + Only Winter + Only Spring + Only 2 Sems + All 3 Sems = Total

$\Rightarrow (78 - x - a - b) + (82 - x - a - c) + (96 - x - b - c) + (a + b + c) + x = 191$

$\Rightarrow 256 - (a + b + c) - 2x = 191$

$\Rightarrow 256 - 29 - 2x = 191$

$\Rightarrow 227 - 2x = 191$

$\Rightarrow 2x = 36$

$\Rightarrow x = 18$

Therefore, 18 students take FL in Fall, Winter, and Spring.

Question #43: In a certain ethical group of 150 people, every person speaks at least one of the three foreign languages; 50 speak French, 75 speak Spanish, and 100 speak Italian. If 35 people speak exactly two foreign languages, how many people speak all three languages?

Solution: Let: No. of people who can speak in all three languages $\Rightarrow x$

No. of people who can speak in French & Spanish $\Rightarrow a$

No. of people who can speak in French & Italian $\Rightarrow b$

No. of people who can speak in Spanish & Italian $\Rightarrow c$

No. of people who can speak in exactly two languages $\Rightarrow a + b + c = 35$

Total No. of students $\Rightarrow 150$

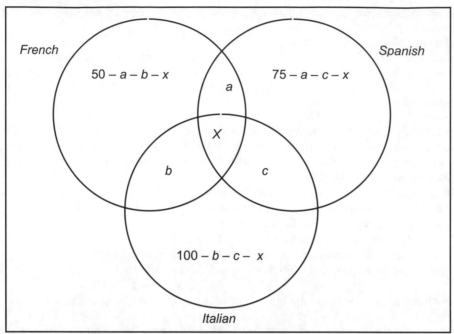

Then, No. of people who can only speak in French ⇒ $50 - x - a - b$
And, No. of people who can only speak in Spanish ⇒ $75 - x - a - c$
And, No. of people who can only speak in Italian   ⇒ $100 - x - b - c$
EZ Problem Set-Up ⇒ Only French + Only Spanish + Only Italian + Any 2 + All 3 = Total
$$\Rightarrow (50 - x - a - b) + (75 - x - a - c) + (100 - x - b - c) + (a + b + c) + x = 150$$
$$\Rightarrow 225 - (a + b + c) - 2x = 150$$
$$\Rightarrow 225 - 35 - 2x = 150$$
$$\Rightarrow 190 - 2x = 150$$
$$\Rightarrow 2x = 40$$
$$\Rightarrow x = 20$$
Therefore, 20 people can speak in all three languages.

SEQUENCE & PATTERNS:

Question #44: There were 125 days between two major hurricanes. If the first hurricane was on a Saturday, how many Sundays were there between the two hurricanes?

Solution: In this question, it's important to realize the fact that the 7 days of the week repeat indefinitely in recurring pattern.
When 125 is divided by 7, the quotient is 17 (7 × 17 = 119) and the remainder is 6.
Therefore, the first 119 days are just the days: Saturday, Sunday, Monday, Tuesday, Wednesday, Thursday, Friday, repeated 17 times.
Thus, the 125th day after the first hurricane was Friday, the same as the 6th day after the first hurricane.
The 119th day in the sequence is simply the 17th Saturday in the sequence.
After the 119th day, the pattern repeats again: the 120th day is Sunday, the 121st day is Monday, the 122nd day is Tuesday, the 123rd day is Wednesday, the 124th day is Thursday, and the 125th day is Friday.
Therefore, during the 17 full weeks between the two hurricanes, there were 17 Sundays, and there was 1 more during the last 6 days, for a total of 18 Sundays.

Question #45: Consider the following infinite sequence: 1, 5, 2, 8, 7, 9, 6, 1, 5, 2, 8, 7, 9, 6, ..., where the seven digits 1, 5, 2, 8, 7, 9, and 6, keep on repeating in that order indefinitely. What is the sum of the 900th through 907th terms of the sequence?

Solution: The same method shown above can be applied to find the 900th term and then determine the rest of the terms; however, you really don't have to waste time doing all that.

Any seven consecutive terms of the sequence, in some order, consists of exactly the same seven numbers: 1, 5, 2, 8, 7, 9, and 6.
So, simply add them $\Rightarrow$ 1 + 5 + 2 + 8 + 7 + 9 + 6 = 38.
Therefore, the sum of the 900th through 907th terms of the sequence is 38.

Question #46: In a sequence of numbers, each term after the first one is twice the preceding term. If the difference between the 5th and the 1st term is 18, what is the value of the middle term?

Solution:
Let, the first term $\Rightarrow n_1 = x$
Then, the second term $\Rightarrow n_2 = 2x$
And, the third term $\Rightarrow n_3 = 4x$
And, the fourth term $\Rightarrow n_4 = 8x$
And, the fifth term $\Rightarrow n_5 = 16x$
EZ Problem Set-Up $\Rightarrow$ Difference between the fifth term and first term = 18
$\Rightarrow$ Fifth Term – First Term = 18
$\Rightarrow n_5 - n_1 = 18$
$\Rightarrow 16x - x = 18$
$\Rightarrow 15x = 18$
$\Rightarrow x = \dfrac{18}{15} = \dfrac{6}{5}$

Therefore, the value of the middle term in the sequence $\Rightarrow 4x = 4 \times \dfrac{6}{5} = \dfrac{24}{5}$

Question #47: The first term is the sequence given below is 2, and each term after the first term is determined by multiplying the preceding term by m and then adding n. What is the value of $m + n$?
2, 9, 23, 51, 107, ...

Solution:
This problem can be solved just by trying a few easy numbers by logical reasoning, like, by asking yourself, 2 times what plus what equals 9, or 9 times what plus what equals 23; or it can also be solved algebraically as shown below:

To find the second term from the first term $\Rightarrow (2 \times m) + n = 9$
$\Rightarrow 2m + n = 9$ $\Rightarrow$ Equation #1

To find the third term from the second term $\Rightarrow (9 \times m) + n = 23$
$\Rightarrow 9m + n = 23$ $\Rightarrow$ Equation #2

Subtract Equation #1 from Equation #2 $\Rightarrow\quad 9m + n = 23$
$\Rightarrow \underline{-(2m + n = 9)}$
$\Rightarrow\quad 7m\quad\ = 14$
$\Rightarrow\quad m\quad\ = 2$

Substitute $m = 2$ in Equation #1 $\Rightarrow 2m + n = 9$
$\Rightarrow 2(2) + n = 9$
$\Rightarrow 4 + n = 9$
$\Rightarrow n = 5$

Value of $m + n \Rightarrow 2 + 5 = 7$

Question #48: There is a sequence of 5 numbers. A number is chosen for the first term, and each successive term is found by adding 8 to the preceding term and then doubling it. If the fifth term is 1,200, what is the value of the first term?

Solution:
Let, the first term in the sequence $\Rightarrow x$
Then, the second term in the sequence $\Rightarrow 2(x + 8) = 2x + 16$
And, the third term in the sequence $\Rightarrow 2(2x + 16 + 8) = 2(2x + 24) = 4x + 48$
And, the fourth term in the sequence $\Rightarrow 2(4x + 48 + 8) = 2(4x + 56) = 8x + 112$
Finally, the fifth term in the sequence $\Rightarrow 2(8x + 112 + 8) = 2(8x + 120) = 16x + 240$
EZ Problem Set-Up $\Rightarrow$ Value of the Fifth Term = 1,200
$\Rightarrow 16x + 240 = 1,200$ [Set up the equation]
$\Rightarrow 16x = 960$ [Subtract 240 from both sides]
$\Rightarrow x = 60$ [Divide both sides by 16]

Question #49: What is the sum of the units digit of 2^{79} and the units digit of 5^{68}?

Solution: To answer this problem, it's important to know that the units digit of any number has a set pattern as the exponent increases.

Write the first few exponents of $2^n \Rightarrow$ 2, 4, 8, 16, 32, 64, 128, 256, 512,.......
Pattern of Units digit of 2^n $\Rightarrow$ 2, 4, 8, 6,   2, 4, 8, 6,....... (repeating sets of four elements)
Value of the Units digit of 2^{79} $\Rightarrow$ 79 divided by 4 is 19 with remainder 3, this means the pattern fully repeats 19 times, and then goes 3 more places, and ends at 8.
Write the first few exponents of $5^n \Rightarrow$ 5, 25, 125, 625,.......
Pattern of Units digit of 5^n $\Rightarrow$ 5, 5, 5, 5, 5, 5, 5, 5,.......
Value of the Units digit of 5^{68} $\Rightarrow$ the units digit of any exponent of 5 is 5
Sum of the units digit of 2^{79} and the units digit of $5^{68} \Rightarrow$ 8 + 5 = 13

Question #50: What is the sum of the units digit of 9^{60} and the units digit of 6^{90}?
Solution: To answer this problem, it's important to know that the units digit of any number has a set pattern as the exponent increases.

Write the first few exponents of $9^n \Rightarrow$ 9, 81, 729, 6561, 59049,.......
Pattern of Units digit of 9^n $\Rightarrow$ 9, 1, 9, 1,   9, 1,   9, 1,....... (repeating sets of two elements)
Value of the Units digit of 9^{60} $\Rightarrow$ every odd exponent of 9 ends with a 9 and every even exponent of 9 ends with a 1, this means the 60th exponent of 9 ends with a 1
Write the first few exponents of $6^n \Rightarrow$ 6, 36, 216, 1296,.......
Pattern of Units digit of 6^n $\Rightarrow$ 6, 6, 6, 6, 6, 6, 6, 6,.......
Value of the Units digit of 6^{90} $\Rightarrow$ the units digit of any exponent of 6 is 6
Sum of the units digit of 9^{60} and the units digit of $6^{90} \Rightarrow$ 1 + 6 = 7

Question #51: In a certain restaurant, a jukebox plays songs in a regularly repeated cycle of 20 different songs. If a dime buys 1 song, then, in dollars, what is the minimum amount of money that must be spent before the same song is played five times?
Solution: Since we want to find the minimum cost of paying the same song five times, let's assume we want the first song to play five times.
The jukebox plays sets of 20 different songs in a repeated pattern – the first song and rest of the 19 songs played will be all different songs.
In the first set of 20 songs, from 1st through 20th song – the 1st song is the one that we want to repeat five times. Total cost for first 20 songs = 20 dimes = $0.10 × 20 = $2.00
Now in the next set of 20 songs, from 21st through 40th song – the 21st song will be the same as the first song. Total cost for next 20 songs = 20 dimes = $0.10 × 20 = $2.00
Likewise, in the next set of 20 songs, from 41st through 60th song – the 41st song will be the same as the first song. Total cost for next 20 songs = 20 dimes = $0.10 × 20 = $2.00
Again, in the next set of 20 songs, from 61st through 80th song – the 61st song will be the same as the first song. Total cost for next 20 songs = 20 dimes = $0.10 × 20 = $2.00
Finally, in the next set of 20 songs, from 81st through 100th song – the 81st song will be the same as the first song. Total cost for next 1 song = 1 dime = $0.10
Note that after playing the 81st song, the 1st, 21st, 41st, 61st, and 81st song will be all the same song and we'll have the first song already played five times, and there'll be no need to play any more songs.
Total Cost $\Rightarrow$ $2.00 + $2.00 + $2.00 + $2.00 + $0.10 = $8.10

MISCELLANEOUS PROBLEMS:

Question #52: A certain clock chimes one note at 10 minutes past every hour, two notes at 20 minutes past every hour, three note at 30 minutes past every hour, four notes at 40 minutes past every hour, and five notes at 50 minutes past every hour. On the onset of every hour, it chimes six notes plus the number of notes equal to that hour. How many notes will the clock chime between 6 P.M. and 11 P.M., inclusive?
Solution: This is a simple problem but it is very easy to make a mistake by miscounting.
The best way to tackle this problem is by systematically putting everything in a grid.

		:00	:10	:20	:30	:40	:50
6 P. M.	$\Rightarrow$	6 + 6	1	2	3	4	5
7 P. M.	$\Rightarrow$	6 + 7	1	2	3	4	5
8 P. M.	$\Rightarrow$	6 + 8	1	2	3	4	5

9 P. M.	$\Rightarrow$ 6 + 9	1	2	3	4	5
10 P. M.	$\Rightarrow$ 6 + 10	1	2	3	4	5
11 P. M.	$\Rightarrow$ 6 + 11	0	0	0	0	0
	$\Rightarrow$ 87	5	10	15	20	25

Total Chimes $\Rightarrow$ 87 + 5 + 10 + 15 + 20 + 25 = 162

Note $\Rightarrow$ Make sure to include the chimes at the hour of 6 P.M.

$\Rightarrow$ Make sure not to include the chimes at 10, 20, 30, 40, 50 past the hour of 11 P.M.

Question #53:   If all the letters represent single digits in the correctly worked computation shown below, what is the value of $X + Y + Z$?

```
  X  2  6  9
  8  Y  2  1
  2  1  Z  2
+ 1  7  1  5
-----------
1 7  7  7  7
```

Solution: Add the digits vertically down, form equations, and solve for the missing digits:

Sum of units digits $\Rightarrow$ 9 + 1 + 2 + 5 = 17

Carry over to tens digit = 1

Sum of tens digits $\Rightarrow$ 1 + (6 + 2 + Z + 1) = 17

$\Rightarrow Z = 7$

Carry over to hundreds digit = 1

Sum of hundreds digits $\Rightarrow$ 1 + (2 + Y + 1 + 7) = 17

$\Rightarrow Y = 6$

Carry over to thousands digit = 1

Sum of thousands digits $\Rightarrow$ 1 + (X + 8 + 2 + 1) = 17

$\Rightarrow X = 5$

Carry over to ten-thousands digit = 1

Sum of ten-thousands digits $\Rightarrow$ 1

Sum of $X + Y + Z$ $\Rightarrow$ 5 + 6 + 7 = 18

STATS – AVERAGES:

Question #54:   The average (arithmetic mean) rating of the students in the south campus is 150 points and the average rating of the students in the north campus is 120 points. There are no common students between the south and north campus. If the average rating of all the students is 132 points, and if there are 50 students in the south campus, how many students are in the north campus?

Solution: Let the number of students in the north campus = n

EZ Problem Set Up: $\Rightarrow$ *Sum of products $\div$ Sum of Weights = Weighted Mean*

$\Rightarrow \dfrac{150(50) + 120(n)}{50 + n} = 132$ [Set up the equation]

$\Rightarrow 150(50) + 120(n) = 132(50 + n)$ [Cross multiply]

$\Rightarrow 7,500 + 120n = 6,600 + 132n$ [Apply distributive property]

$\Rightarrow 7,500 = 6,600 + 12n$ [Subtract 120n from both sides]

$\Rightarrow 12n = 900$ [Subtract 6600 from both sides]

$\Rightarrow n = 75$ [Divide both sides by 12]

Question #55:   In a certain technology company, a senior programmer can execute 5 web applications in 2 hours and a junior programmer can execute 2 web applications in 5 hours. If a senior programmer and a junior programmer, each execute the same number of applications, what is the average amount of time, in minutes, to process one web application?

Solution: For the senior programmer $\Rightarrow$ 5 applications in 2 hours $\Rightarrow$ 10 applications in 4 hours

For the junior programmer $\Rightarrow$ 2 applications in 5 hours $\Rightarrow$ 10 applications in 25 hours

Senior Programmer & Junior Programmer $\Rightarrow$ 20 applications in 29 hours

$\Rightarrow$ 1 application in $\dfrac{29}{20}$ hrs

$$\Rightarrow \frac{29}{20} \times 60 \text{ min} = 87 \text{ minutes}$$

Question #56: If the average of 17 consecutive odd integers is 685, what is the least of these integers?
Solution: The average of a group of evenly spaced numbers is equal to the middle number. There are odd numbers of terms in this group, 17, so the average is the middle most term, i.e., the 9th term. This tells us that the 9th consecutive odd integer here will be the same as the average, which is 685. Now that we have the 9th term, we can count backward to find the first term.
$\Rightarrow$ 9th term: 685 $\Rightarrow$ 8th term: 683 $\Rightarrow$ 7th term: 681 $\Rightarrow$ 6th term: 679 $\Rightarrow$ 5th term: 677
$\Rightarrow$ 4th term: 675 $\Rightarrow$ 3rd term: 673 $\Rightarrow$ 2nd term: 671 $\Rightarrow$ 1st term: 669.

Question #57: If the average of 18 consecutive odd integers is 876, what is the least of these integers?
Solution: The average of a group of evenly spaced numbers is equal to the middle number. There are even numbers of terms in this group, 18, so the average is the midway between the two middle most terms. i.e., the 9th and 10th term. This means that the 9th consecutive odd integer will be the first odd integer less than 876, which is 875. Now that we know the 9th term, we can count backward to find the first term.
$\Rightarrow$ 10th term: 877 $\Rightarrow$ 9th term: 875 $\Rightarrow$ 8th term: 873 $\Rightarrow$ 7th term: 871 $\Rightarrow$ 6th term: 869
$\Rightarrow$ 5th term: 867 $\Rightarrow$ 4th term: 865 $\Rightarrow$ 3rd term: 863 $\Rightarrow$ 2nd term: 861 $\Rightarrow$ 1st term: 859
Therefore, the least of the integer is 859.

Question #58: What is the median of the following set: $\{n, 2, 5, 11, 11, 15, 19\}$, where n is a positive number.
Solution: Let's consider three possibilities for n, it can be less than 11, or equal to 11, or greater than 11.
If $n < 11$, let's say $n = 1$: $\{1, 2, 5, 11, 11, 15, 19\}$ Median = 11
If $n = 11$, let's say $n = 11$: $\{11, 2, 5, 11, 11, 15, 19\}$ Median = 11
If $n > 11$, let's say $n = 25$: $\{25, 2, 5, 11, 11, 15, 19\}$ Median = 11
So regardless of what n is, the median will always be 11.

Question #59: If A is the average (arithmetic mean) of the first 25 positive multiple of 2 and if B is the median of the first 25 positive multiples of 2, what is the value of $A - B$?
Solution: In this problem, you must notice one of the properties of average. If "n" numbers form an arithmetic sequence of evenly spaced numbers (one in which the difference between any two consecutive terms is the same) and if "n" is odd, then the average of the numbers is the average of the smallest and the largest terms or simply the middle term in the sequence. And the median, is also the middle term. This means that in such a case, the mean and the median are the same number.
$\Rightarrow A - B = 0$
It would be a waste of time to calculate the mean and the median, but if you have extra time, you can try to check your answer.

Question #60: If the average (arithmetic mean) of 8, m, and n is 6, and the average of 9, m, and $-n$ is 7, what is the value of m?

Solution: Mean of 8, m, and n is 6 $\Rightarrow \dfrac{8 + m + n}{3} = 6$ [Set up the equation]

$\Rightarrow 8 + m + n = 18$ [Cross multiply]
$\Rightarrow m + n = 10$ [Subtract 8 from both sides] $\Rightarrow$ Equation #1

Mean of 9, m, and $-n$ is 7 $\Rightarrow \dfrac{9 + m - n}{3} = 7$ [Set up the equation]

$\Rightarrow 9 + m - n = 21$ [Cross multiply]
$\Rightarrow m - n = 12$ [Subtract 9 from both sides] $\Rightarrow$ Equation #2

Add Equation #1 & #2 $\Rightarrow m \quad + n = 10$ $\Rightarrow$ Equation #1
$\underline{\Rightarrow m \quad\quad - n = 12}$ $\Rightarrow$ Equation #2
$\Rightarrow 2m \quad\quad = 22$ [Add Equation #1 and Equation #2]
$\Rightarrow \quad m \quad\quad = 11$ [Divide both sides by 2]

Question #61: If the average (arithmetic mean) of x and y is 85 and the average (arithmetic mean) of y and z is 80, what is the value of $(x - z)^2$?

Solution:

Mean of x & y is 85	$\Rightarrow \dfrac{x+y}{2} = 85$	[Set up the equation]
	$\Rightarrow x + y = 170$	[Cross multiply]
	$\Rightarrow x = 170 - y$	[Subtract y from both sides] $\Rightarrow$ Equation #1
Mean of y & z is 80	$\Rightarrow \dfrac{y+z}{2} = 80$	[Set up the equation]
	$\Rightarrow y + z = 160$	[Cross multiply]
	$\Rightarrow z = 160 - y$	[Subtract y from both sides] $\Rightarrow$ Equation #2
Value of $(x - z)^2$	$\Rightarrow [(170 - y) - (160 - y)]^2$	[Substitute value of x & z from equations above]
	$\Rightarrow [170 - y - 160 + y]^2$	[Eliminate parentheses]
	$\Rightarrow [170 - 160]^2$	[Combine like-terms]
	$\Rightarrow [10]^2$	[Do the subtraction]
	$\Rightarrow 100$	[Solve the exponent]

Question #62: If the average (arithmetic mean) of m, n, and 7 is 25, what is the average of $m + 2$, $n - 9$, and 8?

Solution:

Mean of m, n, and 7 is 25	$\Rightarrow \dfrac{m+n+7}{3} = 25$	[Set up the equation]
	$\Rightarrow m + n + 7 = 75$	[Cross multiply]
	$\Rightarrow m + n = 68$	[Subtract 7 from both sides]
Mean of $m + 2$, $n - 9$, & 8	$\Rightarrow \dfrac{m+2+n-9+8}{3}$	[Set up the mean]
	$\Rightarrow \dfrac{m+n+1}{3}$	[Combine like-terms]
	$\Rightarrow \dfrac{68+1}{3}$	[Substitute $m + n = 68$ from above]
	$\Rightarrow \dfrac{69}{3}$	[Do the addition]
	$\Rightarrow 23$	[Do the division]

Question #63: The average (arithmetic mean) of $2a + 12$ and another number is $5a$. What is the average of the other number and $6a$?

Solution:

Average of two numbers	$\Rightarrow 5a$
One number	$\Rightarrow 2a + 12$
Let the other number	$\Rightarrow x$

EZ Problem Set-Up:	$\Rightarrow$ Average of two numbers $= \dfrac{\text{one number} + \text{other number}}{2}$	
	$\Rightarrow 5a = \dfrac{2a+12+x}{2}$	[Set up the equation]
	$\Rightarrow 10a = 2a + 12 + x$	[Cross multiply]
	$\Rightarrow 8a = 12 + x$	[Subtract $2a$ from both sides]
	$\Rightarrow x = 8a - 12$	[Subtract 12 from both sides]
Mean of $8a - 12$ and $6a$	$\Rightarrow$ Sum $\div$ Number	[Write the formula to calculate arithmetic mean]
	$\Rightarrow \dfrac{8a-12+6a}{2}$	[Substitute the known values]
	$\Rightarrow \dfrac{14a-12}{2}$	[Combine like-terms]
	$\Rightarrow \dfrac{2(7a-6)}{2}$	[Factor out 2 in the numerator]
	$\Rightarrow 7a - 6$	[Cancel-out common terms]

Question #64: A students' average score for a series of test was 95. However, after taking one last test, in which the student scored a score of 50, it lowered the overall average score to 90. How many tests were there in the series before taking the last test?

Solution: Before taking the last test:

Mean score	$\Rightarrow$ 95	[Given]
No. of tests	$\Rightarrow N$	[Assumption]
Sum of tests	$\Rightarrow$ Mean × Number	[Write the formula for mean]
	$\Rightarrow 95N$	[Substitute the known values]

After taking the last test:

Score on last test	$\Rightarrow$ 50	[Given]
No. of tests	$\Rightarrow N + 1$	[Add 1 to N tests]
Sum of tests	$\Rightarrow 95N + 50$	[Add the score on last test]
Mean score	$\Rightarrow$ 90	[Given]
EZ Problem Set-Up	$\Rightarrow$ Mean of $N + 1$ tests is 90	

$$\Rightarrow \frac{95N + 50}{N + 1} = 90 \quad \text{[Set up the equation]}$$

$$\Rightarrow 95N + 50 = 90(N + 1) \quad \text{[Cross multiply]}$$

$$\Rightarrow 95N + 50 = 90N + 90 \quad \text{[Apply distributive property]}$$

$$\Rightarrow 5N + 50 = 90 \quad \text{[Subtract } 90N \text{ from both sides]}$$

$$\Rightarrow 5N = 40 \quad \text{[Subtract 50 from both sides]}$$

$$\Rightarrow N = 8 \quad \text{[Divide both sides by 5]}$$

Therefore, there were a total of 8 tests in the series.

Question #65:   During a group vocation, the average (arithmetic mean) daily expense of 10 members was $90. If 2 of the members had no expenses at all, and each of the others had a daily expense of at least $75, including one member, who had a daily expense of exactly $170 dollars, what is the maximum possible daily expenses, in dollars, that any one of the members in the group could have?

Solution:
No. of people in the group	$\Rightarrow$ 10
Mean daily expenses per member	$\Rightarrow$ $90
Sum of daily expenses for group of 10	$\Rightarrow$ No. of people in group × Mean daily expenses per member
	$\Rightarrow$ 10 × $90 = $900

Out of the 10 members, 2 had $0 expense, and 1 had $170 expense, and the rest of the 7 members had at least $75 expense. Let's assume that the 6 of the remaining 7 members had the minimum expense of $75.

Now the total expense for 9 members $\Rightarrow$ $0(2) + $170(1) + $75(6) = $0 + $170 + $450 = $620

Maximum possible expense for the 10th member $\Rightarrow$ Expenses of 10 – Expense of 9 members
$\Rightarrow$ $900 – $620 = $280

Question #66:   The average (arithmetic mean) weight of a group of five people is 175.2 pounds. If no two people weigh less than 155 pounds and if no two peoples' weights are within 5 pounds of each other, then, in pounds, what is the maximum possible weight that any of the five people can have?

Solution:
Mean weight of five people	$\Rightarrow$ 175.2 pounds
No. of people in the group	$\Rightarrow$ 5
Sum of the weights of 5 people	$\Rightarrow$ 175.2 × 5 = 876 pounds

Since we are asked to find the maximum possible weight that any one of the five people can have, we'll have to minimize the weight of four people.

Since the minimum possible weight that any person can have is 155 pounds, and the minimum difference between the weights of two people is 5 pounds, let's assume that the weights of the first four people are 155 pounds, 160 pounds, 165 pounds, and 170 pounds.

Sum of the weight of four people $\Rightarrow$ 155 + 160 + 165 + 170 = 650 pounds

Weight of the fifth person (heaviest possible) $\Rightarrow$ Sum of weights of 5 ppl – Sum of weights of 4 ppl
$\Rightarrow$ 876 – 650 = 226 pounds

Question #67:   A certain student's average (arithmetic mean) score on six tests is 70. Assuming that the students can't earn more than 100 on any one test, what is the least the student can score on the seventh test and still have a chance of getting an average score of 75 after taking nine tests?

Solution:
For 6 Tests	$\Rightarrow$ No. of Tests = 6	
	$\Rightarrow$ Mean = 70	
	$\Rightarrow$ Sum of scores of six tests	$\Rightarrow$ Mean × Number

$\Rightarrow 70 \times 6 = 420$

Since the maximum possible score on any one test is 100, let's assume that the student scored 100 on the eighth and ninth tests.

For 8 Tests: $\Rightarrow$ Sum of scores of eight tests $\Rightarrow$ Sum of scores of six tests + Score on 8th & 9th tests

$\Rightarrow 420 + 100 + 100 = 620$

For 9 Tests $\Rightarrow$ No. of Tests = 9

$\Rightarrow$ Mean = 75

$\Rightarrow$ Sum of scores of all nine tests $\Rightarrow$ *Mean × Number*

$\Rightarrow 75 \times 9 = 675$

Least possible score on the seventh test $\Rightarrow$ Sum of scores of 9 tests – Sum of scores of 8 tests

$\Rightarrow 675 - 620 = 55$

Therefore, the student must at least score 55 on the seventh test and still have a chance of getting an average score of 75 after taking nine tests.

Question #68   A student has taken seven math tests so far this semester. If he gets a 60 on his next test, that score will lower his average (arithmetic mean) by 2 points. What is his average now?

Solution: Before taking the 8th test:

No. of tests	$\Rightarrow 7$	[Given]
Mean of tests	$\Rightarrow A$	[Assumption]
Sum of tests	$\Rightarrow$ *Mean × Number*	[Write the formula for mean]
	$\Rightarrow 7A$	[Substitute the known values]

After taking the 8th test:

Score on 8th test	$\Rightarrow 60$	[Given]
No. of test	$\Rightarrow 7 + 1 = 8$	[Add 1 to 7 tests]
Sum of tests	$\Rightarrow 7A + 60$	[Sum of 7 test plus new score]
Mean score	$\Rightarrow$ Mean on seven tests – 2	[Given]
	$\Rightarrow A - 2$	[Substitute mean on seven tests = A]

EZ Problem Set-Up $\Rightarrow$ Mean of 8 tests = $A - 2$

$\Rightarrow \dfrac{7A + 60}{8} = A - 2$ [Set up the equation]

$\Rightarrow 7A + 60 = 8(A - 2)$ [Cross multiply]

$\Rightarrow 7A + 60 = 8A - 16$ [Apply distributive property]

$\Rightarrow 60 = A - 16$ [Subtract $7A$ from both sides]

$\Rightarrow A = 76$ [Add 16 to both sides]

Therefore, the students' average score now is 76.

Question #69:   In a certain store, the average (arithmetic mean) daily sales for the last n days was 70 units. If today's sale of 160 units increases the average to 75 units per day, what is the value of n?

Solution: For the last n days:

No. of days	$\Rightarrow n$	[Given]
Mean daily sale	$\Rightarrow 70$	[Given]
Total sales	$\Rightarrow x$	[Assumption]
Mean sales	$\Rightarrow$ *Mean = Sum ÷ Number*	[Write the formula for mean]
	$\Rightarrow 70 = \dfrac{x}{n}$	[Substitute the known values]
	$\Rightarrow x = 70n$	[Cross multiply]

For the last n days plus today:

No. of days	$\Rightarrow n + 1$	[Add 1 to n days]
Total sales	$\Rightarrow x + 160$	[Add 160 to x]
Mean daily sale	$\Rightarrow 75$	[Given]

EZ Problem Set-Up $\Rightarrow$ Mean sale of last n days plus today = 75

$\Rightarrow 75 = \dfrac{x + 160}{n + 1}$ [Set up the equation]

$\Rightarrow 75 = \dfrac{70n + 160}{n + 1}$ [Substitute $x = 70n$]

$$\Rightarrow 75(n + 1) = 70n + 160 \qquad \text{[Cross multiply]}$$
$$\Rightarrow 75n + 75 = 70n + 160 \qquad \text{[Apply distributive property]}$$
$$\Rightarrow 5n + 75 = 160 \qquad \text{[Subtract } 70n \text{ from both sides]}$$
$$\Rightarrow 5n = 85 \qquad \text{[Subtract 75 from both sides]}$$
$$\Rightarrow n = 17 \qquad \text{[Divide both sides by 5]}$$

Question #70: There are 7 books placed on a certain bookshelf. Each book is at least 90 pages long, and the total number of pages of all 7 books is 777 pages. If the average number of pages of the first 5 books is 105 pages, what is the greatest possible number of pages of any of the 7 books?

Solution:

Total No. of books	$\Rightarrow 7$
Total No. of pages of all 7 books	$\Rightarrow 777$
Mean No. of pages of 5 books	$\Rightarrow 105$
Sum of the No. of pages of these 5 books	$\Rightarrow$ Mean No. of pages of 5 books × 5
	$\Rightarrow 105 \times 5 = 525$
No. of pages in the remaining 2 books	$\Rightarrow$ No. of pages of 7 books – No. of pages of 5 books
	$\Rightarrow 777 - 525 = 252$

Since the minimum number of pages that any book can have is 90 pages, let's assume that one of the two remaining books has 90 pages.

The maximum possible number of pages for the other book $\Rightarrow 252 - 90 = 162$

EZ BOOK STORE: ORDERS & SALES:

ORDERS & SALES INFORMATION: EZ Solutions books can be ordered via one of the following methods:

🖳 ON-LINE ORDERS:
On-line Orders can be placed 24/7 via internet by going to: www.EZmethods.com

✉ E-MAIL ORDERS:
E-Mail Orders can be placed 24/7 via internet by emailing: orders@EZmethods.com

☎ PHONE ORDERS:
Phone Orders can be placed via telephone by calling: ++301.622.9597

📠 FAX ORDERS:
Fax Orders can be placed via fax by faxing: ++301.622.9597

🖃 MAIL ORDERS:
Mail Orders can be placed via regular mail by mailing to the address given below:
EZ Solutions
Orders Department
P.O. Box 10755
Silver Spring, MD 20914
USA

OTHER OPTIONS: EZ Solutions books are also available at most major bookstores.

Institutional Sales: For volume/bulk sales to bookstores, libraries, schools, colleges, universities, organization, and institutions, please contact us. Quantity discount and special pricing is available.

EZ BOOK LIST:

LIST OF EZ TEST PREP SERIES OF BOOKS:

EZ Test Prep Series books are available for the following sections:
- EZ Solutions – Test Prep Series – General Test Taking Strategies
- EZ Solutions – Test Prep Series – Math Strategies
- EZ Solutions – Test Prep Series – Math Review – Arithmetic
- EZ Solutions – Test Prep Series – Math Review – Algebra
- EZ Solutions – Test Prep Series – Math Review – Applications
- EZ Solutions – Test Prep Series – Math Review – Geometry
- EZ Solutions – Test Prep Series – Math Review – Word Problems
- EZ Solutions – Test Prep Series – Math Review – Logic & Stats
- EZ Solutions – Test Prep Series – Math Practice – Basic Workbook
- EZ Solutions – Test Prep Series – Math Practice – Advanced Workbook
- EZ Solutions – Test Prep Series – Verbal Section – Reading Comprehension
- EZ Solutions – Test Prep Series – Verbal Section – Sentence Correction/Completion
- EZ Solutions – Test Prep Series – Verbal Section – Critical Reasoning
- EZ Solutions – Test Prep Series – Verbal Section – Vocabulary
- EZ Solutions – Test Prep Series – Verbal Section – Grammar
- EZ Solutions – Test Prep Series – Verbal Section – Writing Skills

Note: Some of these books have already been published and others will be released shortly.

EZ Test Prep Series books are available for the following standardized tests:
- EZ Solutions GMAT Test Prep Series of Books
- EZ Solutions GRE Test Prep Series of Books
- EZ Solutions SAT Test Prep Series of Books
- EZ Solutions ACT Test Prep Series of Books
- EZ Solutions PRAXIS Test Prep Series of Books
- EZ Solutions POWER MATH Test Prep Series of Books